recalling 'the sce[...] :
celebrating 100 issues of
feminist review

edited by | **100**

Irene Gedalof and Nirmal Puwar

palgrave
macmillan

100

contents

editorial

100 | recalling 'the scent of memory': celebrating 100 issues of *feminist review*

Irene Gedalof and Nirmal Puwar

Our hundredth celebration issue of *Feminist Review* (*FR*) has taken inspiration from a 2009 colloquium entitled 'Race', Gender, Postcoloniality, organised by Yasmeen Narayan (in collaboration with the journal *Ethnic and Racial Studies*), to celebrate the work of Avtar Brah on the occasion of her retirement from Birkbeck, University of London. As the day unfolded, one contributor after another made reference to a particular example of Avtar's work, her 1999 article 'The Scent of Memory' published in Issue 61 of *FR*, *Snakes and Ladders: Reviewing Feminisms at Century's End*. As those of us in the audience who were members of the FR Collective listened, one of the day's contributors, Gail Lewis, reminded us that Avtar invites her readers to 'write back' to the questions she poses in that remarkable piece: questions about racialisation and diaspora, about home and belonging, about politics and personal lives, about the psychosocial dynamics of subjectivity and identity. In that moment, the idea for this issue was born.

Avtar is the longest-standing member of the current *FR* Collective and has been central to the Collective's historic and ongoing conversations and contestations about a feminist knowledge production that is always attentive to the challenges of intersectionality, and one that combines scholarly rigour with political commitment. 'The Scent of Memory', published at the turn of the new millennium, is exemplary of that kind of academic labour. And yet we, the Collective, had not yet explicitly taken up Avtar's invitation to write back to her compelling article. What better moment to do so than in celebration of our hundredth issue?

The issue begins with a reprint of 'The Scent of Memory', followed by two contributions from that 2009 colloquium, Les Back's interview with Avtar on her life and work, and Stuart Hall's closing address, 'Avtar Brah's Cartographies: Moment, Method, Meaning'. Following on from these, members of the Collective and other contributors take off from and write back to different aspects of 'The Scent of Memory'.

(1–5) © 2012 Feminist Review. 0141-7789/12 www.feminist-review.com

Avtar was, in one sense, herself 'writing back' in this article to Tim Lott's autobiography *The Scent of Dry Roses* and to its inclusion of a suicide note his mother Jean had written at the age of 57 in March 1998, describing her alienation at what the new Southall (in West London) had become for her, a white woman — a space of hate and ontological anxiety. Southall connected Avtar to Jean. The changing landscape of Southall has been a key anchor in Avtar's work, as a place of political creation, agitation and contemplation of diaspora space. Moreover, the fear, resentment and loss experienced by white people at the arrival of South Asian and Afro-Caribbean residents into the area was a key element of Avtar's doctoral research in the area in the 1970s, which included qualitative interviews with white families — a study of whiteness long before the establishment of this subfield of ethnic and racial studies. How boundaries are drawn and the possibilities of crossing them beyond closed identitarian notions of 'us' and 'them', or as Avtar puts it in Punjabi, the *ajnabi* (other, different), *ghair* (strange) and '*apna/apni*' (ours), remains a central concern of not only the article, but also Avtar's broader work. She has continued to activate an openness to new formations and collectivities, while recognising the lived nature of the violence of race, gender and class. What is perceived as the *taking* of public space in Southall (and the UK more broadly) forms a part of the mediations sparked by Avtar's reading of Jean's suicide note. The response to the Dominion Centre, which became a South Asian Cinema after it was bought by the Indian Worker's Association, exemplifies the visceral reaction to the new arrivals as a threat to existing origin stories of local community (Brah, 1999: 14–15). Brah's contemplations are layered by the political memory of the racist stabbing of Gurdip Singh Jaggar, a 15-year-old boy, outside the Dominion Centre in 1976. Avtar takes us to the National Front march through Southall in 1979 and the galvanisation of anti-fascist forces, bringing together white, South Asian and Afro-Caribbean protesters, both in the counter march and at the funeral of Blair Peach, killed at the event by the police, where elderly South Asian women grieved for him as 'our son'. This white teacher became for them an *ajnabi*, a stranger who has different ways but holds the promise of becoming a friend, or even *apna*, 'one of ours' (*ibid.*: 19). The political mobilisation generates new positionalities that work across the hard closed-in lines of insiders and outsiders, and the violence that seeks to push 'them' out and away from 'us'. 'Us' and 'them' are changing and shape-shifting associations and categories, with deep emotional and material consequences. Indeed, Avtar's own search for what the contours of Jean's pain were in her life (both familial and suburban), as well the complications and the intimate everyday exchanges she may have shared with the new settlers of Southall, does the work of making Jean *apni* (of her own) for Avtar.

Southall is also the focus of two contributions to this issue, each exploring the existence of those who migrated, faced racism but were not defined by racism

(Hall, 2002). In 'The Sound of Memory', Tej Purewal conducted a rare interview with her aunt and world-renowned singer Mohinder Kaur Bhamra. We hear how she sang, performed and made music albums from Southall in the post-war period. Listened to across the global South Asian diaspora, her lyrics included newly written verses on migration, nights of labour in the UK, as well as the togetherness produced in *gidda* sessions between women. Southall also features in Nirmal Puwar's discussion of a little known film, *Aaj Kaal*, made by Asian elders within a community education project that Avtar directed over 20 years ago. She reflects on the mediations that informed this performative ethnography, as well as the dynamics and practices of telling with film, offering a different enunciation of British social scenes and public spheres. The social and affective properties of *gidda* feature as an aspect of scenes produced in British front rooms, as do the meeting places generated in British seasides and day centres for the elderly. By excavating Avtar's project, Puwar pushes us to consider the creative possibilities of the work we do. Steeped though we are in ethical dilemmas of exchange, *Aaj Kaal* reminds us that we don't only have the flat page of paper available to us as a mode of pedagogy.

The entangling of auto/biographical memory with broader processes of gendered racialisation in 'Scent' becomes a starting point for a number of pieces in the issue. In 'Working-class Whiteness from Within and Without', Lyn Thomas provides an auto-ethnographic response to 'Scent of Memory'. Writing through a series of memory scenes, she connects out from Southall to her white working class routes in Wolverhampton, the constituency of Enoch Powell, whose 'Rivers of Blood' speech presented a heavy spectre of doubt over the right of 'immigrants' to exist in the UK. In 'The Sense of Memory', Suki Ali both contrasts the diaspora space of her own upbringing in a mixed-race family in a southern seaside English town with that of the Southall explored in 'Scent' and digs deeper into the complex workings of memory suggested by Brah's piece. In 'Acrid Text: Memory and Auto/biography of the "New Human"', Joan Anim-Ado revisits the bitterness of not-belonging and the painful possibilities of resistance through a powerful assemblage of memory 'graffiti'.

The complex spaces and processes of belonging in diaspora space explored in 'Scent' are taken up in different ways by other pieces in the issue. In 'Racialisation, Relationality and Riots: Intersections and Interpellations', Ann and Aisha Phoenix take inspiration from 'The Scent of Memory's' discussion of gendered/racialised interpellation to consider the ways in which these psychosocial processes are at work in two contemporary spaces — a maternity ward in Tower Hamlets and the media coverage of the 2011 riots. In 'Interruption, Reproduction and Genealogies of "Staying Put" in Diaspora Space', Irene Gedalof starts from the figure of the mother that Brah evokes at the beginning, returns to throughout and ends with in 'Scent', to stage a series of interruptions to the ways in which the reproductive is thought in contemporary accounts of Britishness and belonging. Nira Yuval-Davis' contribution 'An Autochthonic Scent of Memory?' revisits and offers a new conceptualisation of the dynamics of defining places of belonging and not-belonging that run through Brah's meditations on Southall of the 1970s and 1980s. Creative responses to the themes of 'Scent' are offered in Laleh Khalili's poem 'In Exile' and in Catherine O'Flynn's short story 'Blossomtime', in which the embodied sense of living in places of exile and of diaspora space are evoked.

The diversity of the modes of response to Avtar's invitation to write back also attests to the rich methodological complexity of the article that inspired them: psychosocial readings of the diaspora space of Tower Hamlets and of the recent riots; retheorising the figure of the mother in contemporary accounts of Britishness; auto-ethnographic accounts of memory in relation to whiteness and mixed-race identities; creative riffs on home and not-belonging; revisiting and revaluing the place of diasporic cultural productions in film and music in the space of Southall. Together they reflect on the different ways of being in academia. While Avtar worked on her PhD in Southall, she was also becoming an activist, going on to co-found Southall Black Sisters. She saw the importance of political mobilisation without romanticising this work or espousing an anti-intellectual stance. She has called on different disciplines in her work — stretching from stratification studies to psychoanalysis and cultural studies. Her 'slow burn' approach to pedagogy and community education is quite a contrast to the speeded-up production chain that academia is heading towards in the contemporary context. Academic positionality in relation to the writing of political events is a complicated issue. It can be a view from afar or caught up in ethnographic romanticisation. Where and how does it intervene? What are the stakes? How can we deepen comprehension of difficult times while working towards change without gesturing towards 'saving the natives' (Chow, 1993)?

While writing back to 'The Scent of Memory', the pieces in this collection also speak to each other, producing echoes in both substance and style. The autobiographical is a key aspect of Thomas's and Ali's articles, as it is in the discussion of the film *Aaj Kaal* by Puwar. The ethics of research and writing don't go away with the use of creative methods, using film or by engaging in personal biographical stories. Memory work is always of the now, as much as of the then, an active form of remembering and practical recollecting.

The unruly and multi-vocal figure of the mother reappears across the issue in different guises. Her material practices of mothering can make her an agent of racialisation as explored by Phoenix and Phoenix, of grappling with the after-effects of racialisation as evoked by Anim-Addo, of entanglement in the reproduction of raced, classed and gendered subjectivities and identities as remembered by Thomas, Khalili and Ali. As metaphor, she can be pressed into service in the work of tracing exclusionary and restrictive genealogies of belonging, as an emblem of sameness; conceptualised from a different point of view, as Gedalof argues, she might be seen as confounding that logic of the same and offering a messier, more promising genealogy.

How we understand genealogies of 'staying put' is another recurring theme. Unpicking the discursive, experiential and theoretical instabilities and complexities of the white British/English 'we' is a preoccupation for Thomas, Gedalof, Phoenix and Phoenix, and Yuval-Davis, and each offers insights into the different ways and different levels at which this work of producing a 'we' operates in the diaspora space of Britain. A further set of echoes are produced by working through the entanglement of not-belonging with emplacement — in Anim-Addo's evocative term, of being 'new-in-*dis*-place' — as explored in different ways by Ali, Puwar, Purewal, Khalili and Anim-Addo herself.

Stylistically, there are also some interesting echoes across the issue — from Anim-Addo's 'graffiti' to Gedalof's 'interruptions', from Thomas's 'memory fragments' to Phoenix and Phoenix's staging of two sets of discourses and practices against each other, the issue offers a series of refusals to present seamless stories, smooth narratives that offer closure and resolution. This refusal of the seamless is fitting in an issue inspired by 'The Scent of Memory', which is itself a stylistically innovative 'meditation through a series of questions'. It is also fitting for an issue more broadly inspired by Avtar, whose work on diaspora space has been consistently committed to defying 'the search for originary absolutes, or genuine and authentic manifestations of a stable, pre-given, unchanging identity; for pristine, pure customs and traditions or unsullied glorious pasts' (Brah 1996: 196).

We hope that this resistance to closure, and the spirit of Avtar's original invitation to 'write back', are also reflected in this issue, and will inspire further answers to her question 'What do you think'?

references

Brah, A. (1996) *Cartographies of Diaspora*, London and NY: Routledge.

Brah, A. (1999) 'The Scent of Memory: strangers, our own and others' *Feminist Review*, Issue 61: 4–26.

Chow, R. (1993) *Writing Diaspora: Tactics of Intervention in Contemporary Cultural Studies*, Bloomington: Indiana.

Hall, S. (2002 [1984]) 'Reconstruction work: images of postwar Black settlement' in Highmore, B. (2002) editor, *The Everyday Life Reader*, London: Routledge, 251–261.

doi:10.1057/fr.2011.67

100 | the scent of memory: strangers, our own and others

This article first appeared in 1999 in Issue 61 of *Feminist Review* and has been reprinted here as originally published.

Avtar Brah

abstract

Using, as a point of departure, Tim Lott's recent autobiography where he attempts to make sense of his mother's suicide of 1988 through a reconstruction of his family genealogy, this article tries to map the production of gendered, classed, and racialized subjects and subjectivity in west London. It addresses the tension between Lott's discourse of his own white working-class boyhood during the 1970s where questions of 'race' are all but absent, and the racialized 'commonsense' that pervades the interviews with other local white contemporaries of Lott and his parents. These narratives are analysed in relation to the socio-economic context and the political activism of the period. Theoretically, it analyses the 'diaspora space' of London/Britain, interrogating essentialist 'origin stories' of belonging; reaching out to a glimmer on the horizon of emerging non-identical formations of kinship across boundaries of class, racism and ethnicity; and exploring the purchase of certain South Asian terms — 'ajnabi', 'ghair' and 'apna/apni' — in constructing a nonbinarized understanding of identification across 'difference'.

keywords

biography/autobiography; memory; interpellation; posthumanist subject; whiteness; class; gender; ethnicity; racism; Asians; Blacks

They all crossed into forbidden territory. They all tampered with the laws that lay down who should be loved, and how. And how much.

(Arundhati Roy in *The God of Small Things*)

This essay is a meditation through a series of questions. A meditation, by definition, cannot pre-suppose answers or conclusions. I hope that this one develops into an open-ended conversation — a kind of graffiti without finite beginnings and endings — with *FR* readers responding, interrogating, critiquing, agreeing or disagreeing, and extending its main concerns through the pages of this journal. The question: 'What do you think'?, which is scattered throughout this text, is, therefore, offered as a genuine invitation to write back. My own meditation is in pursuit of what Donna Haraway so aptly designates as the need to consider how humanity might have a figure outside the narratives of humanism. What language, she asks, would such a 'posthumanist' figure speak?

> I want to set aside the Enlightenment figures of coherent and masterful subjectivity, the bearers of rights, holders of property in the self, legitimate sons with access to language and the power to represent, subjects endowed with inner coherence and rational clarity, the masters of theory, founders of states, and fathers of families, bombs, and scientific theory … and end by asking how recent intercultural and multicultural feminist theory constructs possible postcolonial, nongeneric, and irredeemably specific figures of critical subjectivity, consciousness, and humanity — not in the sacred image of the same, but in the self-critical practice of 'difference', of the I and we that is/are never identical to itself, and so has hope of connection to others.
>
> (Haraway, 1992: 87)

This would seem to be one of the most important tasks facing feminisms at this point.

triggers

In late 1996, the British Sunday newspaper *The Observer* carried a review of a book titled *The Scent of Dried Roses*. The newspaper contained some excerpts from this autobiographical account by a son of his mother's suicide. What caught my eye were the contents of the mother's suicide note, especially the following line: 'This will be so bad for everybody but I hate Southall, I can see only decay. I feel alone'. This sentence reverberated in the quiet of the Sunday morning compelling me to read the book. But why?

The word 'Southall' — ringing loud and clear in my ears — connected me across diverse, even disparate, life worlds to 'Jean' — this 57-year-old white woman who took her own life in March 1988. But, what kind of a *connection* was it that beckoned me inexorably into her world? What clues did I expect to pick up about this woman by reading her son's account of her life? This was not really a question about the reliability of his account, not least because, there is no guarantee that Jean's own account of her life would have rendered her any more transparently 'knowable' to me. The extent to which she becomes 'knowable' is not simply a matter of putting together fragments of information available about her according to some pre-given formula; nor can the task of making sense of Jean's universe only be an issue about the conceptual frameworks available to us for interpretation. Knowing is not so much about the assemblage of existing knowledge as it is about recognizing our constitution as 'ourselves' within the fragments that we process as knowledge; 'hailing' and being 'hailed' within the discourses that produce us and the narratives we spin; directing our socially, culturally, psychically and spiritually marked focus of attention upon that which we appropriate as 'data' or 'evidence'. Hence, 'data' are neither more nor less reliable simply because of the nature of their source: whether the source in question is autobiography, biography, history, religion or science. The boundaries between cosmology, history, religion and science are far from clear cut as they are no more, and no less, than different ways of *trying* to know *that* which defies transparency. For example, what is 'history' if not an on-going contestation of the very terms whereby the *term* itself emerged as a technology of eurocentric gaze. So that, a *specifically* embodied European subject such as Hegel could assert without an iota of self-doubt that Africa had no 'history'? What kind of a 'knowing' is this, where all human history is reduced to 'history'?

My point is that, what is humanity if not an intricate mosaic of *nonidentical* kinship?

Who was Jean? Is this a question about her alone? Why am *I* so exercised about this woman's fate? How am I implicated in *her world and she in mine*, by *my* asking of this question? Is my interest in her driven by a sense of affinity with her or by a sense of difference? Indeed, do these have to be bi-polar alternatives? Clearly, these are not questions that can easily be accommodated within the frame of modernity's imperatives of rationality. As I tried to understand my agenda for reading the book, I gradually became aware that my reasons for wanting to 'read' Jean could in turn be 'read', at least in part, as an alibi for a certain desire: the desire of colonialism's Other to 'know' how differential forms of 'whiteness' are 'lived'? In a way, I was (am?) constructing her as my window on to 'working-class English whiteness'. But it was not just that. Which other, more intimate, cords had she touched in me?

What made Jean *hate* Southall?, I asked myself. Could one of the reasons be that it is one of those localities of London where the post-Second World War immigrants from Britain's former colonies — especially those from South Asia — came to settle in significant numbers? Was she among the white parents who in 1965 campaigned for bussing Asian children out of Southall schools if their numbers rose to one-third of the school population, because they were thought by these parents to 'hold back' white children? Was she at all like some of the white parents whom I interviewed as a research student in 1976? I had spent a considerable part of 1976 talking with 15-year-old students in three schools and their parents at home while trying to study the interplay – in the lives of 'whites' and 'Asians' – of the discourses of race, ethnicity and class in *naming* identity (Brah, 1979). For several months I had sat in classrooms, observed what went on in school grounds, walked the streets and visited homes in Southall, Ealing and Greenford. All this had left indelible impressions of this heaving, bustling, culturally thriving locality of west London which was 'home' to a range of groups: Irish, Welsh, Polish, South Asian and Caribbean descent groups alongside the 'English'. Jean was certainly within the same age-group as most of the white parents I had spoken to. Most of these parents had been incredibly outspoken and forthright in recounting what they thought about Asians in Southall. In some cases, my face-to-face presence during interviews seemed to be completely obliterated, as if I did not exist, while they heaped a variety of stereotypic constructions upon Asian populations. Did Jean experience them/us/me as a 'threat' in the same way as politicians such as Powell and Thatcher had been making out? Or could it be that her daily contact with Asian children through her job as a 'dinner lady' in a primary school with a predominantly Asian school population, fostered bonds of connection and affection which served to refute the appeals of an essentialist Britishness of the Powellian–Thatcherite variety?

origin stories

One 'white' mother whom I interviewed in 1976 had said to me: '"Where did *they* come from"?, my father used to say, "they were here, and then the shops opened up"'.

The 'they' in this locution signified 'Asians'. 'She means people like me', I had thought to myself, feeling acutely 'othered', as my efforts at maintaining 'objectivity' (which my supervisor at university had insisted was critical for gaining academic credibility for my research) fast receded. I could not be a disinterested listener, although I listened attentively. My intellect, feelings and emotions had all been galvanized by my respondent's discourse. I was framed within it, whether I liked it or not. What was it that made her referent 'they' instantly recognizable as 'Asians' to us both? I did not know her ethnicity. She could have been English, Irish, Welsh, Polish or anything else in terms of her own 'background'. South Asians or 'people of colour' in general were not the only substantially large 'immigrant' group in Southall. Nor were they necessarily the most recent. The Southallian population at the time was continually renewed by, for instance, Irish immigrants. So, what was it that 'rang a bell' in the core of our sense of ourselves or 'interpellated' us relationally, simultaneously, with the result that we both understood who the 'they' in our conversation was? What non-logocentric discursive spatiality produces such electric moments of 'recognition'?

***

a digression through the idea of 'interpellation'

With regard to this question, I believe that there is much that is still of value in the Althusserian idea of 'interpellation', the concept that struggles with some of what I am trying to grapple with here, namely the making sense of being situated and 'hailed' socially, culturally, symbolically and psychically, all at once. I am mindful of the critiques of Althusser's conceptual framework (cf. Hindess and Hirst, 1975; Laclau and Mouffe, 1985). Indeed, I too have some serious reservations about aspects of this discourse, including its economic determinism 'in the last instance', its class-centricity and its structuralist formalism. Yet, to hold such reservations is not to deny the importance of economic and class relations.

A significant strength of the Althusserian discourse is that it takes seriously the relationship between the social and the psychic in the production of class subjects. It tries to stage a critical and non-reductive dialogue between and across 'consciousness' (or 'conscious agency'), 'subjectivity' and 'identity'. The analytical reach of the *combined* Althusserian theoretical repertoire is profound, with its key concepts ranging from the notion of 'historical conjuncture', as the outcome of *articulation* of contradictions that defy simplistic reductionism; through the idea of 'overdetermination', as the *modes of articulation* incorporating a symbolic dimension and a plurality of meaning; to the concept of 'articulation' itself, as a metaphor used to indicate relations of linkages and their effects across different levels of socio-cultural formation such that, as Stuart Hall notes, 'things are related, as much through their differences as through their similarities' (Hall, 1980: 320). The concept of articulation also embodies Saussure's insight that language is not a reflection of the world but produces meaning.

Hence, Althusser's claim that everything in the social is overdetermined highlights the processes whereby the social constitutes itself in and through the symbolic. And, therein lies the importance of the Althusserian reworking, following Gramsci, of the concept of ideology as signifying, not false consciousness, but referring, instead, to the complex matrices of meaning, concepts, categories and representations in and through which individuals make sense of the world. That is to say that, individuals are 'hailed'/'interpellated' within and across universes of representations and discourses of meaning in the process of our constitution into cultural/social subjects. The importance of the poststructuralist critique of the concept of ideology notwithstanding, I read interpellation as the process of signification whereby we come to 'live' (albeit largely unconsciously) our symbolic and psychic relationship to the social. I have sympathy with those critiques of the Althusserian paradigm which take issue with the functionalism embedded in his discussion of the relationship between 'interpellation' and the 'Ideological State Apparatuses', but the concept of interpellation itself remains pertinent and useful. It places the question of the relationship between effects of capitalist social relations and subjectivity into the realm of productive interrogation.

A far more serious limitation of Althusserian structuralist Marxism, in my view, resides in its lack of attention to questions of women's gender (for the male gender is its norm), racism, ethnicity and sexuality. My encounter with Jean within the pages of a Sunday newspaper and later in her son's autobiography, or with the white mother whom I had interviewed two decades earlier, cannot be understood outside of these 'other' contexts.

***

'... "Where did *they* come from"?, my father use to say ...'.

One straight answer would be that which was encapsulated in the contemporary political slogan: 'We are here because you were there'! This slogan referred to the history of British colonialism and imperialism, which resulted in Britain turning to its former colonies for the recruitment of workers to meet the post-Second World War labour shortages that befell capitalist economies of western Europe. Was my 'research respondent' familiar with this history? She easily might not have been, given, as I discovered during my research, a spectacular amnesia on this matter within the curriculum of Southall schools of the period, and presumably earlier. More worryingly, the school library in one of the three secondary schools still stocked reference books which discussed the anti-colonial Rebellion of 1857 in terms of the 'Indian Mutiny' and the 'Black Hole of Calcutta', without any evidence indicating that such texts were being subjected to critical scrutiny. But even if we assume, for the sake of argument, that my interviewee was singularly familiar with the history of British imperial adventures abroad, we cannot automatically deduce *how* such evidence would have been interpreted by her. Facts do not speak for themselves. How was she 'interpellated', as a working-class white woman with her *unique* autobiography, within the imperial discursive formations? Indeed, how did colonial discourses figure in the production of her subjectivity? How did they mark the minutiae of her everyday life? How and when did her father's rhetorical question, and the sense of threat and discomfort it conveys, become her own sense of her self?

We do not have the detail necessary to attempt any definitive answers (if, indeed, such a thing were ever possible). But some clues are available from the combined narratives of working-class white parents and school-students I interviewed. A local (but not entirely localized) form of Gramscian 'common-sense' — fragmentary, fragmented and contradictory but one that could not be dismissed as irrational within the terms of its own internal logic — may be gleaned from their commentaries. The refrain of 'too many coloureds', 'within a month they were here like bees', and 'they have taken over' and so on is a major theme within these representations. As one 15-year-old white boy said to me:

> Southall is too overpopulated with them. Such a lot of them. It is alright if they move up to
> Birmingham, somewhere different because they all like to come in one place ... It makes

some people not like them and they move out of the area. Some people can't afford to move and they are stuck by themselves.

What economists, sociologists or geographers described as the 'white flight' from declining inner- or outer-city areas by upwardly mobile sections of the white working class in a period of economic boom, is experienced by those who remain as a sense of having fallen behind those able to leave, 'stuck by themselves'. The resentment towards the upwardly mobile fellow whites is projected on to Asians and other 'people of colour' who are now blamed for the departure. The reams written about the role of global capitalism and unequal development in underpinning contemporary labour migrations have little resonance in this explanation. They do not form part of the 'commonsense' of this beleaguered identity.

A 15-year-old white girl confessed:

> I think they have taken over Southall. I suppose people just don't like the way they live, the smell of their food, it gets down your throat because you are not used to it. It is not so tidy as it used to be. I think they have mucked it up a bit really. A lot of old people, they complain, they say it used to be a nice country place and everything, and they have taken over all the shops, and it is horrible round here now.

Here we encounter feminized commonsense with its fantasy of tranquil and tidy rural domesticity which is 'mucked up', disrupted by the 'intruders' with their alien foods and unfamiliar smells. There is an overwhelming feeling of being 'taken over', of being soiled and defiled, of things being 'horrible'. The 'intruder' is discursively embodied as a form of aggressive masculinity. This discourse constructs Southall in terms of a vulnerable feminized space and displaces female anxiety about male aggression into a fear of the colonialism's 'Other'. This is partially achieved by transmuting colonial immigrant labour into the figure of 'colonizer': Asians come to be represented as having 'taken over', as the discourse converts the transgressed-against into the transgressors.

In contrast to the somewhat 'indirect workings' of racialized discourses in the girl's narrative, a father–son pair, conversing with me at their home, are positioned within an explicit and overt discourse of 'racial' superiority:

> Father: We have emigrated to other countries. Educated them, raised their standard of living, but they are allowing in too many. The black man is getting more educated and the white man doesn't like it. I was brought up to believe that the black man was a slave. Now they want the same standard as us! We don't like it.

> Son: We resent them and we will influence our children. Even when I was five, you'd mix with them in school but never have them in your house. It is colour, not culture. You always feel you are white, you are are brown, you are black.

Far from being understood as a source of regret, the tales of colonial exploits and exploitation are refracted here through the ideology of 'civilizing mission' and absolutist racialized difference, and *experienced* as an inter-generational form of male-bonding between father and son, while holding at bay the painful reality of the inferiorized position of working-class masculinity: 'the black man is getting more educated (i.e., getting ahead in class terms), and the white (working-class) man doesn't like it'. The discourse of racial superiority may be understood here as *displacing* class antagonism while the father and son are transported into the realm of imagined and imaginary class-less and unified Englishness.

Similarly, a three-way discussion between myself and the parents of another student, steers into focus the inconsistencies, dissonance, disavowal and contradiction within the logic of narratives marked by racialized discourse:

> Mother: I am moving out because there is no future for my children in Southall. There are no shops or other facilities.
>
> Father interjects: The facilities are there but proprietors have changed.
>
> Mother: Indian shops are over-run by mice. We never used to get mice in our house until the Asians moved in next door. Look at their garden. It is filth.
>
> Father protests: Our own garden too is over-run by weeds!
>
> Mother: *Ours is just overgrown. Theirs is filth and dirt.* (emphasis added)

The imagery of vermin, dirt and filth is common enough in representations of all kinds of 'Others'. Here, it would seem to feature as a way of disavowing one's own sense of failure symbolized by the unkempt 'garden' while the neighbour's garden becomes the bearer of this self-disgust: 'Ours is just overgrown. Theirs is filth and dirt'. The very fact of having Asians as neighbours itself serves as a signifier of decline in this discourse. As regards future prospects for the children, it is arguable that the future of all children in this working-class London suburb in the throes of a recession at the time was far from sanguine. But the term 'future' may be understood as holding a double meaning here: referring to general prospects as well as to 'racial' destiny. A deeply felt concern that the more 'successful' white person was in a position to exercise the option of moving out is at the heart of this expression of acute anxiety. The father's interjection highlights inconsistencies within the discourse, but such contradictions are shored up by the mother's denial.

On the other hand, disavowal and denial are not the only vehicles for 'othering' processes. A subjective sense of resentment may persist even when the 'conditions underlying the recruitment of immigrant workers' and their 'contribution to the economy' is fairly explicitly invoked. Invocation, after all is not always the same as acknowledgment. Another mother, for example, observes:

> I was in Southall when the Indians came. They were brought in as cheap labour. They don't want to mix with us; don't try to learn the language. We try to get on. We feel resentful. My mother says that we were kicked out of India, now they are all here. People blame them for the economic crisis. But, our economy would fall down if they all went home. Who would run our buses, and our hospitals?

This discourse references the economic context within which workers from former colonies were recruited as replacement labour for jobs that white workers had abandoned in response to better opportunities provided to them by the post-war economic boom. It is couched within an acceptance, no matter how ambivalently articulated, of the proposition that the economic crisis of the late 1970s could not be blamed upon Asian or Caribbean descent people in Southall. Nonetheless, these populations come to embody the site of difference and unfamiliarity where 'old ways of doing things' are in crisis. English ambivalence towards mixing with 'outsiders' and learning 'a new language' of communication is projected onto groups who, if the contemporary evidence of a thriving programme of classes in English as a Second Language is to be taken seriously, were exceedingly busy trying to learn English, as well as the wider cultural language of a rapidly changing late capitalist social formation. But everyday commonsense of this discourse is not especially concerned about these seemingly 'distant' issues: 'we feel resentful', and a (mis)reading of the process of decolonization, 'we were kicked out of India, now they are all here', legitimates the logic of resentment.

How do we change this 'distanciation' of the 'macro issues' into more intimate conversations that foster connectedness and understanding?

This brief foray into excerpts from certain narratives — recorded in the 1970s Southall Jean would have been familiar with as the mother of teenage sons — is not intended to suggest that there was a coherent, homogeneous or unidirectional racialized discourse circulating in Southall; or to argue that the respondents involved were misinformed, irrational, bigots. On the contrary, the point is precisely that the white young people and their parents were 'ordinary' (in Raymond William's sense of the term), everyday folk like you and me. Several admitted to having Asian and African-Caribbean descent friends, and a few counted individuals with these backgrounds as among their relatives. But none of this can be taken to work as a necessary inoculation against states of mind, emotions, values and practices which may have ethnicist or racist effects. For example, a white mother with an Asian child is not, by definition, immune from positionality within racialized discourses and practices. Rather, the issue is much more about the position that we politically (in the widest sense) come to *practise*, and not merely *espouse*, as we 'live' (both consciously and unconsciously) the vicissitudes of our lives.

And, is this not one of the most difficult things to do, positioned, as each and everyone of us is, in some relationship of hierarchy, authority or dominance to another? How do we construct, both individually and collectively, non-logocentric political practices — theoretical paradigms, political activism, as well as modes of relating to another person — which galvanize identification, empathy and affinity, and not only 'solidarity'?

'... Where did they come from? ...'

Stories of origin abound in Southall as elsewhere. The local library stocks a pamphlet which holds that the 'Saxons' were one of the first to leave a permanent mark on this area (Kirwan, 1965). The name 'Southall' is said to be of Saxon origin, meaning the south corner of a stretch of land. Were they not a linguistic group then, instead of a separate 'race' as racial typologists claim? The Saxon invaders, according to this chronicle, were followed by the Danes, and later by the Normans. (And, '... Where did they come from? ...', I ask you). Until the nineteenth century, the majority of the inhabitants of Southall depended on agriculture for their livelihood. It is suggested that the farmers in the area were probably converted to Christianity by the missionaries of St Augustine in the eighth century. About this time, parishes were marked out and Southall became part of the 'Precinct' of Norwood. Southall began to lose its rural character during the late seventeenth century. The process would seem to have been initiated in 1698 when an influential local family succeeded in gaining a charter to hold a weekly market in the area; even today a market is still held on the same site. With the construction of a canal between Uxbridge and Brentford, and the building of the railway in 1838–1839, Southall rapidly developed into an industrial town. The growth of industry and the availability of good transport facilities have played a critical role in attracting mobile labour to the area. Before the Second World War, the Irish and the unemployed from south Wales and the north of England constituted the major source of outside labour; immediately after the war, sizeable Polish enclaves also developed alongside South Asian and African-Caribbean groups. During the 1990s, the existing populations have been augmented by refugee groups, most notably from Somalia.

Who, in this fragment of global migrations, can claim to be 'native' of Southall?

The reason generally offered by academic discussions for the arrival of Asians in Southall during the 1950s was the availability of work at a rubber reconditioning plant, the Woolfs rubber factory, in Hayes, very close to the border of Southall. Owing to the unpleasant working conditions and the need for shift work, the company found it difficult to recruit white labour. During the Second World War, the personnel officer at Woolfs had apparently fought alongside Sikhs in the Middle East, and had been impressed by them. This ironical encounter between the colonizer and the colonized, away from 'home' on an imperial battlefield, was often cited to me by professionals working in the area as a watershed in the policy of hiring Asians. Soon, these workers were to combine into the Indian Workers Association and engage in a very British trade union activity of the period, mounting campaigns for unionization and improvement in working conditions (Harrison, 1974). Yet, as we have seen above, class solidarity did not figure strongly in the white parents' accounts. A few of the white parents were born during the economic depression of the 1930s, and several recounted family and neighbourhood stories of hardship and scarcity. They spoke of the tradition of fierce pride with regard to skilled work which meant that a skilled worker would rather remain unemployed than engage in unskilled forms of work. In academic-speak the working class was internally fractured by the hierarchy marked by occupation skill and the ambition to succeed in life. It was also equally differentiated by gender and other modes of differentiation. But these internal fissions would be subsumed within the boundary of 'us' when facing comparison with the middle classes. As a working-class locality, Southall was overshadowed by the more affluent, middle-class suburb of Ealing. As a community worker explained:

> Oh, yes there has always been a feeling of 'Us against Authority' — that the rules were imposed from outside and pushed onto them. There was very much the element that Southall was the back-end of Ealing. Southall residents would get angry, would resent it. It was a dig and it made them even more united.

According to the women, Southall was a close-knit community and social control was stringent. One woman told me:

> Most people lived and worked here. A lot of your relatives were in Southall. Most people knew one another. You couldn't do anything without everyone knowing about it. We wouldn't dream of going into Ealing when we were youngsters — right up till I was 21. Sunday night it used to be the community center ... I don't have a clue what they do there now. Saturday we used to be at the Dominion Cinema. That used to be a cinema for us, with a dance hall at the top which my aunty used to be the manageress of.

The point about not having a clue as to what 'they do there now' and, that the Dominion 'used to be a cinema for us' is a reference to the fact that when the popularity of television during the 1960s resulted in a drop in the cinema-going white audiences, the Dominion was bought by the Indian Workers Association to hold Asian community events, including the showing of Indian films. Notwithstanding the fact that it was the play of economic markets which governed this 'take-over', what registers with segments of the white population is the fact that the Dominion was now owned by an Asian organization. Asians are thus constructed as having usurped what is perceived by the white residents as *their* community resource. If previously, intra-class boundaries were the primary signifier of 'difference', it is a racialized form of ethnicity that now moves centre-stage as the major axis of differentiation. The 'pub', a classic gendered signifier of working-class sociality, becomes the point of condensation in naturalizing such 'difference':

> You don't find the white people going into the Victory. The Victory is for the Asians, the Black Dog is for the Jamaicans. We wouldn't dream of walking into the Victory or the Black Dog. That's just not on — we don't do that. We used to go to the White Swan — now it is mixed. We go to the White Hart over the bridge, which is ours, and the George is Irish. It's all segregated.

This multilayered discourse embodies the contradictory relationality of 'race', gender, class and differentialized ethnicity in the post-colonial spatiality of Southall. The figure of the 'pub' articulates 'power-geometries of spatiality' (Massey, 1999) along these different signifiers of 'difference'. Its symbolism, partially communicated through the semiology of animal imagery, simultaneously demarcates, transgresses and erases a multiplicity of borders. The 'we' here is a certain Englishness, differentiated from Irishness, with the 'difference' of the latter signalled by 'The George'. The discourse marks the heterogeneity of 'whiteness', but it is a malleable boundary compared to that constructed against the 'Other' colour(s): 'we wouldn't dream of walking into the Victory or the Black Dog'. But, the 'Other' colour(s) is/are both similarized and differentiated: the Asian emerges as the victor, viewed as the 'colonizer', as we have already seen. The 'Jamaican' referring to African descent black people, on the other hand, is 'interpellated' across the long established racist imagery of the African as closer to animals: the image of 'Black Dog', saturated with racialized meanings, conveys a sense of domesticated savagery. While this commonsense discourse consciously invokes a situation where 'it's all segregated', it simultaneously undoes this claim by foregrounding subconscious anxieties about what might be going on at the 'White Swan', the feminine figure of racial and sexual purity, where the clientele is now 'mixed'. The White Swan was also the site of class ambivalence, for it attracted a higher class of 'racially' mixed clientele, 'not the general run', as one woman explained to me, to be found at the Victory, the Black Dog, the George, or, more significantly, at the White Hart — the very heart within this representation of this *particular* variety of working-class Englishness.

'... Where have they come from? ...'

The immediate context for the question was the summer of 1976. Which 'other' genealogies of Southallian Englishness, the ones in which my own Africaness/ Asianess/Californianess/Englishness/Panjabiness, are allusions/illusions in this question? I can only sketch a few features here. As I retrace, certain contours begin to take shape: bodies, landscapes, sights, smells; sensations of fear and threat, of belonging, unbelonging and sometimes alienation; of familiarity and estrangement, of love and hate; memories of blood on the streets, excitement of political mobilization and optimism that comes in the wake of daring to imagine futures of hope when confronted with despair. Some memories, in particular, stand out. In Southall, Gurdip Singh Chaggar, a 15-year-old boy returning home from school is stabbed to death in front of the Dominion Cinema in April 1976. His death sends shock waves among Asian communities of Southall, and it produces a resounding response as they (we) came out in force to demonstrate on the streets of Southall. At first, the media reports suggest that the attackers are three 'white' teenage boys. Some political activists discuss the incident as primarily a question of class — working-class communities torn apart by the dominance of the ruling classes. Then the media refer to one of the three as being 'mixed race' — in this case, meaning that he had one black and one white parent. His colour, light brown, becomes quite a significant political talking point. For some people this boy's involvement was a signal that this was not a racist murder, as if racism is coded in our genes. This position is not surprising, however, given that even in the late 1990s certain eminent socio-biologists continue to champion their troubling and troublesome theses about 'selfish genes', 'homosexual genes' and so on (cf. Rose, 1997 for a brilliant critique). For other commentators, this was a racist murder except that the brown boy had been deluded into thinking that he was white like his friends. But, while all positionality within discourse involves some disillusion on all our parts, racist or other *effects* of practices, whether they be scholarly treatise or actions such as stabbing, do not depend for their effectivity on the agent necessarily having to be white, gentile, male or heterosexual (although of course these subject positions are implicated in the construction of racialized, gendered or sexualized forms of power). If this were the case, we would not have any hope of, say, a white person ever being non-racist, or someone engaged in heterosexual practice ever being non-heterosexist.

While the political commentators, media pundits and community activists debated the murder, the dead boy's mother wailed in agony the question: 'Why'? This is a question that no feminism worth its salt, can refuse to address.

In East London, the proverbial 'gateway' into the 'heart' of London for a variety of immigrants over the centuries, incidents of racist attacks and violence continue to escalate throughout the 1970s resulting in several cases of death. Two male students from Mile End are killed in 1976. During 1978, three men — Altab Ali in Whitechapel, Kennith Singh in Newham and Ishaque Ali in Hackney — all die from wounds inflicted during street attacks. These deaths galvanize the East London Asians as well as some Left organizations into public demonstrations (Bethnal Green and Stepney Trades Council, 1978). In Notting Hill, there are massive confrontations in the summer of 1976 between the police and Black young people as the latter try to stake their claim to this inner-city enclave of central London where dire poverty jostles with fantastic wealth. The summer of 1976 was dubbed by the media as the 'long hot summer' as they relayed reports, television footage and photographs of African and Asian descent protesters demonstrating publicly their anger and frustration at overt and covert forms of racism that were all but ignored by agencies of the state and rarely debated in public policy or other political forums, aside from certain research organizations. These public demonstrations were conspicuous, among other things, for the involvement of British-born young Blacks and Asians who were asserting a new British political identity. Britain 'turned a different colour' in a million senses of this phrase, as Powellian constructions of 'whiteness' — British=White — were publicly interrogated, challenged and decentred: a gesture that wordlessly, but not silently, declared 'we are not just "in Britain" but rather are "of Britain", and we don't even care whether or not you agree'.

'... and then the shops opened up ...

The high street of Southall in the late 1970s, as today, is indeed peppered with Asian-owned shops selling dazzling saris, beautiful salwar-kameez, exquisite gold jewellery and restaurants offering all manner of delicious South Asian cuisine. To a casual visitor, of whom there are frequently many in Southall, the street exudes an atmosphere of wealth and prosperity. To the local white residents, the majority of whom are working class, this apparent example of Asian entrepreneurship can easily seem, as we have already seen, like a 'take-over' because Britain in the 1970s is awash with constructions of 'the Asian' as an outsider *par excellence*. In the processes that mark the play of these signifying practices, local Asian shops become a sign of white working-class failure, a site of envy and desire. The 'Asian shop' assumes such a magnified visibility in the popular imagination that the presence on the high street of corporate businesses such as Marks and Spencer or Woolworths passes without comment. Even Woolworths, the chain-store owned by a USA-based firm, becomes 'our own' as against 'these Asian outsiders'. That is to say that chromatism of the racialized imagination spotlights Asian-owned small business as a threat while rendering global operations of corporate business colourless and invisible. Yet, contrary to what this defensive 'Englishness' of a beleaguered subordinate class imagines, the grass is not greener on the other side. The shops are a facade. Behind the cheer and sparkle there is the grim 'Asian reality' of high levels of unemployment, rampant low pay, with many businesses — often set up under the noose of high debt in order to avoid unemployment — teetering on the verge of liquidation; overcrowding, a general lack of public amenities and a growing presence of fascist organizations such as the National Front.

Which fragments of this reality did Jean connect with? With the glitter *as if it were a transparent sign of wealth* or with its opaqueness, signalling the much more complex and difficult terrain of hope, dreams, despair and desire eked out on the margins of low income and poverty, where lack of money can easily come to stand for personal failure. What kind of 'puzzle' of loss and desire is figured in her suicide?

And the National Front comes marching in ...

1979 is the election year and the National Front is fielding enough candidates nationally to win prime-time on television for a political broadcast. Although the National Front had little support in Southall, they wished to hold an election rally in the local Town Hall. Despite petitions to the contrary made by local residents opposed to the fascists, the local authority grants them permission to hold their meeting. Escorted by the police, they begin their march shouting inflammatory slogans, calling for the repatriation of 'immigrants', a term that by now had become synonymous in popular consciousness with 'people of colour'. Their opponents have arranged a show of strength by planning a counter-march for the same day and a route is agreed with the local police. In the event, the anti-fascist marchers are blocked from following the agreed route by the Special Patrol Group Units of the Metropolitan Police. During the confrontations that ensue, nearly 700 (predominantly Asian) men and women of all ages are arrested and bussed out to police stations all over London. Of these, 344 are charged and tried in courts. The building occupied by a Black musicians' co-operative, including the band 'Misty in Roots', is raided by the police and the music equipment is all destroyed. The lawyers and the medical staff present are, according to their own accounts, forced out of the building amidst a barrage of racist and sexist abuse. Clarence Baker, the lead singer of Misty in Roots, is wounded and lies unconscious in hospital for some time. As a report notes:

> 2,756 police, including Special Patrol Group units, with horses, dogs, vans, riot shields and a helicopter were sent in ... the evidence of hundreds of eyewitnesses shows that ... police vans were driven straight at crowds of people, and when they scattered and ran, officers charged at them, hitting out at random. ... A *Daily Telegraph* reporter saw 'several dozen crying, screaming coloured (*sic*) demonstrators ... dragged bodily along Park View Road to the police station ... nearly every demonstrator we saw had blood flowing from some sort of injury; some were doubled up in pain. Women and men were crying'.
>
> (Campaign against Racism and Fascism/Southall Rights, 1981: 2)

On that day, Blair Peach, a white teacher from East London, died from head injuries suffered, according to evidence presented to the courts, when he was hit by police officer(s) attached to the Special Patrol Group. I saw older Asian women file past his coffin, calling him 'put' (my son) as tears streamed down their agonized faces. He was no 'outsider', as far as they were concerned, although they did not know him. He was very much 'our own', laying his life down for a future where racist and fascist activity would not stalk their neighbourhood. The women's lament was no superficial gesture of sentimentality, as some forms of 'hard politic' might maintain. It was a profound expression of love and inclusion. One of the many creoles spoken on the South Asian subcontinent is Urdu which makes a distinction between 'ajnabi' and 'ghair'. An 'ajnabi' is a stranger; a newcomer whom one does not yet know but who holds the promise of friendship, love, intimacy. The 'ajnabi' may have different ways of doing things but is not alien. She could be(come) 'apna'; that is, 'one of our own'. The idea of 'ghair' is much more difficult to translate for its point of departure is intimacy; it walks the tightrope between insider/outsider. The difference of the 'ghair' cannot be fully captured by the dichotomy of Self and Other; nor is it an essentialist category. Yet, it is a form of irreducible, opaque, difference. Although these three terms may often be used in contradistinction to each other, they do not represent opposites. To the women who mourned Blair Peach, he was an 'ajnabi' but not a 'ghair'. He was 'apna'. The distinction is politically important. The world is full of ajnabis. There are feminists, for instance, whom I may never meet. They are 'ajnabi' but not 'ghair' because they are part of my imagined community. Unless, of course I meet one and she treats me as if I am 'ghair', because of, say, my colour. At that moment she steps out of my boundary of 'apne' (plural of 'apna': own kind) and begins to *feel* 'ghair'. We may continue to share political views. May even engage in common political projects. Yet, we will be divided by the boundary of 'ghairness' and our relationship will feel hollow. But, then again, her positionality could change — as has often happened through anti-racist projects — and the ghairness may be transformed.

In the aftermath of the events described above, Southall became the site of intense feminist, anti-racist and other forms of political activity. Southall Black Sisters was formed. The Southall Youth Movement (a predominantly male organization) fought fascists but also came into conflict with feminist politics. Southall Rights and Southall Monitoring Group continue their advocacy work. A variety of Marxist groups, and various community organizations continue still to maintain their presence. But, political shifts marked by such terms as 'Thatcherism' (and now 'Blairism') have produced a significantly changed political terrain. This period, however, is not my focus of concern here, although I have discussed some features of this phase elsewhere (cf. Brah, 1987, 1996; Southall Black Sisters, 1989).

'... Where did they (we) come from? ...': an origin story of the late 1990s

13 July 1997, *The Observer* carries the headline 'How I braved academic derision to prove we're really Africans'. The subject of this headline is Chris Stringer, a paleontologist. Addressing the *Observer* readers, he writes how he was vilified when he first proposed the idea that 'they [the Neanderthals] are not our [read Europeans'] ancestors and humans are all Africans under the skin' (p. 12). So, are all *Observer* readers Europeans? That is an interesting presumption, or perhaps a subversive act begging the question about Europeaness. We are all, he says, Africans under the skin? The differences are only skin-deep? What does one do with the skin itself? What is the 'truth of the matter'? What is the matter of truth? The report outlines the controversy. Evidently it was generally accepted during the early 1980s, that early humans known as *Homo erectus* had indeed emerged from Africa but nearly a million years ago. *Homo erectus*, the story goes,

wandered the world evolving into Neanderthals in Europe, Java Man in the Far East and Peking Man in China (what a spectacle of male cloning, long before our very own dear 'Dolly', the sheep, came to fame in 1997!). Chris Stringer accepted this hypothesis but only partially. Yes, *Homo erectus* had indeed evolved into the above eminent trio (where was women's lineage among all these men?), but they were not our immediate ancestors. Instead, Stringer contended that present day humans are all descended from a second wave of humans who also emerged from Africa but approximately 100,000 years ago and replaced all the rest.

Stringer's thesis was based on the study of bones. The occasion for Stringer's *Observer* article is research published the previous week using DNA samples from bones. These studies by Alan Wilson's team at the University of Berkeley would seem to confirm Stringer's hypothesis that Europeans could not claim a separate line of descent from Neanderthals. This new evidence appears to establish that we must all have had a common ancestor: 'an African Eve, that had strolled *our* homeland a mere 200,000 years ago'. The image of a beautiful African woman walking tall and strong across thousands of miles we today call Europe is gloriously appealing. What was her name? Was she called Eve? Is it important what she was called? What would she feel if she returned today to find that some of her ancestors were enslaved, colonized, ethnically cleansed, subjected to rape, murder, holocausts, and reduced to impoverished masses, largely because they were assumed to be 'different'. With which mother's tears would she cry? What collective achievements or acts of love, kindness, compassion, sensuality, beauty or creativity could we name that would bring a smile to her face? 'Mother, are we all the same or different?' How would she/you reply?

the enigma of Jean

Jean unexpectedly entered my universe one Sunday morning nearly 2 years ago. Today we 'inhabit' Southall together as she 'lives' in the intimacy of my memory. I never met her. She was clearly an 'ajnabi'. But, somehow she had not felt like 'ghair'. I wanted to know what had made her hate Southall, a place which I had experienced so differently. I was also deeply touched by her words: 'I feel alone'. I had heard that note on the lips of several Asian mothers I had interviewed that summer so long ago as they traced memories of rural Punjab or East Africa, places where they grew up. They spoke of the pain of separation from family, friends and the land they had known as 'home'; recounted the hardship of manual labour in London factories combined with the demands of 'woman's work' in the household; and, they described the pleasures as well as the trials and tribulations of having teenage children, just as Jean did. Their lives changed so radically when they boarded that plane to England. Stepping into Jean's neighbourhood was pretty traumatic for them. But, in time, Southall had become home and their locally born children were now approaching school leaving age.

There was so much that all women in Southall 'objectively' shared. But we do not 'live' lives objectively, nor is this a straightforward question of false consciousness, as we have seen.

Tim Lott's book, as one might expect, is not so much about his mother as it is about his own attempt to make sense of her suicide. Within its own terms, this is an honest, meticulous, deeply moving account of a son's inquest into his mother's death through a reconstruction of his family biography. It is a gripping narrative of the changing features of class during this century as 'lived' by an extended family. It is a chronicle of the upper or well-off sections of the working class who are listed as C2 on the Registrar General's classification of occupation, a group with more money than the Ds and Es, and a whole lot more ambition to succeed. Jean had been an attractive young woman with a beautiful cascade of chestnut brown hair which she loses in the early years of her married life due to alopecia. From then on, she wore a wig and never let anyone, including her husband and her children, see her without the wig. She even slept with a head scarf knotted tight in 'gypsy style'. What must it have felt like to live in fear of the 'wig' coming off? What constructions of female 'beauty' did Jean's mind occupy that she lived in terror of her 'camouflage' being discovered? It is only after her death that her son discovers how, as part of the treatment for alopecia, Jean had been prescribed a tranquillizer that was powerful enough to be used in serious cases of epilepsy. Later, for years, she was put on drugs normally used in cases of schizophrenia. The doctor's note speaks of 'emotional factors playing a part' in the condition that resulted in her hair loss.

What *was* Jean's condition?! The wider ramifications of this question are such that the question itself becomes virtually impossible to answer. Her suicide note points to a deep sense of alienation:

> I cannot keep up with this pretense. We have had so many happy year's (unhappy years?) and I can see the strain this is having on you (the husband), in the end you will grow to hate me. So it is time to get out of your life. You have so much to give such a bright mind and I am holding you back. (comments in parenthesis added)

How far was the husband's 'lived' masculinity implicated in Jean's demise? This is not a question of apportioning blame, but rather a point about the psychological and emotional fallout of 'living' social relations of gender where the trope of 'good wife' works to make the woman feel so hopelessly inadequate that she must feel that she is 'in his way'.

In all this, Jean still remains an enigma, as she properly should. Who am I to 'analyse' Tim Lott's memory of a kindly and devoted mother? I still do not know how 'my kind' — the Asians — featured in her life world. *The Scent of Dried Roses* is largely silent about the questions that exercise me, which 'interpellate' me as a racialized gendered subject. Following Ruth Frankenberg, one could easily 'read' this book as a form of 'whiteness' that is blissfully oblivious of the 'social geographies of race' (Frankenberg, 1993: 54) which constitute 'white' as a privileged signifier. What are the implications of this repression? I believe that the effects of both 'writing out' and 'being written out' are devastating for all concerned. The *repressed* eventually returns.

There is such a great deal of, otherwise complex and sophisticated, writing published today that still continues to 'forget' its own constitution in and through the discursive interstices of 'race'. Lott is very aware of the nuances of how class colours life but without acknowledging the 'colour' of his own class as compared to that of 'people of colour'. He knows that, as Annette Kuhn argues, class is not only about income, the nature of your job, your accent, how you dress or how you furnish your home. It is more than that for: 'it is something under your skin, in your reflexes, in your psyche, at the very core of your being' (Kuhn, 1995: 98). Precisely! But, class does not operate independently of other axes of differentiation. It is gendered, raced, sexualized and so on, in precisely the same way. Accept that colour-based racialization is not merely *under the skin*. The colour of our skin is exactly what 'colours' us, our very being, across assymetrical power relations. Lott speaks of how he and his two brothers loathed Southall, mentions the Asian presence in passing and declares that the Whites and Asians were insular communities who were merely indifferent to one another. Is it mere indifference that leads to narratives such as those quoted above? Lott says that he and his brothers did not leave Southall 'because we disliked Asians':

> No, we bolted because Southall was a dump, because it was nowhere, like most of subtopian England. We hated it for the reasons we imagined our parents liked it — because it was predictable, safe, conservative and limited in scale and possibility. We hated because we could see that it didn't know what it was, or where it belonged, or what it was for.
>
> (Lott, 1996: 29)

There is not the space here to fully address this perfectly plausible commentary on 'escapes', but can it really be understood independently of the resentful Englishness, discussed earlier, articulated by his peers and their parents who could not 'bolt'; or, indeed, outside the context of his mother's attempt at 'final escape'. In any case, with regard to Jean here, I am far more concerned about the genealogy of 'staying put' in the 'diaspora space' (Brah, 1996) of Southall. Lott continues:

> But Jean stayed, tending her isolated front garden, as the other gardens were paved over for car-parking space, as Sikh traditional styles — saris, turbans, salwar and kameez, dhupatas and guths — became more familiar sights than Aran sweaters or M&S belted raincoats. She would nod and say hello, always be polite and friendly, chat over the fence to Mr and Mrs Mukhrejee at No. 29. Perhaps, she was secretly prejudiced, although she never said anything.
>
> (Lott, 1996: 29)

Perhaps, she was not 'prejudiced' at all, if she never expressed any such sentiment even to her loved ones. This is important to me. Like many of you, I have read scholarly treatises on prejudice and racism. I even confess to writing them! But, I have this fantasy that some disclosures — especially in relation to deep-seated feelings about issues of such unmentionables as racism or homophobia — are shared as secrets within the intimate space of friendship, family and 'community'. My study in Southall had offered me some glimpses, but I did not have access to the 'intimate' history of such phenomena. I think I had hoped that Tim Lott's book would provide me that entrée. I am none the wiser about Jean, except for what is contained in the above quite telling observation by her son. Her map of suburban England had radically changed, due to a million reasons: global and local economic restructuring; major political changes such as the impact of Thatcherism; the impact of new information technologies on daily life; and the broader social influence of late twentieth-century formations of globalization. There had been major cultural shifts rendering her kind of femininity in crisis (cf. Steedman, 1986; Hall, 1992; Skeggs, 1997). All this clearly had a deep and profound effect on her. The growing presence of Asians might have been disconcerting to her; they (we) might have assumed iconic significance within her understanding of these topographies of change. But, Jean did not demonize Asian presence. She did not blame 'us' for everything that had gone wrong in her life. OK, we did not become intimate. But, nor did she treat me as a 'ghair'. In my story she becomes 'apni' (the feminine form of the term).

I began this meditation with an invitation for you to write back. I hope that you will respond and participate in this discussion. It has taken me nearly 2 years to reach this point in the narrative. I have managed to complete other projects since then but 'Jean' and her pain (my pain?) has been much more difficult to write about. Why? I keep thinking about how equally painful it had been to read Tony Morrison's *Beloved*. But, what a wonderful title — *Beloved*! Wonderful because it heals even as it opens all the intimate wounds. So, as Ann Michaels says:

> Questions without answers must be asked very slowly ... It's Hebrew tradition that forefathers (sic) are referred to as 'we', not 'they' ... This encourages empathy and a responsibility to the past (all our pasts, I hope, for this is crucial if we are not to collapse into ethnic cleansings of all kinds) but, more important, it collapses time ... If moral choices are eternal individual actions take on immense significance no matter how small: not for this life only.
>
> (Michaels, 1998[1996]: 159; comment in parenthesis added)

notes

Avtar Brah teaches at Birkbeck College, University of London. This article arises out of material presented in 1997 at the conference titled 'Feminist

Transformations', convened by the Women's Studies Institute at the University of Lancaster. I wish to thank Ann Phoenix for her insightful conversations about points raised here, and for her helpful comments on an earlier version of the article.

references

Althusser, L. (1965) *For Marx*, London: Allan Lane.

Althusser, L. (1971) *Lenin and Philosophy and Other Essays*, London: New Left Books.

Bethnal Green and Stepney Trades Council (1978) *Blood on the Streets*.

Brah, A. (1979) *Inter-Generational and Inter-Ethnic Perceptions: A Comparative Study of English and Asian Adolescents and Their Parents in Southall*, PhD thesis, University of Bristol.

Brah, A. (1987) 'Journey to Nairobi' in Grewal, S. *et al.* (1987) editors, *Charting the Journey: Writings by Black and Third World Women*, London: Sheba Press.

Brah, A. (1996) *Cartographies of Diaspora, Contesting Identities*, London and New York: Routledge.

Campaign Against Racism and Fascism/Southall Rights (1981) *Southall: Birth of a Black Community*, London: Institute of Race Relations and Southall Rights.

Frankenberg, R. (1993) 'Growing up White: feminism, racism, and the social geography of childhood' *Feminist Review*, No. 45.

Hall, C. (1992) *White, Male, and Middle Class: Explorations in Feminism and History*, London: Verso.

Hall, S. (1980) 'Race, articulation and societies structured in dominance' in *Sociological Theories: Race and Colonialism*, Paris: UNESCO.

Haraway, D.J. (1992) 'Ecce homo, ain't (ar'n't) I a woman, and inappropriate/d others': the human in a post-humanist landscapes' in Butler, J. and Scott, J.W. (1992) editors, *Feminists Theorize the Political*, New York: Routledge.

Harrison, P. (1974) 'The patience of Southall' *New Society*, 4 April, Vol. 28, No. 600.

Hindess, B. and Hirst, P. (1975) *Pre-Capitalist Modes of Production*, London: Routledge & Kegan Paul.

Kirwan, P. (1965) *Southall: A Brief History*, Middlesex: Southall Public Libraries.

Kuhn, A. (1995) *Family Secrets: Acts of Memory and Imagination*, London: Verso.

Laclau, E. and Mouffe, C. (1985) *Hegemony and Socialist Strategy: Towards a Radical Democratic Politics*, London: Verso.

Lott, T. (1996) *The Scent of Dried Roses*, Viking.

Massey, D. (1999) 'Imagining globalisation: power-geometries of time-space' in Brah, A., Hickman, M.J. and Mac an Ghaill, M. (1999) editors, *Future Worlds: Migration, Environment and Globalisation*, London: Macmillan.

Michaels, A. (1998[1996]) *Fugitive Pieces*, London: Bloomsbury Paperbacks.

Morrison, T. (1987) *Beloved*, London: Chatto & Windus.

Rose, S. (1997) *Lifelines: Biology, Freedom, Determinism*, London: Allen Lane Penguin Press.

Roy, A. (1997) *The God of Small Things*, London: Flamingo.

Skeggs, B. (1997) *Formations of Class and Gender: Becoming Respectable*, London: Sage.

Southall Black Sisters (1989) *Against the Tide*, London: SBS.

Steedman, C. (1986) *Landscape for a Good Woman: A Story of Two Lives*, London: Virago.

doi:10.1057/fr.2011.73

Avtar Brah's cartographies: moment, method, meaning

Stuart Hall

abstract

The following draws out a few points that suggest an inner coherence in the midst of the rich diversity of questions Avtar Brah addresses. One critical factor is that Brah's work appears at a specific historical 'moment' — a simultaneously political, historical and theoretical conjuncture — the diasporic. The diaspora — as an emergent space and an interpretive frame — unpicks the claims made for the unities of culturally homogeneous, racially purified identities, and constitutes the moment of the problematic of the subject — when critical thought comes face to face with the perplexing interface between the social and the psychic. Brah confronts the necessarily complex and contradictory specificities of differentiated subjectivities in the diasporic frame within a distinct 'methodology' — analytic and interpretive. The very structures 'out there', which have so often been thought of as determining, are understood as themselves providing frameworks of meaning, as having an internal psychic and discursive dimension. Avtar Brah is one of the few who have begun to capture such a double inscription through ongoing research. Such is particularly evident in 'The Scent of Memory', and it is through a reading of that essay that Brah's distinct 'methodology' is presented — an approach which is sensitive to the always already contradictory condition of 'reality'. What I suggest of Brah's 'methodology' is that it is a practice that has significant consequences for the meaning and value placed on social contexts, for the 'presence' and 'absence' of information and knowledge in interpretation and analysis, a practice that we might call diasporic reasoning.

keywords

diaspora; subject; interpretive method

(27–38) © 2012 Feminist Review. 0141-7789/12 www.feminist-review.com

concluding remarks at the end of a day celebrating her work[1]

1 Keynote presented at '"Race", Gender, Postcoloniality: A colloquium for Avtar Brah' on 3rd July 2009.

Is there anything more to say? This has been an extremely thought-provoking, multifaceted day, and that's only appropriate because of the work, life and politics, of the person whom we are celebrating. Much has already been said about the richness and the originality of Avtar Brah's work: one thinks especially in the sociological fields of the studies of social inequality and ethnically and gendered labour markets; and in relation to wider issues, her important theoretical contributions to debates on feminism, race/ethnicity and multi-culturalism. Much has already been said, in particular by her sisters, her intellectual peers and interrogators, about the fruitful intersection in her work between politics and theory. I personally would have liked to hear more about one key, troubling and recalcitrant problem to which she has given long and considered attention — the question feminist theorists call 'inter-sectionality': the tensions and contradictions set in motion among groups involved in social movements and the practice of politics by competing claims, and sometimes contradictory interests, commitments and forms of identification. (The most startling example is the dilemma posed for black women who stand with other feminists in critiquing the sexist and patriarchal practices of (black) men while identifying with the latter's struggles against racism — a source of searching reflection by women during recent decades and a key example of the new 'politics of difference', which emerges with the new social movements.)

In short, it's impossible to try to effect a summary. So, in closing the day, I can only try to draw out a few points in the course of acknowledging the many ways I have learnt from Avtar's work, understood it in my own way and tried to practice it in so far as I understood it. And to remark that, despite the many differences in life experience — and she and I have talked about and thought a lot about difference — how deeply I've felt connected to and implicated in her project.

I won't attempt to refer in detail to what many other people have said during the day. But I've been looking again at the range of approaches and ideas brought together by her wonderful book, *Cartographies of Diaspora*. The title itself gives a clue to the many themes, foci and frameworks of analysis that have characterised her thinking; above all, the non-essentialised, non-reductive ways they have intersected, and displaced one another at different stages of her work. What I'm looking for is an underlying figure to characterise what pulls these elements together. There's a wonderful story by one of my favourite novelists, Henry James (on whose international novels, believe it or not, I started to work for my DPhil.) called *The Figure In the Carpet*. Of course, there is in fact no single pattern, nothing that draws all the threads together. But as you read the work, you can't help but feel there's an underlying 'figure of thought' here, which is shared by all that Avtar says and has written. I don't want to reduce the work to it, but I do want to insist that this sense of an inner coherence in the midst of the diversity of questions she addresses is not just incidental. I would argue that there is a 'figure in the carpet' at work across many levels and periods of her work, across many moments of her political intervention and in other ways. I'm going to try to characterise, briefly, some of the elements that go into the making of that figure.

One critical factor is that her work appears at a certain specific historical moment and is an intervention in that moment. She speaks of it and simultaneously is formed by it. She develops it, in practice and in thought, above all, wrestles with its difficulties. She is not, of course, a monument to it. But her particular way of thinking belongs to this 'moment', which is simultaneously a political, historical and theoretical conjuncture. This is the moment of *the diasporic*.

This is a new, emergent space of inquiry. This is 'diaspora' as a specific structure of transformations, displacements and condensations, which gain a historical specificity in the moment of post-war global migration. 'Diaspora' defines a new emergent space. It is one of the interpretive frames, as she put it herself, for analysing the economic, political and cultural modalities of historically specific forms and sites of migrancy. The word both responds to and goes beyond the reductive boundaries of what at the time we knew as identity politics. Identities are summoned up, mobilised, transformed and interrogated in this process. But the search, and even more, the discovery of an essential identity that would condense all the diasporic lines and provide a warrant for their trans-historical authenticity is doomed to failure.

Diasporas — always in formation, with their origins and sources always already elsewhere, and their futures still emergent — are not amenable, either in theory or practice, to the 'logic of the same'. With positive and negative consequences, both diasporic communities and ways of thinking are permanently shadowed by the question of differences, which stubbornly refuses to go away. We have to go on thinking and acting, not against, but *with* difference — without, of course, simply collapsing into it in a riot of relativism.

Kobena Mercer (1998) calls the diasporic a 'syncretic dynamic' set in motion by de-colonisation and trans-global migration. It takes place, not 'after' in a simple chronological sense, but *in the aftermath of* — that is, 'post' — colonisation/de-colonisation. It arises from the transformation of power relations between 'the west' and 'the rest', which for so long stabilized the shape of the global system. It references the way in which people and communities in the poor two-thirds of the world have been broken up and displaced — by the rampant poverty, hunger, disease, worklessness, civil war, environmental disasters, the corruption and venality of leading elites associated with global inequality and underdevelopment. This process is driven by the new forms of global capitalism that have emerged with globalisation, by so-called 'structural adjustment programmes' and pressure from the so-called 'international community' to open vulnerable economies to 'free trade', 'market forces' and unstoppable trans-national investment flows and to expose other ways of life to the full force of western culture. Working together, these forces have precipitated one of the greatest global movements of people we have ever seen in modern history.

The modern idea of diaspora is rooted in the inevitable 'clash of cultures', which is one of its inevitable consequences. A new stage of capitalist globalisation unsettles and reconfigures not only earlier imperial settlements, older structures of economic, cultural and ideological power, it also destroys homes, settled communities and ways of life and precipitates vulnerable minorities into what the philosopher, Agamben, calls the 'bare life' conditions of the *favellas* and refuse dump 'cities', the dollar-a-day sweatshops, the transit and refugee camps, the twilight asylum encampments, the detention centres and low wage, invisibility of the black economies of the advanced world.

What's more, the idea of diaspora troubles the notions of cultural origin, of 'roots', of primordial identities and authenticity. It unpicks the claims made for the unities of culturally homogeneous, racially purified national cultures and identities. It reaches naturally for the messy territory of the multicultural. It introduces the logic of translation and entanglement. As Kobena Mercer put it, it 'critically appropriates elements from the master codes of the dominant culture and "creolizes" them ... re-articulating their symbolic meaning otherwise'. It is the moment of the 'here' *and* 'there', of the double inscription, of double consciousness and multiple belongingnesses.

It is also the context in which no one social division is able to explain or account for power relations in 'the social totality'. It is the moment when the politics of race, gender and class come together in a new, powerful, unstoppable, but unstable and explosive articulation, displacing and at the same time complexifying each other. It transforms the nature of social forces and social movements. Accordingly, it bypasses existing forms of theorising. It does not provide us with ready-made answers, but it sets us new questions, which proliferate across older frames of thought, social engagement and political activity.

It's also the moment of the problematic of the subject — when critical thought comes face to face with the perplexing interface between the social and the psychic, the objective and the subjective in the historical play of difference. That's almost a quote from Avtar too. Neither side of this framework can ever be given a wholly determining priority over the other. Neither can be thought in exclusion of the other. Neither is the same as the other. No methodology attuned to the one can have a singular totalising effect or authority over the field as a whole. The whole can only be grasped conceptually in its double-sided, complex, combined and uneven, unsettled and displaced character.

At the centre of this diasporic frame emerged the idea of a gendered 'subject', which was simultaneously social and psychic, interpretive and engaged; and a 'politics of the subject' that depended on the idea, not that subjectivity determined us 'in the last instance', but that subjectivity was constructed; and that the production of subjectivity is itself a complicated and contested process, implicating and implicated in the social, the psychic and the political, and always unfinished.

Some current trends in psychoanalysis anxiously set up what is in effect a 'Berlin Wall' between the psychic and the social, between the psychoanalytic and the discursive unconscious. The former concerns the 'forgetting' of the rules, which govern the production of the inner life of psychic subjectivity; the latter is the 'forgetting' of the rules by which social subjectivity is constituted. It is true that the two sides cannot be directly read off against one another. The bar of the unconscious has fallen. The challenge is nevertheless to find ways of thinking them in their interconnections. Psychoanalysis has done tremendous work in teasing out the processes of internalisation, projection, symbolisation, condensation and displacement, by which, as it were, an inner psychic world comes into existence, and of courageously charting the inevitable success and failures of the process. But the 'politics of the subject' also crucially depends on how this still-emerging subject is interpellated into, 'hailed' by or invited to take up subject positions in social, political and ideological discourses. No doubt the 'failures' of the one relate to those of the other and shape how those positions are inhabited. But it cannot be thought as a relation of one-way determination. (What would be the value in critiquing base-up economic reductionism only to collapse into inside-out psychoanalytic reductionism?) Thinking the relation between the psychic subject and social subject requires that double inscription which both Althusser and Foucault — in their different ways — identified. Judith Butler calls it 'the ambivalence of subjection' — on the one hand the processes of subject formation and the emergence of subjectivity, and on the other the process by which the subject is 'subjected to' discourses that have an intrinsically social character. (One might be tempted to call the latter process 'the formation of the social subject proper' — except that, in Freud's terms, the 'social' is already inside!)

The preoccupation with difference in this double-sided diasporic perspective produces a concern with questions of class, gender and race, with the social as always a gendered, classed and raced terrain. Every social relationship or problem takes place in a social space that is socially, sexually and economically differentiated. However, just to take one example, the approaches that conceptualise racism — a massively important historical force — through simple black/white binaries, negativity and positivity, superiority and inferiority, inclusion and exclusion, are certainly real enough, necessary and have to be addressed in their own terms, even if they are not sufficient. It is important not to fall into the post-structuralist trap of thinking that because we have exposed binary forms of conceptualization, then binary structures in the 'real world' have somehow been dispersed. But we cannot deny that these processes also give rise to deeply imprinted but often unconscious or disavowed racialised practices, which nevertheless inhabit spaces of deep ambivalence within us and have profound social consequences. These require – in thought, at least – our getting beyond the binaries.

Let us, for a moment, think of what has been called a politics of race and racism from that double point of view. Neither racialised or gendered politics and structures have unitary consequences. We can only really understand what they are when we can tease out their specificities, their intricate complexities and contradictory effects.

It is the necessary complexity, the necessary contradictoriness, which Avtar's work courageously and rigorously confronts. This demonstrates at one and the same time how her powerful analytic and sensitive interpretative skills work together. They're not, of course, applied in a linear way, one after another, because that would destroy the whole point. There is no sense that the analytic impulse replaces or substitutes for the interpretative or vice versa. Indeed, one of the key things that she is saying is that the very structures 'out there', which we have thought of as in some way determining, can only be understood as themselves providing frameworks of meaning; that's to say, as having an internal, psychic and discursive dimension at all times.

What interests me is how these different emphases are deployed differently at different moments in Avtar's work. The earlier work – on employment, on the labour market, on class and gender divisions, on working women and youth unemployment – was of immense sociological importance in its own right. However, in later work, they return as the frameworks through which at every point Avtar's subjects are making sense of the world they inhabit. There is no discourse or discursive element that is not at the same time a structure that positions us. There is no transitive independence for the subject. I am not saying there is no free thought or unsponsored ideas – though I'm not sure there are ideas that have no presupposition, no conditions of existence. At least, I don't know many [laughs]. However, whether there are or are not, these two processes are absolutely locked into one another. Think of race or of patriarchy, of their internal, compulsive shapes and external structures; of how at the same time they are what we 'live' and how we make our own kind of sense of life. They frame ways of thinking and feeling and experiencing, which are not always cognitively or consciously available. The 'maps of meaning' that enable us to become subjects are what in another context we would call the 'culture'. And yet at that very moment when these structures of exclusion, of superiority and inferiority, of marginalisation, of otherness are operating, the troubled subject comes to life. I think Avtar Brah is one of the few people who has begun to capture that double inscription in an actual, ongoing body of research and thinking.

I would like to demonstrate this briefly with a concrete example. I said to Gail Lewis when we came in, 'the one thing I would really like to say to the audience is, go home and read Avtar's essay on "The Scent of Memory" '. In fact, everybody seems to be reading 'The Scent of Memory'. I can't help feeling this is because, if you read it, you come as close as you can to feeling on your pulse, rather than just knowing rationally, what it is like to think complexity in this intricate multi-layered way. I know you all know it well, but I do recommend that you have another look, particularly at *how* it works — what we used to call its 'methodology'.

It's a formidable piece of work; formidable because its claims for itself are so modest. It doesn't have the requisite theoretical sections, which underpin scholarly credentials. I love the fact that the theoretical section, beautiful though it is, is locked into one and a half pages — *exemplary for all of your graduate students!* [laughter]. It doesn't bristle with trendy references. It identifies only a few, selective theoretical sources. I am particularly interested in that because, in fact, they are theoretical sources, which she and I came to share, though from very different starting points. They include Althusser's notions of contradiction, overdetermination and interpellation — the way in which the subject is hailed into place inside structures and discourses; Gramsci's ideas about 'common sense' and 'conjuncture' — the coming together of different forces and contradictions, which 'fuse' in a ruptural unity. So I was glad to see them there. But I'm not recommending you re-read the piece just in order to go back over that long, winding road to rediscover the gurus of the past!

You'll remember that the trigger for 'The Scent of Memory' is a review in *The Observer* of an autobiography of a young white man, Tim Lott, in which he tries to make sense of his mother's suicide. She was a respectable, white, working-class woman who lived in Southall. There are very few clues, which suggest that these memories and reflections are a fruitful starting point for a profound examination. But there are words she says that hint at and express her loneliness, her sense of isolation and her mourning. And they do conjure up, on the edge or horizon of language, her sense of loss of a space, especially a loss of the Southall, which she and other people of her age knew. That's all there is. And then there is Tim Lott's reflection on all that.

What sort of discourse is this? Is it the informal, unthinking language of racist 'common sense'? Is it, even in its contemporary, tidied up form, the pseudo-neutral language of immigration, with all its treacherous currents? Is it a reworking of an old working-class structure of feeling about 'Us' and 'Them'? Why is it different from the discourses of the BNP? Is it an innocent but misplaced nostalgia for 'the good old days', which – as Raymond Williams pointed out – have always just passed away? Isn't it what Paul Gilroy (2004) calls an example of British postcolonial melancholia – the unrequited mourning for a lost object of desire? It is interesting that both Tim and his mother, in different ways and from different positions, speak of a Southall that is 'gone' and whose disappearance has something to do with what has come in its place. Are the two actually the same? Do they inhabit the same structure of feeling?

How do we start to make sense of this – or rather the end of this – life? How are we to understand her sadness and how this relates in turn to the largely unspoken way she responds to the Southall she perceives to have changed? Taken over, taken away by the presence of large numbers of 'other' kinds of people. What is the nature of the 'sameness' that is being mourned? What is the nature of the difference that has intruded? To put that more mundanely, how do we analyse these 'data'? Where are the skills? What is the method?

These symptomatic bits and pieces are the materials Avtar works from in this essay. She doesn't want to discover more about the family and their socio-economic background, or how they love one another, or don't, as most families do and don't. Class is relevant, but it doesn't automatically explain how things are seen: despite all they share in terms of background, Tim and his mother see things differently. What is gained by simply labelling it 'racist talk'? There doesn't seem much point in simply denouncing or unmasking it. We know all about that already. What Avtar is doing is trying to *get inside* the way external social change reverberates on the inner strings of the heart.

So she looks for the connections, the resonances. Fortunately there are some. They connect her – the interviewer – to the many interviews she conducted in Southall, often with white parents, Asians and children in the mid-70s, which formed part of her PhD thesis. This is the kind of good fortune that researchers rarely are permitted to experience.

Something connects because something troubles her about the way the pieces don't fit together. And so she goes analogically to evidence of a similar kind – conversations, discussions, interviews with a range of other people all responding to roughly the same situation. This is what *contextualisation* means. It is not an inert background sketch, of 'the-history-was-like-this' or 'this-is-what-the-period-was-like' kind. This is the contextualisation that takes seriously the task of showing concretely the mediations between one set of subjective under-standings with or operating from inside another set. This procedure constitutes the analysis as an interpretive field. She draws on a 'structure of feeling' – a range of meanings and feelings that seem to be shared between various people whom she's talked to before. These understandings and feelings always carry in part unconscious meanings and investments. They are always embedded, not just in the things people do or say, but in the way they say it and so often in what they do not or cannot say at all. The absent/presences are key parts of the 'data' too.

At this point, Avtar draws a distinction — which I think is seminal to her work — between the kind of knowledge which these interpretive observations produce, which can only be 'read' in order to be understood, which speak through indirection and silence as much as anything they record, and what we might expect a more 'rational', empirical process of scientific reflection to do. I don't know how much Avtar is attached to Sociology as a 'scientific discourse'. That is one of the secrets between us that I hope she retains forever! [laughter] I want to say the narratives in the interpretive work done here — the interplay between what is said and not said, the silences of the son about the mother and of the mother about the world that makes her isolated and desperate enough to commit suicide, but which she cannot name — is subtle, insightful, in the best sense, *explanatory*. Yes, but is it sociological analysis? The fathers of the discipline would say, probably not ('Corrupted by Cultural Studies', they might add). And, in this instance at least, thank God for that. [laughter]

What does this approach tell us? Where is the defeat? Why do people think there is one? I won't attempt an answer here. I just want to remind you that Southall is a typical inner city area colonized especially by Asian families: a poor, struggling, mixed up place — but also full of life, colour and activity. How does one come to feel that this complex multi-cultural reality is a defeat? Well, it depends who for? Understanding is relational. It follows the logic of positionality, of a 'politics of location'.

It is also profoundly shaped by a structure of memory. What Avtar begins to tease out is the particular perception of the past and the structure of memory, which sustains this troubled sense of change and how it's experienced. But how much do they know about the past? How are the intruders seen? Who are they? How are they received or othered? How are the larger social processes, which have positioned them, like immigration, like the break-up of working-class communities, understood? Can they be understood within the old colonial relationship between Britain and the colonial work? Or can they only be understood and explained within the changing experiences of social classes and ethnicities. A multi-layered discourse is the only approach that can come to terms with this kind of complexity. It's different, of course, from enlightenment rationality, but it isn't a form of analysis that is without its reasons. It has a 'logic' to it — a way of connecting one thing to another. It has a way of reading between the lines; reading otherwise, against the grain. It is a hermeneutic discourse, which embodies in its actual operations the contradictory rationales of race, gender, class and ethnicity in the postcolonial specificity of a place called Southall.

Another framework she introduces is the *politicisation* of these contradictory frames in the late 1970s and 1980s: the rise of the National Front, the formation of the Indian Workers Association, the arrival of new migrant groups, the confrontations, both on racism and on gender, the death of Blair Peach, the thirtieth anniversary of which we've just 'celebrated' (if you can call it that). I don't want to speak at length of this politicisation. We're still trying to make sense of a moment in a life and of a passing remark the woman makes about the environment, which she has chosen to leave, symbolically, through her suicide. That is all. It's virtually the only clue we have. We don't have a plethora of empirical evidence. There isn't much background information. We must make as much use as we can of information and knowledge. But for the purposes at hand here, they have to be understood as interpretative structures, which organise the meaning of a life and give shape to the relationships between groups of people who are subjected to them. These interpretive structures cannot depend entirely on objective background knowledge. We must find ways of using that knowledge, but in itself it cannot explain what is going on. The background is not the end of the story.

The end of the story is to return to where she began — the enigma of Jean; to return to that enigma with the sense that how much of what we think we know may be an illusion. Avtar has tried to read what evidence we have, and she's tried to read *through* even the evidence we don't have. But the idea that at the end we've come to be able to fully read Jean is not the case. We don't ever *fully* understand, or completely totalise, the thing that has triggered off an inquiry in our minds. She cannot finally be read, and nor can Southall. It is not an unfinished project. It is not a question of what we think of it or whether we approve. That is for another occasion and — when it comes — political responsibility requires that we do not miss or evade it. However, *this* moment of the analysis constitutes a return to a complex but still finally undisclosed, undecided life, and the subject who is the bearer of all these processes, structures, positions and feelings.

I'm not describing a methodology in the proper sense. It's not a set of procedures that you can take home and apply to the next problem on the desk. In part, this is because it is an approach, which, against the sociological consensus, regards reality as *always contradictory*. Contrary to expectations, so-called 'reality' always present a face to us, which is this-and-that, double-sided. So our approach must be one that refuses to take comfort from the 'recognition' of what we already know (Sartre once called this the sign of a lazy Marxism!). Nor can we take pride from some form of patriarchal theoretical 'mastery'. Instead, the language breaks on you. And the language breaks, in my view (and I've been listening to language break throughout the day), because it has to address, without final resolution, the inevitable complexity of the world constructed as it is, materially, politically, socially, psychically and culturally.

This requires the courage, from time to time, to think 'both/and'. Where else could a body of work, research and reflection like hers be expected to end?

To close, I want to return to what we can learn from the modesty of the critical theoretical intervention, which I've referred to. As I've said before, I am particularly stimulated by the fact that the theoretical scaffold section is so short. I can't think of anybody in the room, who approaches structural Marxism, Gramscianism, interpellation, post-structuralism, psychoanalysis, discourse analysis, feminism, postcolonialism and so on, who would be satisfied with a page and a half! But she is, because it is not the main purpose of this work to produce critical thought in the form of a self-sufficient Theory (big T). This is not what the exercise is about.

Of course, the task cannot be done without theorising, because we've got to think behind or get beyond the chaotic way experience — reality — presents itself. Foucault thought concepts were tools to think with. Marx said concepts are like microscopes. They allow us to alter the magnification so that we can look behind the 'obvious' ways society offers itself to us, and penetrate its deceptive surfaces. He advised that the only way to do this was to add what he called 'more and more determinations' — greater historical specificity — in order to produce 'the concrete in thought'.

I want to end by urging you to read her essay again [laughter]. Go home, and read it now! It's in *Feminist Review* — where else? Submit yourself to what the way of reading produces. It produces an understanding of what is going on in the minds of the Southall postcolonial diaspora. Simultaneously, it produces a kind of methodology of reading who this woman is, why she positions herself and is positioned in this particular way, why she perceives social change in the way that she does, and perhaps why she is partly destroyed by it. When you've done that, don't apply to the Economic and Social Research Council for another grant [laughter]. Your PhD supervisor will insist that the first chapter of the thesis must give us the methodology and review the literature. Well, tough luck, you only have a page and a half to do it in [laughter].

However, you may also come to appreciate what I think is an essential part of Avtar's 'logic of inquiry'. It has to do with the way her modesty of approach, her submission to the difficulty of reading and interpreting a social situation, a historical path, an individual life and so on, runs side by side with the most ambitious and adventurous project of engagement and political commitment. She and I have shared many of the moments I've discussed, but most of all we have shared this practice of 'diasporic reasoning'. I know her 'moment'. I've not lived it in the way in which she has. But I know how hard it is to try to understand it, and I know what an achievement it is to have done that.

author biography

Stuart Hall is Emeritus Professor of Sociology, The Open University, and has lived in the United Kingdom since 1951. Born in Jamaica, educated at Oxford, he was founder-editor of *New Left Review*, Director of the Centre for Cultural Studies, Birmingham University, chair of boards of Iniva: The Institute for the International Visual Arts and Autograph: The Association of Black Photographers and was on the lead team of Rivington Place, the Diversity Visual Arts centre. Publications include essays on race, identity, multi-culturalism, politics and cultural theory in many publications, including *Stuart Hall: Critical Essays in Cultural Studies* and *Difference: Contemporary Photography and Black Identity*.

references

Gilory, P. (2004) *After Empire: Melancholia, or Convival Culture*, London and New York: Routledge.

Mercer, K. (1988) 'Diaspora Culture and the Dialogic Imagination', in Chant, M.B. and Andrade-Watkins, C. (1988) editors, *Blackframes: Critical Perspectives on Black Independent Cinema*, London and Cambridge, MA: MIT Press.

doi:10.1057/fr.2011.65

activism, imagination and writing: Avtar Brah reflects on her life and work with Les Back

Les Back and Avtar Brah

abstract

Avtar Brah (AB) was interviewed by Les Back (LB) on 3 July 2009 at a colloquium held to mark her retirement where, *inter alia*, her work was discussed. The interview is a reflection on her politics, activism and scholarship. It touches on some key moments of her life.

keywords

gender; race; ethnicity; politics; solidarity; difference

(39–51) © 2012 Feminist Review. 0141-7789/12 www.feminist-review.com

introduction by Les Back

Before we hear from Avtar, I would like to offer a few preliminary thoughts. So much of today's event has been a tribute to Avtar Brah's work as a writer and activist and also the values she has given us and shown us by example. I have been struggling to think of what I might say myself by way of introduction to our conversation. It occurs to me that perhaps one of the greatest compliments that can be bestowed upon a writer is if her books are stolen from the library. More than one copy of Avtar's *Cartographies of Diaspora* (Brah, 1996) has disappeared from Goldsmith's College library where I have been teaching her work for over a decade. In preparation for today, I thought it would be good to reread *Cartographies*, but then I realised that I'd loaned the book to a student. The book had not been returned. So I dutifully found my way to Goldsmith's library and found this copy of Avtar's important and wonderful book. I'm not sure whether people at the back will be able to see this, but this book has been bruised by so many sets of eyes and handled by so many keen readers that its spine barely holds the pages together and it is almost falling to pieces. I think it is a symbol of the careful attention of your readership and just how many of us have found your thought useful, relevant and essential. One of the characteristics of Avtar's writing is her ability to combine political commitments with social investigation but she also combines artistic sensibilities with theoretical engagement. Perhaps, that is also why your book is read so intensely almost to the point of disintegration.

LB: *Could you start by telling us a little bit about the things in your early life that affected you and led you to your intellectual and political commitments?*

AB: Well, that question makes me think about the place where I grew up. I grew up in Uganda. It was still a British colony when I was a child there and we got political independence when I was a teenager. So one of the early things that influenced me was what we today call the social structure of a colonial society. I obviously didn't call it that then, but certainly it was a social structure in which you had Europeans at the top, you had Asians in the middle and Blacks at the bottom. This 'colonial sandwich' began to make me think about the ways in which inequalities in social life articulate and take shape. I didn't theorise it but I was beginning to be aware of that.

And then some of the early influences were novels and poetry, especially in my own mother tongue Punjabi. One of the influences was a Punjabi novelist called Nanak Singh. He wrote about Punjabi society in India. He was really a feminist writer because he wrote about the patriarchal, caste and class divisions in Punjab. And that made me think critically about what was going on in Punjab and also made me start considering my own position as a woman.

There was also an eighteenth-century poet, Waris Shah, who wrote a renowned book called *Heer Ranjha*, which somewhat resembles *Romeo and Juliet* in the sense that the central characters are two young people whose relationship is opposed by their families. The text is a historical, legal and moral narrative about Punjabi society. It uses Sharia for addressing questions of transgression of moral codes, as well as the issue of personal choice and liberation. It teaches you about the possibility and the limitations of transgression. The text is recited or sung and I grew up listening to it on the radio. It made quite an impact on me. It is a highly complex text, which touched me to the core. It is not straightforwardly a feminist text, but Heer's critique of her position as a woman had a singularly feminist message for me.

And then last but not least, there was a woman poet called Amrita Pritam. She writes as a feminist and she wrote a very famous poem about the Indian partition of 1947, and what happened to women during that partition. She talks about women who were abducted on both sides of the border between India and Pakistan, and how some of their families disowned them afterwards because they were 'soiled goods'. It's a very, very powerful poem, and it left a deep impression with me. So those are some of my earlier influences.

LB: *I think it's already been mentioned that you weave together your love of literature, your commitment to politics and your sociological imagination in your writing and research. I wanted to ask about your own experience of education. What was it like to study in the United States?*

AB: That was an important early influence as well, because I went to America as a scholarship student and I distinctly remember that when I was being interviewed for the scholarship I was asked by a member of the panel how I described myself and I said that I saw myself as a Ugandan of Asian descent. And I think that was my first experience of enunciating a political identity. This was in the context of a post-independence Uganda with a history of colonial relations in its immediate background. Hence, it was very, very important to me to have that kind of identity, to proclaim that identity. And later, when I've thought about questions of subjectivity, such experiences helped me to clarify in my mind the difference between subjectivity, with its unruly psychoanalytical connotations, and political identity, which is an avowed identity — you know, it's something you make your own in a conscious kind of way. So some of these early experiences helped me to think through theoretical and political concerns.

And when I went to America, during the late 1960s, it was, as we all know, a period of student politics, of the civil rights movement, the Black Power movement, the Flower Power movement and so on. And the political energy at the time just really swept me along with it and I was involved quite a lot in student politics. I was attracted both to the Flower Power politics, which were all about love and peace, and the Black Power movement, which was speaking about the harsh realities of, you know, class inequality and racial inequality. So I was kind of veering between the two, but never quite 'dropped out', as the Flower Power people were saying. All that was quite a formative experience for me in America.

LB: *I wonder if you could talk a little bit about that and your connection to Southall and also your bearing witness to those key political moments particularly 1979.*

AB: Well, I came to Britain in the early 1970s when, like America, Britain too was in the throes of protest politics. There was the anti-Vietnam War movement, the Campaign for Nuclear Disarmament, the Workers Industrial struggles, and the Women's Liberation Movement was just getting underway. I started working as a researcher at the Ethnic Relations Unit in Bristol University. But for that job I might never have worked in the academic field of race and ethnicity. Due to Idi Amin's expulsion of Asians from Uganda, I was made a stateless refugee. I suddenly found myself having to make a new life in Britain. And I had to start from scratch – all my friends, all my connections were in America. I started to look for a job and I saw this interviewer's post at Bristol and of course my knowledge of Punjabi and Urdu helped me to get that job. And through that I became involved in the whole area of race and ethnicity, both as an academic enterprise and as a politics. There was a senior colleague at Bristol for whom doing objective research meant that you did not have anything to do with the communities you were researching. So he was actively discouraging us from having any involvement in community politics. I found that hugely problematic and moved away from that kind of academic perspective on research.

I remember in 1977 a busload of us came from Bristol to Lewisham where there was a huge demonstration against the National Front. There was a major confrontation between the police and the protestors. It was frightening when the police charged at us on horseback. And of course the 1970s was also a period when there were all kinds of industrial strikes and some of them were led by Asian women, such as the ones at Imperial Typewriters in Leicester, the Chix Factory in Slough and the well-known massive struggle at Grunwick in London.

When all of that was happening, it really politicised me and gave me an insight into the workings of British society. I started my PhD in the middle of the seventies and came to Southall to do research as a PhD student. And then, a year later I came there to work as a community worker, because my research contract at Bristol University had ended. I gained quite a different insight from being a community worker and an activist rather than an academic. It just gave me a completely different lens onto social life. And that's how I was in Southall in 1979. The Asian and Black youth movements were beginning to emerge and there was an active Asian youth movement in Southall. But it was predominantly, not predominantly, but exclusively a male youth movement. On that historic day, the

National Front marched into Southall and the local community organisations decided to have a peaceful sit-in to demonstrate against the fascist organisation. But there was a massive police operation and I think something like 777 people were arrested and 344 were charged. So we were all involved in the campaigns to free the 344. And it was in the throes of that politics that Southall Black Sisters, a feminist collective of Asian and African-Caribbean descent women, was born. I was one of the founding members of Southall Black Sisters. A group of us had been meeting together to look at the particular issues that affected young Asian women and we were also sort of contesting the masculinist ethos of the Southall Youth Movement. We were trying to create a space where we could raise feminist issues as a Black women's group, using the term Black to highlight the specificity of the experience of racialisation in a postcolonial situation. But at the same time, we also worked with White women on common issues and with men. However, there were debates between Black and White feminists about a variety of exclusions, about theorising women's experience, and the whole question of the heterogeneity of the category woman and the power dynamics between different groups of women. So it was a kind of solidarity, but we also explored the things where we didn't agree, so both contestation and solidarity. 1979 was a deeply formative experience both politically and theoretically, because I was writing my PhD at the time. So it was a very, very important moment.

LB: *In many respects, that moment is the political touchstone of your influential essay 'The Scent of Memory'. But I just wondered what you had to say about your involvement with politics around that time which you just mentioned and how you reflect on that now.*

AB: Yes. Well, black politics was very important in my life as a young researcher with Asian people and people of African and Caribbean descent coming together and naming a colour that had been seen as a derogatory thing, giving it in turn a positive evaluation. But it was a different moment from America. Of course there were black politics going on there but the term 'black' had very different connotations in Britain. Black politics genuinely posed a serious challenge to the chromatism of the time and probably does so even today. But in the academy, these politics brought us into conflict with, how can I put it, some of the big professors within race relations. There was a conference, I think it was at Southampton, where there was a great deal of contestation between the scholars from the Centre for Cultural Studies at Birmingham University together with those from the Institute of Race Relations on the one hand, and some of these professors on the other. Analytically such debates were crucial to furthering academic and political knowledge and practice.

And I was very much part of that politics struggling all the time to think politically but also theoretically and empirically about the complexity of the issues involved. How do we theorise 'difference'? How do we work through 'difference' without creating divisions? How do we differentiate between theorising difference and celebrating difference? I don't have that much against multiculturalism when it talks about celebration. I think we do need to celebrate difference. But when does difference become a social division? I have learnt a lot from Stuart Hall in terms of thinking about difference and owe him a great debt for that. Questions of difference and questions of solidarity and questions of politics, these have been very much the cornerstone of my life.

LB: *You wrote in 'The Scent of Memory' about that time: 'I couldn't be a disinterested listener although I listened attentively' (Brah, 1999: 7). Another thing I wanted to ask you about is the kind of debt that we owe to a generation of writers and scholars including yourself. What was thinkable in those days is not what is thinkable now, and the debt that we owe is that your work among others makes thinkable a critique of racism within the post-imperial British social formation. You mentioned a few things about the struggles around the frameworks of knowledge and the politics of that and I just wondered how you reflected on that?*

AB: Well, leaving aside research centres like the Ethnic Relations Unit, which was specifically created to look at questions of race and ethnicity, generally it was not easy in those days to talk about race in sociology. Race was not seen at the centre of sociological analysis, and so one struggle was to get this subject included as an important area of study. But more importantly, it was a problem as to how the subject was actually analysed. Often, it was seen as an epiphenomenon. Class was obviously at the heart of sociological analysis. Other areas such as racism and gender, you had to theorise them as ideology. Even within feminism the study of racism was marginal. And of course gender was not seen as critical to the analysis of race and ethnicity. So there was a struggle at the level of knowledge formation. Overall, there was a failure to see that these subjects were at the heart of the formation of modern Britain. And I think that was when Stuart Hall's work became very important for me because he actually put those issues at the centre. He looked at British social crisis and said that this crisis actually filters through race and that you actually live your race through class and class through race and we can extend that perspective to every other axis of differentiation. And those struggles affected not just me, but a lot of my colleagues here in the room and yourself included. We were all collectively engaged in changing frameworks of knowledge.

LB: *Well, I think that is true and in part it is what we owe you actually. I think that is true, although the politics of the academy is something that maybe we can come back to at the end. But I wanted to also ask you a little bit about the struggle to combine your commitment to attentiveness with a version of empirical sociology that is not disinterested and at the same time is holding onto political and theoretical sensibilities, because I think that's something that has very much characterised the work that you've done.*

AB: Well, you've written a lovely book called *The Art of Listening* and I think listening is very important; I don't think we listen enough to what people are saying. And I think we don't listen often enough to words other than our own, at all different levels. At the global level, we don't listen to it because if we did listen then maybe we wouldn't have all these wars that are going on. And so the politics of listening I think are quite, very important in that sense.

LB: *What was it about the notion of diaspora that caught your imagination?*

AB: Well, it is a different way of exploring migrancy and the position of categories of people such as immigrants and ethnic minorities. I'm not against the terminology of immigrants and ethnic minorities *per se*. Rather, I tend to de-centre instead of replace these labels. But I think that the concept of diaspora offers you a way of conceptualising the kind of global mobilities today and the ways in which, economically, politically, culturally and psychically, we cross all kinds of borders all the time. And we are having to think about questions of home and belonging. The concept of diaspora helped me think through some questions that I had been preoccupied with under different headings for a long time. But, you know, diaspora is about globalisation and dispersal, but at the same time it's also about location and 'staying put'.

LB: *I'm just going to read a passage and ask you to think about it. I teach one of my first year undergraduate lectures with just one quotation from you, which is from the 'Difference, Diversity, Differentiation' essay. We spend a whole hour on this one quotation. It goes: 'The search for grand theories specifying the interconnections between racism, gender and class has been less than productive. They are best construed as historically contingent and context-specific relationships' (Brah, 1993: 208). I wanted to ask you about how you think those relationships might have shifted and how you think about that task, that profoundly difficult task to really make that sensibility into a way of thinking about the world?*

AB: Well, I was strongly influenced by Marxist thought. The difficulty arose when along with other feminists, I tried to think about race and gender in relation to class within a framework like Marxism or for that matter any other grand narrative. There were foreclosures within those frameworks that were very, very difficult to open up to the analysis of gender, sexuality, ethnicity. I remember there was a long feminist debate about domestic labour, how to theorise it within a Marxist perspective, but in the end it didn't come to much. And so we were all beginning to look for other explanations, other ways of thinking, and that's where post-structuralism did open up some new avenues for some of us. Others thought we were going bonkers, you know. But it did certainly make sense to me. And post-structuralist thought really comes from an engagement with, and critique of those grand narratives and with thinking about these issues of sexuality or class or gender in relational terms, in contingent terms, and in ways that don't foreclose but open up spaces, to think differently.

LB: *I would like to go back to that wonderful essay 'The Scent of Memory', which I think brings together so many of your concerns. In it you use the notion of interpellation and how others interpellate us as a way of understanding racism and multiculture. You do this very through the figure of Jean, whose story is told in an autobiographical account by Tim Lott and who was from Southall? [AB: Yes, it is] I wonder if you could say a little bit about that?*

AB: Well, it was the enigma of Jean, which was also the enigma of the encounter between whiteness and othernesses, you know, Blackness, Asianness, whatever. Or any other form of encounter between people who are located within different cultural formations. I was trying to consider the structural features in society alongside the subjective dimensions, about subjectivity itself and its kind of unpredicted and unruly mechanisms. You never really fully understand the Other. I never really fully understood Jean, and in the essay I say that she remained opaque to me but I could actually empathise with her. I found a connectivity with her figure so to speak. And I think these issues are very important. This goes back to the politics of the nineties: there were the 'hard' politics, and then there were these so-called softer areas — about subjectivity and so on — which those involved in 'hard' politics didn't want to engage with. And I think feminists were trying to do the latter. You know, we were trying to bring together the subjective with the structural; the social with the cultural.

LB: *And I suppose too the psychic with the social.*

AB: The psychic definitely, the psychic and the social. Definitely. And I was trying to bring the psychic together with the social in that essay. I wasn't consciously doing it. That was another thing. Because I found there was also the spiritual dimension that I think underpins that piece. And although I've always been a little bit at a distance from organised religion — I've always had some problems with organised religion — but nonetheless spirituality attracts me. And so in that sense it's a very spiritually informed essay.

LB: *Another thing that several people have said from the audience, which was great to hear, was the importance of you as a teacher too. I wonder if you could say a little bit about teaching, the teaching that you did, given that I do think we live in a time that there is a kind of institutionalised selfishness in the academy, which we need to fight and resist and refuse in response to the questions we address. I just wondered if I could ask you a little bit about your teaching, what your teaching methods meant to you.*

AB: My teaching meant a lot to me. I loved teaching. And my students were very important to me. And I mean, we're actually lucky at Birkbeck College — we have wonderful students, you know, all mature students. And many of my students were returning to education after a long time so their life experience was very, very rich. And I found them very receptive. Although some of the ways of thinking that we were trying to introduce them to about race and ethnicity were a bit difficult, at first, they worked hard and did well.

Those were very productive years as Jane Hoy said. Apart from the Master's level programme, we produced many courses for non-traditional students. We were again lucky to be at Birkbeck's Faculty of Lifelong Learning where there weren't that many bureaucratic obstacles to innovation. If you thought of an idea that was good, you could actually produce a course. And some of the courses we developed would today be called Diaspora Studies. For instance, we had courses in Irish Studies, Jewish Studies, Palestinian Studies, Caribbean Studies, Asian Studies. We had a course in Black Theatre. We produced courses in Women's Studies and Lesbian Studies. And actually our Lesbian Studies programme was one of the first in London and Jane was very centrally involved in that.

And we were also working with part-time lecturers. We had about forty, fifty part-time lecturers. And that was amazing because, you know, although it was hard work supporting a large panel of part-time lecturers, we had these wonderful people who were specialists in their field who would come and teach on our programmes. So I found that a very, very creative period in my life.

LB: *You also spent a couple of periods in America.*

AB: Yes, I did. Two years.

LB: *Can I ask you a little bit about that time in America at Santa Cruz and then Cornell?*

AB: Well, some of the chapters in *Cartographies* were written in California. It was quite good to have the space to write because when I said we were doing all these wonderful things at Birkbeck College I didn't add that our primary role at the time was to create these courses, and that left very little time to write. And going to California gave me the time and the space to do some reading and to think and write. And in the 1990s feminism was very alive and very active. I always find going to America — I wouldn't want to live there [laughter] — but it's intellectually very, very exciting. Every time I go there, I feel intellectually energised, you know. And that was great. And I had a lot of support from all kinds of people. People like Angela Davis was a colleague, Donna Haraway was a colleague. James Clifford was a colleague. All these wonderful people. It was really marvellous. And then with Cornell too, I went to the Humanities Centre there and again it was a wonderful intellectual environment. 9/11 happened while I was there, and I was involved in the campus activities to deal with its political and personal aftermath.

LB: *And what do you think about America now and the hopes that cling to Obama?*

AB: America now, well, that's a big question, isn't it.

LB: *It is a big question but I just wondered given that you're probably qualified more than anyone to answer.*

AB: Well, I feel that the social movements of the sixties and the seventies, those earlier social movements and those of the eighties, nineties, feminism, and civil rights, the Black Power movement, all those kind of political movements made an impact. There were times when we were critical of them and sometimes we say oh, have we really made a difference? I think they did make a difference. I think that in complex ways they have actually created the space for an Obama to emerge. So in that sense I feel quite good because there are times when you feel a bit despondent, did we really achieve anything? And I think we did achieve things.

Obviously like everybody else, I was thrilled that we were going to have a black president. I didn't think that I would see that in my lifetime, you know, so it was wonderful. And I still retain some optimism that maybe things will be different but I also have deep scepticism as well, because he's an individual who is part of a whole kind of machinery so to speak. And certainly I'm disappointed with his foreign policy, very much so. So at the moment, that's what I'm thinking about, the war in Afghanistan, and what is going on in Iraq still. I'm worrying about the sort of new imperialisms of today, which can casually speak the language of democracy.

LB: *I wonder about the imperialisms of now and how that affects the notion of diaspora, the diasporas of today and it seems that the replay of those imperial kind of forays are the driving force for all kinds of movements and I wondered what you think about that?*

AB: Yes, of course the globalisation that we witness is producing all different kinds of diasporas, or different kinds of migrations. Capital is so mobile now that it can go anywhere for labour, internally as well as externally, and people migrate here while multinationals relocate overseas. So a lot of things are happening that were not happening in the same way 30, 40 years ago. And at the same time the inequalities, that is, global inequalities, persist as the global market integrates different countries differentially, and so some countries are far worse off than others. Hence, we've got these poverty-stricken countries from which people are leaving, and at the same time we've got in those countries fairly repressive regimes that may be bolstered by the democracies of the West. So there are people who are migrating as refugees, as asylum seekers, and their plight is dire. But the thing is that capital desperately needs that cheap labour, but people in Britain or in other parts of the world of the advanced economies don't want these migrants here. As a result, we have all these anti-immigrant, anti-refugee, anti-asylum seeker discourses and politics that are hugely problematic.

LB: *Yes, I suppose added to that is the whole discourse about the death of multiculturalism.*

AB: Absolutely, yes. We spent years critiquing multiculturalism [laughter], and now we actually find ourselves defending multiculturalism because, you know, there were of course critiques from the political left, which talked about multiculturalism being too culturist and that multiculturalists were not taking issues of racism and issues of class on board, whereas now of course we've got critiques from the political right. Today there is talk about community cohesion, which is a sort of, implicit, or sometimes even explicit agenda for assimilation. Roy Jenkins' speech at least had a kind of a liberal view of multiculturalism but that's gone now.[1] Today people blame multiculturalism for things for which really multiculturalism is not to blame. Anyhow, what do we want instead? Do we want monoculturalism?

And that brings me back to the whole question of difference. How do we think about difference? Do we want people to be just all the same, you know? How do we discuss questions of difference, whether it's cultural difference, generational difference or ethnic difference, class difference, all those differences, how do we think about those? So I'm not against multiculturalism in that sense. I think we need a sort of critical multiculturalism that takes on aboard questions of racism, ethnicity, sexuality, class and so on.

LB: *To come back to your work in Southall, wasn't one of the things you tried to do was to map a kind of multiculture that wasn't a multiculturism, that wasn't, you know, a mosaic of compartmentalised cultural units but a form of multiculture that is interpellated across experiences of difference.*

AB: That's right, that's right. No, multiculture is very important. It's obviously what makes life interesting. You're right, it's the difference between how we think about multicultures and multiculturalism. But multiculturalism itself was a state policy at one time. And I know that the Burnage Enquiry[2] argued against the ways in which these policies were implemented in some areas, and quite rightly so, but not all multiculturalism is bad because I think there were some quite interesting and exciting projects that took place under that rubric. It gave teachers permission to do things that weren't possible otherwise because multiculturalism as policy was particularly prevalent in education, in schools particularly. So in that sense, I think multiculturalism itself also did have some positive aspects that have been lost in the recent debates. But of course the New Right — and not even the New Right but the Centre Right and politicians such as Gordon Brown now talk about British values such as fairness as if these are unique to Britain and other societies don't have those values at all.

1 In 1966, Roy Jenkins, the then Home Secretary gave a speech in which he argued against assimilation and in favour of integration, defining it as 'not a flattening process of assimilation but as equal opportunity, accompanied by cultural diversity, in an atmosphere of mutual tolerance' (Roy Jenkins, Address given on 23 May 1966 to a meeting of the Voluntary Liaison Committee: National Council for Civil Liberties).

2 See Macdonald Inquiry (1989).

LB: *Just a very final question before we close: reflecting on what everyone has said today, has anything occurred to you that you would like to add in listening to people talking about this figure, Avtar Brah, in the company of Avtar Brah [laughter]. Are there any final reflections you would like to make?*

AB: I couldn't really, I can't even recognise the figure that ... [laughter]. Such wonderful things have been said today. I'm really deeply, deeply touched. I am glad that some of the ideas that I've had have touched other chords in other people's lives, in their work and their lives. I'm pleased about that because obviously intellectual work is about communication in that sense. So I'm very grateful for that, that that has happened. But I feel very humbled by all the things that have happened today, very humbled. And I am deeply indebted to all the speakers today. And I also want to thank everyone for being here and I also want to thank Claire Alexander and Suki Ali and John Solomos who first came up with the idea of holding this event. Special thanks to Yasmeen Narayan for organising the event. [Applause] But I just really want to thank everyone. And also special thanks to Stuart Hall. I am deeply grateful to him for making the effort to be here despite his health. He has been my intellectual guru. I have actually learnt from him at every inch of my academic career. So I feel really honoured that he's going to end this session with his wonderful words. Thank you.

[Applause]

closing remarks from Les Back

Well, I usually don't take these kinds of liberties but I want to thank you on behalf of all of us here for sharing those thoughts with us. And I think one of the things that is characteristic of not only your writing but also your teaching and pedagogy is how to combine a kind of clear insightful commitment to critique and politics while at the same time practising a form of intellectual generosity, openness and facilitation, which I think amounts to more than just an invitation to follow your example. I think it's almost a demand on us that we should be interpellated by your actions and act similarly. I think this is important in the face of contemporary racism and the threats faced by diasporic communities, but also in relation to the life of the mind and universities as a space for developing an alternative vision of the world.

[Applause]

authors' biographies

Les Back teaches Sociology at Goldsmiths, University of London. His books include *The Art of Listening* (Berg, 2007), *Out of Whiteness*: *Colour, Politics and Culture* (with Vron Ware University of Chicago Press, 2002) and *The Changing Face of*

Football: *Racism and Multiculture in the English Game* (with John Solomos and Tim Crabbe Berg, 2001). In 2011, he published a digital book entitled *Academic Diary* (http://www.academic-diary.co.uk/).

Avtar Brah is Emeritus Professor of Sociology at Birkbeck College. She writes on race, ethnicity, gender, identity and diaspora. Her publications include: *Cartographies of Diaspora/Contesting Identities* (1996, Routledge); *Hybridity and its Discontents*: *Politics, Science, Culture* (edited with Annie E. Coombes, 2000, Routledge); *Global Futures*: *Migration, Environment and Globalization* (edited with Mary J. Hickman and Mairtin Mac an Ghail, 1999, Macmillan); and *Thinking Identities* (edited with Mary J. Hickman and Mairtin Mac an Ghail, 1999, Macmillan).

references

Brah, A. (1993) 'Difference, diversity, differentiation' in Wrench, J. and Solomos, J. (1993) editors, *Racism and Migration in Western Europe*, Oxford: berg.

Brah, A. (1997) *Cartographies of Diaspora: Contesting Identities*, London; New York: Routledge.

Brah, A. (1999) 'The Scent of Memory: strangers, our own, and others' *Feminist Review*, Issue 61: 4–26.

Macdonald Inquiry (1989) *Murder in the Playground: The Report of the Macdonald Inquiry into Racism and Racial Violence, in Manchester Schools*, London: Longsight press.

doi:10.1057/fr.2011.66

100 | racialisation, relationality and riots: intersections and interpellations

Aisha Phoenix and Ann Phoenix

abstract

This paper takes up Avtar Brah's (1999) invitation to write back to the issues she raises in her mapping of the production of gendered, classed and racialised subjectivities in west London. It addresses two topics that, together, illuminate racialised and gendered interpellation and psychosocial processes. The paper is divided into two main sections. The first draws on empirical research on the transition to motherhood conducted in east London to consider one mother's experience of giving birth in the local maternity hospital. The maternity ward constituted a site where racialised difference became salient, leading her to construct her maternal identity by asserting her difference from Bangladeshi mothers and so self-racialising, as well as 'othering' Bangladeshi mothers. The paper analyses the ways in which her biography may help to explain why her experience of the maternity hospital interpellates her into racialised positioning. The second section focuses on media responses to the riots in various English cities in August 2011. It examines the ways in which some media punditry racialised the riots and inclusion in the British postcolonial nation. The paper analyses three sets of commentaries and illuminates the ways in which they racialise the debate in essentialising ways, reproducing themes that were identified in the 1980s as 'new racism' and apportioning blame for the riots to 'black gangster culture'. While these media pronouncements focus on racialisation, they are intersectional in implicitly also invoking gender and social class. The paper argues that the understanding of the mother's self-racialisation is deepened by a consideration of the racialised discourses that can be evoked (and are contested) in periods of social unrest. The paper thus draws on part of the methodology of 'The Scent of Memory' in layering media readings and biographical narratives to analyse the contemporary psychosocial space of racialisation.

keywords

intersections; interpellation; psychosocial; racialisation; racism; riots

(52–71) © 2012 Feminist Review. 0141-7789/12 www.feminist-review.com

introduction

In 'The Scent of Memory', Avtar Brah (1999) takes as her starting point the poignant example of a white, working-class woman, Jean Lott, who committed suicide in the 1990s, leaving a note that identified her hatred of living in Southall. The painful curtailment of Jean's life led her son to analyse her emotional engagement with the shift in the area from one populated by the 'respectable' white working classes in the 1960s to one characterised as 'Asian' in the 1980s. For Brah, the substance of the suicide note was interpellative. It implicated her in Jean's story by hailing her into her own and Southall's racialised, gendered history. Brah's meditation on the questions thus raised for her involved the pursuit and analysis of the 'scent of memory' in different contexts and using different methodologies. The resulting account is theoretically rich, multi-layered, intertextual and psychosocial and links Brah's empirical work with everyday experiences, cultural readings and reflexive engagement with the complexity of her own and others' intersectional positioning. Published at the end of the twentieth century, 'The Scent of Memory' raises numerous issues of relevance to the second decade of the twenty-first century.

In this paper, we take up Brah's invitation to write back to the issues she raises by addressing two topics of contemporary concern that elucidate racialised, gendered interpellation and the importance of looking at both macro (social) and micro (personal) processes. The paper is structured into two main parts, each of which is concerned with contemporary events related to racialisation and its intersection with other social categories. Together, the two parts illuminate the ways in which personal and social histories are imbricated in the present. The paper starts by presenting a fragment of an empirical interview, which gives some insight into the complexity of processes of self-racialisation and othering. It then considers some media commentaries on the English riots of August 2011 to examine processes of racialisation that make general, rather than personal, claims. Each of these issues is central to Brah's analysis of how racialisation disrupted Jean's satisfaction with the area in which she spent much of her adult life. In adopting this structure, we aim to address some of the ways in which the personal and sociostructural are always interlinked in processes of racialisation. We thus aim to complement Brah's (1999) analyses by focusing on the psychosocial and 'writing back' to her concerns.

The first main section of the paper draws on empirical research on the transition to motherhood conducted in Tower Hamlets, an area of London that has become increasingly identified as 'Bangladeshi' over the last two decades and can in some ways be viewed as paralleling the history of Southall's identification as 'Indian'. It considers how one mother racialises herself and others in discussing her experience of the local maternity hospital and, in doing so, interpellates us as authors into racialised positioning. At the same time, the detailed psychosocial attention to the racist discourses she constructs allows openness to the functions served by her biographical narrative. The second section examines media responses to the riots in many English cities in August 2011. It focuses on the ways in which some of this media punditry racialised the riots and inclusion in the British postcolonial nation and the reactions this provoked. The paper argues that the understanding of the mother's self-racialisation is deepened by a consideration of the racialised discourses that can be evoked (and that are also contested) in periods of social unrest. The paper thus draws on part of the methodology of 'The Scent of Memory' in layering media readings and biographical narratives to produce a palimpsest analysis of the contemporary psychosocial space of racialisation.

self-racialising the transition to motherhood

The empirical part of this paper is informed by a study, conducted by Heather Elliott, Wendy Hollway and Ann Phoenix, of first-time mothers from a variety of ethnic groups living in Tower Hamlets.[1] The study is referred to as the 'Becoming a Mother' study and was part of the ESRC *Identities and Social Action* research programme. Tower Hamlets is ethnically mixed and one of the most disadvantaged boroughs in the United Kingdom, but with a mixed social class population since it borders London's financial heartland, the City. It has a long tradition of settlement by successive waves of immigrants and a population that is approximately 33 per cent Bangladeshi, 42 per cent White and 7 per cent African-Caribbean.[2] Eighteen mothers were interviewed on three occasions in 2005 and 2006: in late pregnancy or soon after giving birth, when their infants were 6 months old and approximately a year after giving birth. They were British African-Caribbean (2); British Bangladeshi (8); West African (1); White British (6); and White South African (1). In addition, two focus groups, one of white mothers and the other of Bangladeshi British mothers, were conducted after the interviews were completed. The study explored the identity processes involved in the transition to motherhood. It focused on women's experiences of becoming first-time mothers and the emotional resources and conflicts they bring to the task. It also considered how the mothers negotiate their new identities in intersection with ethnicity, religion, culture, age and social class. The interview questions were designed to elicit 'experience-near' accounts of specific life events.

It is no surprise that the transition to parenthood marks a shift in people's lives and responsibilities that often crystallises for parents how and where they want to live in order to bring up their children in the circumstances they consider optimal, including the areas and schools they would ideally choose. This was the case in the 'Becoming a Mother' study. The mothers were differentiated in their feelings about Tower Hamlets after birth. Some consolidated their

1 ESRC-funded study number RES 148-25 0058: Becoming a Mother.

2 Office of National Statistics. (2001) Census 2001 — ethnicity and religion in England and Wales, http://www.statistics.gov.uk/census2001/profiles/commentaries/ethnicity.asp, last accessed 26 May 2008.

commitment to the area as ideal for childrearing, some moved soon after birth, some moved later and others wanted to move as soon as they could. Nine of the eighteen women moved (two out of London) within the first year of motherhood, while a further two had advanced plans to move and some moved later. Those who moved out of the borough generally viewed Tower Hamlets as fun to live in while they were childless, but less appropriate for children to live in, perhaps partly because of the scarcity of suitable housing. For some of the white mothers and the one West African mother in the study, the Bangladeshi population was not viewed positively, something that the focus group and some individual interviews with Bangladeshi mothers made clear. Many of the sample appeared to feel guarded about speaking of racialised difference. This was perhaps not surprising given that they gave birth soon after the vehement competition between the Labour and Respect parties in the 2005 UK election campaign that became racialised in Tower Hamlets, and the bombings and attempted bombings of 7 July 2005 ('7/7'), two of which took place in Tower Hamlets.

This section focuses on the account of a white mother, given the pseudonym Catherine, who was interviewed by Heather Elliott. For Catherine, the experience of giving birth in the local hospital produced feelings about Tower Hamlets akin to Jean Lott's about Southall. In the extract below, round brackets signify a pause, with the number in brackets indicating the number of seconds the pause lasted and (.) indicating that it was a pause of less than one second. Underlining under a word indicates that it was emphasised, while information in square brackets is information to the reader about either the dynamics of the talk or the transcription.

> *Catherine*: ... the other thing that's strange about that hospital [slower] is that (.) it's a Bangladeshi community, so *most* of the women in there (3) are Bangladeshi. And there was one woman who didn't feed her daughter properly, because it was a baby girl. [text omitted] And they prefer boys, because you have to provide a dowry don't you? [text omitted] I think, it's not racist at all, but because they're Bang- because it's Bangladeshi um (3) their society is different to ours. It's a bit like that in Poplar as well, there is this kind of it does seem like segregation, that's where *you* *get* a lot of the Respect party coming round and everything else, *because* of all of that. [text omitted] Um and it just seems like there's no one there that *you* can relate to, or that could relate to you, because (.) most of the Bangladeshi women there *stay at home* and always <u>have</u> been stay at home women, either mothers or first time mums, but they have always been staying at home. [text omitted] So going in there, being someone who has had a career, and <u>now</u> decided to have (.) a family, there's no one who relates to that.

Following our intertextual engagement with 'The Scent of Memory', an understanding of why Catherine experiences racialised disidentification with Bangladeshi mothers and Tower Hamlets requires both an exploration of Catherine's biography and of the socio-economic context. This section thus locates the account above in the context of what we know about Catherine's life.

biographical 'triggers'

While Catherine is of a much younger generation than Jean and has come to adulthood at a time when Britain is undoubtedly multiethnic, her account gives a similar sense of alienation and loneliness to what Jean seems to have felt. For Catherine, who generally spends her days at work as a sales executive, the maternity ward constituted a microcosm of Tower Hamlets and a site of spatialisation where she experienced racialised difference. In that space, she constructed her identity by asserting her difference from Bangladeshi mothers and generalising from one unfavourable example (of a Bangladeshi mother not feeding her daughter properly). In doing so, she also racialised social class since the lack of a career she criticises, and the suggestion that Bangladeshi women do not wait to decide to have children, is at least partly related to social class and education. Catherine can be said to be self-racialising as well as othering Bangladeshi mothers by positioning herself as clearly very different from them.

The experience of giving birth in the hospital illustrates the ways in which space allows the existence of multiplicity where heterogeneity can coexist in 'throwntogetherness' (Massey, 2005), even as the space is racialised (Westwood, 1990; Räthzel *et al.*, 2008). Space here is not only about practices and relationality, but about trajectories that are always in process and under construction (Massey, 2005), since desires for moving or staying put are relational and dynamic. In this case, Catherine constructed the hospital as a space for Bangladeshis, with the implication that it is not a comfortable site for white mothers like her. In Brah's terms, 'the discourse of racial superiority may be understood here as *displacing* class antagonism' (1999: 11). While Catherine's discourse sets up power relations marked by constructions of superiority over Bangladeshi mothers, there is also a sense that she is excluded because she does not belong.

The structure of this short extract from the interview is familiar to discourse analysts. It constructs a proleptic double hander (Billig, 1991) that defends against possible charges of racism: 'I think, it's not racist at all, but because they're Bang- because it's Bangladeshi um (3) their society is different to ours'. Catherine lays out a case for there being important differences between Bangladeshi people and other people who live in Tower Hamlets. What she says fits with Brah's (1999) analysis of how localities can become 'racially' coded in ways that produce challenges to spatial identities and feelings of belonging. In Catherine's case, this racial coding also serves to 'other' Bangladeshis. That couplet of belonging or exclusion as part of racial coding together with processes of othering makes space itself interpellative.

In analysing the reasons for Jean's dislike of Southall, Brah draws on Althusser's notion of interpellation to produce a psychosocial analysis. According to

Althusser (1977), people are 'interpellated' as subjects when they recognise themselves to have been 'hailed' by ideology. Metaphorically, this process is akin to what happens when someone recognises that they are being hailed by a policeman. In everyday life, institutions such as families, churches and schools 'hail' people by including them in categories that prescribe and enforce particular ways of thinking about themselves and of acting as subjects. Brah meditates on her interpellation as Asian by her Southall research participants in the 1970s and by Jean's avowed hatred of Southall before interrogating the emotion associated with those accounts in the context of Jean's and her participants' lives and gendered, racialised and social class positioning. Brah (1999: 7) gives a particularly powerful example of how interpellation can involve racialised/gendered processes of othering and intense emotions (which in this case are painful):

> One 'white' mother whom I interviewed in 1976 had said to me: 'Where did *they* come from?', my father used to say, 'they were here, and then the shops opened up.'
> The 'they' in this locution signified 'Asians'. 'She means people like me', I had thought to myself, feeling acutely 'othered' .... I could not be a disinterested listener, although I listened attentively. My intellect, feelings, and emotions had all been galvanized by my respondent's discourse. I was framed within it, whether I liked it or not. What was it that made her referent 'they' instantly recognizable as 'Asians' to us both? (Brah, 1999: 7)

Just as Brah (1999: 5) explains that 'The word "Southall" — ringing loud and clear in my ears — connected me across diverse, even disparate, life worlds to "Jean" — this 57-year-old white woman who took her own life in March 1988', so mention of the place name 'Tower Hamlets' was highly evocative and emotionally coded for Catherine and (in different ways) for the women in the 'Becoming a Mother' study.

Catherine was interviewed by a white woman resident of Tower Hamlets and appeared to identify with her as an employed woman. As black readers of this account who do not live in Tower Hamlets and are of different generations from Catherine, we feel interpellated into subject positions as 'other', even though it is Asian culture, not colour that is at issue in Catherine's account. In the UK context, we are framed within Catherine's discourse because of the numerous ways in which 'black' or 'African Caribbean culture' is constructed as pathological (as, for example, in the section below). We are also 'hailed' by the routine linking of 'black and Asian' or 'black and minority ethnic', particularly when difference from the white majority ethnic group is being evaluated negatively. This is not to claim that the process of interpellation Brah describes is either the same, or feels the same, as those we experience on reading this part of Catherine's interview. Nor is there any necessary fellow feeling between different racialised and ethnicised groups. However, racialised interpellations are not neatly confined within socially constructed boundaries. Brah provides a helpful example of how experience can give flashes of insight into other people's experiences in describing her early experiences of living in the United Kingdom:

> Within weeks of being in London I had been called a 'Paki'. I was so taken aback ... that I was struck silent. I now realised ... what it felt like to be called a 'nigger' ... I was now constituted within the discourse of 'Paki' as a racialised insider/outsider, a post-colonial subject constructed and marked by everyday practices at the heart of the metropolis ... it signified the inferiorised Other right here at the core of the fountain head of 'Britishness' (Brah, 1996: 9).

One way in which the concept of interpellation can be extended from Brah's analysis concerns Catherine's *dis*-interpellation by Bangladeshiness, Tower Hamlets as a community and the local maternity ward. The strength of her feelings of strangeness and lack of belonging led her to construct rigid racialised boundaries between Bangladeshis and white mothers (while leaving gender and social class unnamed). This implicitly interpellated her into white English subjectivity. The relational nature of interpellation is thus illuminated by her reaction.

A consideration of interpellation necessarily raises the question of affect (both Catherine's and that of readers positioned in different ways) and its inextricable linking to the socio-economic structures within which we all construct our identities. Interpellation is therefore psychosocial in that it involves the mutual constitution of the personal and the social in ways that constantly transform each other and can be conflictual (Bjerrum Nilsen and Haavind, 2010). 'The Scent of Memory' was ground-breaking in considering the processes through which this happens. Brah's (1999) rich analysis considers history, geography, South Asian concepts that subtly nuance the concepts of 'our own' and 'stranger' and the intersecting relationships produced in London's 'diaspora space' that serve to overdetermine racialised/gendered/social class explanations for Jean Lott's misery and Brah's findings from her Southall study.

The section below addresses some broader sociostructural issues in giving examples of current ways in which racialising discourses (re)produce racisms and make available and justify discourses such as Catherine's. The rest of this section briefly focuses on an area that Brah could not address in 'The Scent of Memory'; the contribution of biographical experience to, in this case Catherine's, spatialised racialisation. Brah (1999) asks early in her paper 'Who was Jean?' and, late in the paper, concludes that Jean necessarily remains an enigma (and perhaps morally ought to). A major aim of the 'Becoming a Mother' study, however, was to find out about the women's identity transitions in the process of becoming mothers from their own perspectives. This more 'personal' under-standing can, hopefully, throw light on Catherine's sociostructural identity positioning within the borough in which she lives. In relation to this, two issues appear to be of particular importance.

First, while social class is evident, but implicit, in Catherine's account it was somewhat ambiguous in that she was recruited into the study by a midwife, who told us that Catherine, who lived in a council flat, was working class. However, it did not fit with either her and her partner's employment status or her father's profession and affluence. She was actually not a council tenant, but was subletting a large council flat for a substantial market rent, probably because private rental accommodation is very expensive in Tower Hamlets and few houses are available for sale or rent. Nonetheless, the midwife's misrecognition of Catherine's class position underlines an ambiguity that Catherine appeared to feel. In an interview that took place in late pregnancy, it became clear that there were conflicts for Catherine about her socio-economic positioning and, in particular, that she experienced some people in her family as judging her for not being married and owning a home before having a baby. She experienced her lack of home ownership as a conflictual issue, but could not afford to move during the first year of her daughter's life when she was on maternity leave. However, at the interview when her daughter was 12 months old, she said that her partner had just heard about a local home ownership scheme in Tower Hamlets that would cost less than their current rent and would enable them to part-own a three-bedroom house. She said 'I'll be *happier* when we have the stability of owning our own place' and that she would not have a second child 'until we own our own house and we're moved out of here'.

Second, Catherine had experienced various troubling life events that she felt left her with 'emotional baggage' that she wanted to 'get rid of' because it could affect her daughter. She had a painful and traumatic birth and a difficult postpartum period in the hospital, as well as fears about having to stay at home on maternity leave when she was used to going out to work. Staying at home could, therefore, be seen as part of what she was seeking to 'other' as much as the Bangladeshi women in whom she vested always staying at home and not having careers. Catherine worked in a highly competitive, male-dominated institution and knew that her professional position would be threatened by time away on maternity leave (which proved to be the case). Giving birth in the local hospital was likely, therefore, to have intensified Catherine's fears about motherhood conflicting with her professional identity, and so her middle class status and social networks. This was particularly the case since she would be spending the next few months at home, in a geographical space she usually only passed through to get to work and which she characterised as Bangladeshi.

A plausible explanation for Catherine's reported experience of outsiderness at the hospital is, therefore, that she displaced the source of feelings of outsiderness and her acute sense of undesirable social class positioning in her family onto Bangladeshi women in the hospital and Bangladeshi people more generally in Tower Hamlets. She projected a condensation of negatively evaluated differences from herself onto the Bangladeshi 'community'. Her claims to difference were thus crucial and salient in allowing Catherine the possibility of feeling more powerful than, and superior to, Bangladeshi women in terms of social class, gendered appropriateness and belonging to the nation. These personal motivations coupled with the ethnicised local history of contestation over resources in Tower Hamlets are likely to have overdetermined Catherine's brief portrayal of Bangladeshis. Her socio-economic positioning and life history are thus both relevant to a consideration of Catherine's self-racialisation and othering of Bangladeshi mothers in the Tower Hamlet's maternity ward.

While the three interviews with Catherine provide more insight into her viewpoints and narratives than were available to Brah (1999) about Jean's, this analysis is necessarily speculative. The implication of such a reading, however, is that, while Catherine's proleptic defence that 'it's not racist at all' is unconvincing, this part of her narrative neither fixes her as racist nor into racist discourses once and for all. Instead, it gives an indication of why a focus on racist discourses, rather than people as racist (e.g. Wetherell and Potter, 1992), allows nuanced, psychosocial readings that reflect the complexities of everyday life. A psychosocial analysis also helps to explain why such a narrative is easily evoked in her particular circumstances and the work it does in Catherine's life. In addition, it produces a holistic and sympathetic reading of Catherine akin to Brah's meditation on Jean because it is rounded and contextual. In so doing, it indicates how racialisation is pervasive and contemporary encounters are deeply psychosocial, interpellating researchers into the stories they hear and the analyses they produce in restorying these accounts (Lewis, 2009; McLeod and Thomson, 2009). These analyses are invaluable in enabling new insights by allowing a space between researchers' own stories and those of their research participants (Elliott, 2011), as well as productive engagement with the emotions evoked (Elliott *et al.*, in press).

The analysis of the above fragment of Catherine's story demonstrates the inextricable linking of personal biography with the socio-economic and political (Mulinari and Räthzel, 2007). The rest of this paper uses contemporary examples to move from the microanalytic focus above to take a broad lens to issues of racism and racialisation similar to those with which Brah was concerned.

writing back: the lingering odour of pathologising discourses

The absence of insider narratives led Brah (1999) to extrapolate from media analyses and analyses of the negative discourses on Asians produced by white research participants in a study she conducted in 1970s Southall. 'The Scent of Memory' includes analyses of political demonstrations against the racist murders of young Asian men in Southall and east London and the riots in Notting Hill in the 1970s. This allowed Brah both to illuminate the ways in which racist discourses about Asians functioned and were deployed by white residents of Southall and to contextualise them in wider social discourses. Brah (1999: 17) highlights how young black people came together in Notting Hill to stake their claim to an area in which 'dire poverty' jostled with 'fantastic wealth'. She argues that British-born black and Asian young people were asserting a new British political identity and interrogating and challenging constructions of 'whiteness' and the notion that British means white, which was popularised by the Conservative politician Enoch Powell in 1968.

The second half of this paper aims to continue the process of 'writing back' to Brah by considering some of the racialised discourses that circulate at times of social tension. It does so by extrapolating, as Brah does, from analyses of riots that are contemporaneous with the personal experiences at the heart of Catherine's analysis. While the riots happened after Catherine had been interviewed, they illuminate the ways in which negative racialised discourses can become widely available and are both legitimated and contested (in much the same way that negative discourses about Muslims and Asians were commonplace following '7/7' at the time when Catherine was racialising Tower Hamlets). This section examines some of the media discourses that followed the 2011 riots, 35 years later than the riots Brah analyses. It argues that while the causes, social context and nature of the twenty-first century riots are different from those in the 1970s, some of the views expressed by media commentators following the riots parallel the narrow constructions of Britishness that Brah argued British-born black and Asian young people were challenging decades earlier. Our concern here is not to analyse the causes of the riots, which have been the focus of much of the political debate and was partially Brah's focus. Instead, we aim to deconstruct a selection of media commentaries on the riots in terms of their racialised inclusions and exclusions from the nation in order to illuminate parallels with, and divergences from, the context Brah describes and some of the discourses available to Catherine. Whereas Brah focused on macro-historical cultural readings of the riots, we take a somewhat narrower view in analysing individual accounts available in the media.

discursively racialising the riots: ahistorical origin stories

In summer 2011, following the fatal police shooting of a young black man, Mark Duggan, in the north London area of Tottenham, multiethnic riots erupted in several parts of England and lasted for several days. The media and general population were preoccupied by the scale, and sometimes violence, of the riots, which were characterised by looting and setting fire to shops and cars, as well as the multiple causes identified by commentators. While the riots were multiethnic, a number of commentators held black people responsible. For example, the historian David Starkey used his appearance on BBC 2's news and current affairs programme, *Newsnight*, to make pejorative, essentialising assertions about blackness and to blame black people and what he constructs as a deviant black culture, which he argues some working class white people have adopted.[3] Starkey suggested that the 2011 riots fulfilled Enoch Powell's prophecy, made in his infamous 'Rivers of Blood' speech, that violent conflict would be the inevitable result of immigration:

3 See http://www.bbc.co.uk/news/uk-14513517 for BBC clip of the programme. Last accessed 18th November 2011.

> His prophecy was absolutely right in one sense. The Tiber didn't foam with blood, but flames lambent wrapped round Tottenham and wrapped round Clapham, but it wasn't inter-communal violence, this is where he was completely wrong. What's happened is that a substantial section of the chavs have become black. The whites have become black.[4]

4 *ibid.*

Starkey's statement gives recognition to the multiethnic nature of the riots and to the unacceptability of old ways of racialising social dissent while determinedly racialising them. As Jones (2011), who opposed Starkey's arguments on the *Newsnight* programme, explains, hatred of the working classes has become so accepted among the middle classes that the pejorative term 'chavs' has become a taken-for-granted negative stereotype. For Starkey, whose professional historical interest lies in the upper classes, the section of the white working classes whose behaviour he finds unacceptable 'have become black'. He thus essentialises whiteness as good (and English) and blackness as its antithesis.

Brah's (1999) reading of the 1976 confrontations of black and Asian young people with the police suggests that the riots were, in part, about redefining and broadening the exclusionary discourses of Britishness that were prevalent at the time. It is striking that Starkey uses the multiethnic riots in summer 2011 implicitly to reproduce the anachronistic, exclusionary, racialised discourses about Britishness and belonging that Brah demonstrates were being resisted by black young people in the 1970s riots.

> A particular sort of violent, destructive, nihilistic gangster culture has become the fashion and black and white, boy and girl operate in this language together. This language which is wholly false, which is a Jamaican patois that's been intruded in England, and this is why so many of us have this sense of literally a foreign country [sic].[5]

5 *ibid.*

By asserting that a 'Jamaican patois' has been 'intruded in England', with the result that 'so many *of us* have this sense of literally a foreign country' (emphasis added), Starkey implicitly constructs African-Caribbean people as 'intruders', outsiders who can be blamed for making the white majority feel like foreigners in their own country. In using 'Jamaican patois' as a signifier of intrusion that has rendered England 'literally' foreign, Starkey is (re)producing an old debate as illustrated by Brah's analysis of the 1970s discourse of white participants who considered Southall to have been taken over by Asians:

> Here we encounter feminized commonsense with its fantasy of tranquil and tidy rural domesticity which is 'mucked up', disrupted by the 'intruders' with their alien food and unfamiliar smells. There is an overwhelming feeling of being 'taken over', of being soiled and defiled, of things being 'horrible'. The 'intruder' is discursively embodied as a form of aggressive masculinity. Asians come to be represented as having 'taken over', as the discourse converts the transgressed-against into the transgressors. (Brah, 1999: 10)

By racialising the nation into black and white (as in the first extract above), Starkey reproduces the discourses Brah highlights. He represents black people, metonymically symbolised by 'Jamaican patois', as having 'taken over' England and converts them 'into the transgressors'. In his *Newsnight* appearance, Starkey argues that 'it's not skin colour, it's cultural' and extends his auditory, linguistic focus to identify MP David Lammy as 'an archetypical, successful black man' whom he suggests one would think 'white' if only listening to him talk. This construction of whiteness as synonymous with education, eloquence and success implies that blackness is devoid of these characteristics and that any black person who has these attributes can be thought of as white. Starkey's *Newsnight* performance thus shows the enduring utility of Brah's analysis and demonstrates the recursiveness of old racialised discourses and hence their availability to be drawn on (often in new ways) by Catherine and others.

A central part of Brah's (1999) analysis was of 'new racist' discourses (Barker, 1981). 'New racism' refers to the ways in which 'immigration was regarded as having brought to Britain a population that destroyed the cultural homogeneity of the nation and that, as it grew in size, threatened to "swamp" the culture of "our own people"' (Miles and Brown, 2003: 61). Starkey presents a 'new racist' argument that had already been deconstructed in the early 1980s (CCCS, 1982). By binarising black and white while pathologising blackness, he creates afresh an old racialised hierarchy of belonging.

If Starkey were alone in treating the riots as an opportunity to produce 'new racist' discourses, this would neither indicate that Brah's analysis retains elements relevant to a contemporary analysis, nor illuminate the discourses potentially available to Catherine. However, while Starkey's *Newsnight* appearance generated a 'storm of protest',[6] numerous supporters praised his views on Twitter and in feedback to other media. Equally, other high-profile commentators expressed views commensurate with Starkey's. For example, John Bird, (one of the founders of a UK social business that offers homeless people the opportunity to earn an income through selling *The Big Issue* magazine), alluded to Britain being 'taken over' by black people. In an article in the *Independent* newspaper, Bird wrote that one of the most significant images from the riots was that of a 'shorter, weaker, white boy being made to

6 Quinn, B. (2011) 'David Starkey claims "the whites have become black"' *The Guardian*, 13 August 2011, http://www.guardian.co.uk/uk/2011/aug/13/david-starkey-claims-whites-black, last accessed 26

strip while a bigger black boy, or man, watches'.[7] He argued that 'supremacy on the street is a black supremacy. It is the uniform of the poor black inner city boldly adopting an identity to say "fuck you" – taking a social position of emptiness and nothingness and making it into a social power statement'.[8] While Bird acknowledged that not all of the rioters were black, he suggested that black people were nonetheless responsible because 'poor inner-city black people are fashion leaders. They are the style leaders. They are the leader. And you follow'.[9] As in Starkey's discourse, Bird presented black young men as powerful 'transgressors' whose 'supremacy' over the streets is problematic. His is a discourse that, to quote Brah (1999: 15), 'embodies the contradictory relationality of "race", gender, class, and ... articulates "power-geometries" of spatiality (Massey, 1999) along these different signifiers of "difference"' in ways that (re)produce old racist discourses in new forms and reinforce racialised black–white boundaries. Bird's use of 'our' interpellates a 'we' into belonging that makes us feel othered and excluded as black people, just as it others 'poor black inner city' young men.

Following the volume of negative criticism he received, Starkey attempted to defend his *Newsnight* position in an article in the *Telegraph* newspaper.[10] He cited an article written in the *Daily Mirror* newspaper by Tony Parsons, which holds 'the gang culture of black London' responsible for the riots in a variety of English cities. Parsons attributed the riots to a 'generation that is good for nothing and yet scared of nothing'.[11] He claimed that 'without the gang culture of black London, none of the riots would have happened – including the riots in other cities like Manchester and Birmingham where most of rioters [sic] were white'. Parsons argued that this is especially sad for 'all the decent, hard working black men and women in this country' who 'do not deserve to see the clock turned back to the Seventies and Eighties, when racism was overt and vicious. But that is what will happen. The images of black youths running wild will not be quickly forgotten'.[12] Parsons' discourse constructs the riots as making possible a return to overt and vicious racism against black people.

Starkey, Bird and Parsons each racialise the riots and blame black young people. Each does so by drawing on 'new racist' ideas comparable to those Brah demonstrates are central to both popular and political racialised exclusions and inclusions from the local and the national. Each implicitly genders their accounts in that they are primarily focusing on black young men, not women. Their explanations are thus intersectional in bringing together racialisation, gender and (implicitly) social class. Their discourses neither fit with current 'post-race' formulations nor recognise that blackness 'has always been an unstable identity, psychically, culturally, and politically. It, too, is a narrative, a story, a history. Something constructed, told, spoken, not simply found' (Hall, 1996: 116). As Paul Gilroy (2004) describes, culturalist, new racist arguments have residual appeal in postcolonial Britain, and while an emphasis on culture in racial discourse may

September 2011.

7 Bird, 2011: http://www .independent.co .uk/opinion/ commentators/ john-bird-fashion-has-become-a-weapon-on-the-streets-of-london-2337838.html. Last accessed 21st August 2011.

8 *ibid.*

9 *ibid.*

10 See Starkey, D. (2011) 'UK riots: it's not about criminality and cuts, it's about culture and this is only the beginning' *The Telegraph*, http:// www.telegraph .co.uk/news/ uknews/law-and-order/8711621/UK-riots-Its-not-about-criminality-and-cuts-its-about-culture-and-this-is-onlythe-beginning.html, last accessed 21 August 2011.

11 See Parsons, T. (2011) 'UK riots: why did the riots happen? Who are the rioters? What can we do to end this madness?' *Daily Mirror*, http:// www.mirror.co.uk/ news/top-stories/ 2011/08/13/uk-riots-tonyparsons-the-britain-we-knew-has-gone-for-ever-115875-23340566/, last accessed 26 August 2011.

12 *ibid.*

seem more benign than the cruder force of biological 'race' theory, it is equally brutal. Gilroy is undoubtedly right that currently 'social and cultural differences are being coded according to the rules of a biological discourse' (2004: 34). However, the commentaries following the 2011 riots show that what is now old 'new racism' continues to be drawn on in popular discourses when this proves expedient, with little attempt to appeal to empirical evidence. Such discourses are, arguably, easily evoked and recognised because they have sedimented into common sense (Gramsci, 1971) and are recursive.

In a *World Have Your Say* programme during the riots, the BBC World Service said that many people who contacted the BBC 'pointed fingers directly at young black men' and the *World Have Your Say* programme asked its audience to respond to the question they posed: 'Is there a problem with young black men, or is society and the media demonising the people at the bottom of the pile?'.[13] While framing the debate in this way reproduces the discourse that Brah described, the reaction to the programme demonstrates that there is also a rupturing of such discursive formations. The BBC was inundated with complaints about this question and apologised for any offence its headline had caused, stating that 'The original headline question that appears online was, in hindsight, too stark and could have been clearer'.[14] However, it is noteworthy that the question ('Is there a problem with young black men?') was a repeat of one asked in 2006 by the same programme following 'an altercation between two groups of black men which had ended in three being shot — and one dying later'.[15] In both cases, the BBC posed a question that invited its international audience to decide whether or not young black men, constructed by the BBC as a homogeneous group, are pathological. This seems an example of how 'new racist' cultural arguments always intersect with gendered constructions (c.f. CCCS, 1982), and/or Gilroy's notion that cultural arguments are being coded into biological discourses.

For Brah, concerned to understand Jean's positioning, an important political question was 'How do we change this "distanciation" of the "macro issues" into more intimate conversations that foster connectedness and understanding?' For us, however, Starkey, Bird and Parsons seem not to be seeking connectedness and understanding, but to assert their viewpoints, which involve pathologising blackness without addressing the underlying political and socio-economic causes of the riots. That their pathologising discourses serve racist ends can be seen clearly in comments made by the far-right British National Party (BNP)[16] that 'multiculturalism' and immigration were to blame for the riots. After Starkey's appearance on *Newsnight*, BNP Chairman Nick Griffin tweeted 'Wondering whether to make David Starkey an honoury [sic] Gold Member for his *Newsnight* appearance'.

In recognition of the concerted opposition to his pronouncements, David Starkey gave an interview to *The Voice* black weekly newspaper (Richards, 2011), in which

13 McGovern N. (2011) WHYS 60: England riots. *World Have Your Say. BBC World Service*, http://www.bbc.co.uk/iplayer/episode/p00j84dk/World_Have_Your_Say_WHYS_60_England_riots/, accessed 21 August 2011.

14 BBC spokesperson cited in Burrell, I. (2011) 'BBC forced to apologise again for riots coverage' *The Independent*, http://www.independent.co.uk/news/media/tv-radio/bbc-forced-to-apologise-again-for-riots-coverage-2338180.html, last accessed 22 August 2011.

15 Atkins R. (2006) 'Is there a problem with young black men?' *BBC World Service, World Have Your Say Blog*, http://www.bbc.co.uk/blogs/worldhaveyoursay/2006/11/is_there_a_problem_with_young.html, accessed 21 August 2011.

16 British National Party. (2011) 'London burning

he claimed that 'I'm a white man not black, therefore I'm not allowed to speak'. The implication that his pronouncements would have been acceptable if voiced by a black man erroneously assumes that those who have criticised his comments are more concerned with essentialist embodiment than with content. His defence of his position also demonstrates how a range of rhetorical devices are frequently marshalled to warrant unpalatable claims. In this case, Starkey denies that he needs to apologise for what he said (although he agrees that it was inappropriate to have mentioned Enoch Powell), and, instead, uses various rhetorical strategies to warrant his version of the causes of the riots:

> I'm absolutely not, in anyway [sic] possible, racist. I think racists are demented. I was born crippled, with two left feet and had to wear surgical boats [sic] until I was in my early teens. I turned out to be gay and I had to wear spectacles from the age of nine.
> I've been on the receiving end as well. I know about prejudice and what hurt feels like. I have been abused by a policeman. It's not about skin colour, it's about how people are brought up. (Starkey, quoted in Richards, 2011: 2)

It appears that Starkey's aim here is to generate sympathy in *The Voice* readership (most of whom are black) by giving personal information designed to position him as relatively powerless and vulnerable. This functions as defensive prolepsis (in much the same way as Catherine denies racism in the previous section), allowing him to deny charges of racism, particularly since he asserts that 'racists are demented' (c.f. Billig, 1991). In addition, Starkey constructs himself as knowing how it feels to be hurt by prejudice. In order to buttress his claims to expert knowledge, he draws on 'situated knowledges' (Haraway, 1991) and intersectionality by presenting his whiteness (which could potentially position him as powerful) as decentred by disability and homosexuality. He does not draw on his disciplinary expertise as a historian, but uses identity as a resource to construct positions from which it is legitimate to pontificate (Antaki and Widdicombe, 1998). In the above extract, Starkey also makes claims that can be read as psychosocial from the vantage point of the social sciences since he brings in the personal and emotional to legitimate his social analyses.

It is important to acknowledge, as Brah recognised in her discussion of the riots in the 1970s, that many people resist pathologising discourses. Arguments such as those explored in this section are far from the only ones that have claimed media attention since the 2011 riots. While the above examples racialise the debate in essentialising and exclusionary ways, other commentators have taken a more nuanced, complex view. For example, Patricia Daley, a black British Caribbean lecturer at Oxford University, who grew up on the Pembury estate in Hackney, London (a borough that adjoins Tower Hamlets), suggests 'In a television debate, the historian, David Starkey, blames the riots on whites becoming black by adopting black culture; thus implying that black culture is dysfunctional. Many commentators have attacked the racism of much of his

after three days of race riots', http://www.bnp.org.uk/news/national/london-burning-after-three-days-race-riots, accessed 21 August 2011.

17 See Daley, P. (2011) 'Recalling 1970s London: has life improved since for the young, poor and black?' Open Democracy, 19 August 2011, http://www.opendemocracy.net/ourkingdom/patricia-daley/recalling-1970s-london-has-life-improved-since-for-young-poor-and-black, last accessed 27 August 2011.

18 Munslow A., Gilroy P., Sayer D., Constantine S., and 99 others. (2011) 'Starkey's ignorance is hardly work of history'. Letter to THE, 25–31 August 2011: 28, http://www.timeshighereducation.co.uk/story.asp?storycode =417236, last accessed 26 August 2011.

19 See Starkey, D. (2011) 'UK riots: it's not about criminality and cuts, it's about culture and this is only the beginning' The Telegraph, http://www.telegraph.co.uk/news/uknews/law-and-order/8711621/UK-riots-Its-not-about-criminality-and-cuts-its-about-culture-and-this-is-onlythe-beginning.html, last accessed 21 August 2011.

retort'.[17] Similarly, in a letter published in *Times Higher Education*, a group of more than one hundred historians, social theorists and graduates argued that David Starkey was a 'singularly poor choice' for the BBC *Newsnight* programme. They censured the 'poverty' of Starkey's 'reductionist argument', which was 'evidentially insupportable and factually wrong' and suggested that this was unsurprising given that 'Starkey has professed himself to be a historian of elites, and his academic work has never focused on race and class'. They also critiqued the way in which the BBC represented Starkey's opinions 'as those of a "historian"' given that 'as even the most basic grasp of cultural history would show' the views Starkey presented on the programme have no basis in research or evidence. 'In particular, his crass generalisations about black culture and white culture as oppositional, monolithic entities demonstrate a failure to grasp the subtleties of race and class that would disgrace a first-year history undergraduate'.[18]

Unlike Catherine's account above, Starkey, Bird and Parsons' pronouncements are public media accounts designed to be opinion (in)forming. It is not, therefore, possible to do biographically-informed psychosocial readings of them. It would, of course, be possible to investigate their lives and biographies with a view to understanding how these accounts function for them. For the purposes of our analyses here and of 'writing back' to 'The Scent of Memory', however, it is more relevant to examine their impact within a postcolonial context that various theorists suggest is melancholic because histories of slavery and colonialism remain unacknowledged (Gilroy, 2004; Flax, 2010). Starkey's proclamation that 'we will not continue, I think, to tolerate being lied to and cheated in the matter of race'[19] can thus be read as a moral pronouncement, which claims that being 'honest' about 'race' requires accepting that a black 'gangsta culture' has been adopted by 'chavs' and lies at the heart of current social ills. This rhetoric ignores both the multiethnic nature of the riots and the multiple and complex reasons they took hold in various locations, as well as the history of racialisation and racism in the United Kingdom. This ignoring of the 'history of the present' serves, in Brah's (1999: 10) terms, to convert 'the transgressed-against into the transgressors' and is racist in effect. Starkey's approach runs counter to current work by narrative analysts, psychoanalysts and social scientists that analyses the interpenetration of 'big' (social) and 'small' (personal) histories (e.g. Davoine and Gaudillière, 2004; Freeman, 2008; Flax, 2011; Walkerdine *et al.*, in press) and to the approach taken in 'The Scent of Memory', which contextualises Jean's personal story historically and socio-economically.

The three sets of discourses presented in this second section of the paper, together with the BBC 'World Have Your Say' discussion topic, work to construct part of the context in which racialisation takes exclusionary, racist forms in ways similar to those identified by Brah (1999). For Catherine, living in contemporary postcolonial London, such pronouncements constitute the context in which her racialised subjectification is enabled. They produce a legible subjectivity for her to occupy (c.f. Butler, 2004) that helps to give her life value and meaning. Discourses of this kind are interpellative, hailing us all into different emotionally-marked subjectivities and so exposing 'the hollowness in the mantra "we are all in it together" '.[20] Thus, while such discourses highlight the ways in which we are all interlinked in complex ways in Brah's (1996) 'diaspora space', they also demonstrate how we are positioned differentially in power relations. From a psychosocial perspective, the ready availability of racist discourses that are repeated across time, but draw on new elements to warrant their claims helps to explain why Catherine's biographical insecurities are linked with her racialisation of Bangladeshi mothers, and hence why 'The Scent of Memory' was innovative in taking what we now recognise as a psychosocial approach.

conclusions

The two sets of analyses in this paper relate to accounts produced in very different contexts for different purposes. Catherine told the story of her pregnancy and birth to a research interviewer in the privacy of her own home. In contrast, Starkey, Bird and Parsons made public pronouncements about the causes and implications of the 2011 UK riots. There are thus important differences in their aims. Nonetheless, our reading of 'The Scent of Memory' and analyses of the interview with Catherine and the racialising responses to the 2011 riots have shown the power of racialised interpellation to 'other' black and minoritised ethnic people in Britain. Although now old, what was identified as 'new racism' in the 1980s is still being evoked in attempts to position black and minoritised ethnic people lower on the hierarchy of belonging than their white counterparts. By focusing on 'culture' as opposed to skin colour or ethnic origin, both Catherine (in her interview) and Starkey, Parsons and Bird (in their post-riot commentaries) seek to avoid critiques of their discourses as racist at the same time as they homogenise and pathologise Asian or black people. Juxtaposing the two sets of accounts highlights the relational nature of interpellation and of the psychosocial space of racialisation.

It is disturbing that in 2011 commentators are predicting a return to the racism of the 1970s and 1980s[21] while reviving racist discourses from that era. Just as Brah (1999) discusses the ways in which class differences were obscured and racialised in the 'new racist' discourses she examined, so the effects of poverty on social cohesion and disaffection, while evident, are left implicit in Catherine's narratives and in Starkey, Bird and Parsons' commentaries. We would have liked to have been able to write back to Brah, meditating on how much the socio-political situation has changed since she wrote 'The Scent of Memory' in 1999. There have undoubtedly been many hopeful changes since the 1970s, so that

20 See Daley, P. (2011) 'Recalling 1970s London: has life improved since for the young, poor and black?' Open Democracy, 19 August 2011, http://www.opendemocracy.net/ourkingdom/patricia-daley/recalling-1970s-london-has-life-improved-since-for-young-poor-and-black, last accessed 27 August 2011.

21 For example, Parsons, T. (2011) 'UK riots: why did the riots happen? Who are the rioters? What can we do to end this madness?' Daily Mirror, http://www.mirror.co.uk/news/top-stories/2011/08/13/uk-

riots-tonyparsons-
the-britain-we-
knew-has-gone-for-
ever-115875-
23340566/, last
accessed 26 August
2011.

some spaces can now be characterised as 'convivial multicultures' (Gilroy, 2004; Rampton *et al.*, 2010). However, the response to the 2011 riots has shown how the scent of pathologising discourses and 'new racism' lingers on.

Brah (1999: 24) draws her meditation to a close, citing the novelist Toni Morrison. 'What a wonderful title – *Beloved*! Wonderful because it heals even as it opens the intimate wounds'. We would like to end our 'writing back' with similar optimism. As much as Catherine's narrative may be painful for those it others and as much as Starkey, Bird and Parsons' racist discourses have incensed, offended and wounded, there is something healing about the challenge to the 'new racist' discourses that the 2011 riots elicited. Starkey, and no doubt Bird and Parsons have their supporters and gain privilege from attempts to impose their partial perspectives (Haraway, 1991). Numerous voices, however, will not stay silent and allow them to distort and monopolise a much-needed debate, one to which 'The Scent of Memory' continues to make a thought-provoking contribution.

acknowledgements

Thanks to Heather Elliott and Wendy Hollway for helpful comments, to the mothers who took part in the 'Becoming a Mother' study and the Economic and Social Research Council who funded it.

authors' biographies

Aisha Phoenix is a PhD student in the Sociology Department at Goldsmiths, University of London. Her research is on Palestinian Muslim young people living in the West Bank. Her particular focus is on how their experiences and readings of the past affect their orientations to the future. Her earlier research was on Somali young women and hierarchies of belonging.

Ann Phoenix is Professor and Co-Director at Thomas Coram Research Unit, Institute of Education, University of London and co-directs the Childhood Wellbeing Research Centre funded by the Department for Education. Her research focuses on psychosocial identities. She has recently completed research for an ESRC Professorial Fellowship on 'Transforming Experiences: Re-conceptualising identities and "non-normative" childhoods'. She is the Principal Investigator on NOVELLA (Narratives of Varied Everyday Lives and Linked Approaches), an ESRC National Centre for Research Methods node (2011–2014).

references

Althusser, L. (1977) 'Ideology and ideological state apparatuses (notes towards an investigation)' in Althusser, L. (1977) editor, *'Lenin and Philosophy' and Other Essays*, London: New Left Books.

Antaki, C. and Widdicombe, S. (1998) *Identities in Talk*, London: Sage.

Barker, M. (1981) *The New Racism: Conservatives and the Ideology of the Tribe*, London: Junction Books.

Billig, M. (1991) *Ideology and Opinions: Studies in Rhetorical Psychology*, London: Sage.

Bjerrum Nilsen, H. and Haavind, H. (2010) 'Personal development and socio-cultural change' Centre for Advanced Studies, Norwegian Academy of Sciences research group 2010/11. Unpublished research application.

Brah, A. (1996) *Cartographies of Diaspora: Contesting Identities*, London: Routledge.

Brah, A. (1999) 'The Scent of Memory: strangers, our own, and others' *Feminist Review*, Issue 61: 4–26.

Butler, J. (2004) *Undoing Gender*, New York: Routledge.

Centre for Contemporary Cultural Studies (1982) *The Empire Strikes Back: Race and Racism in 70s Britain*, London: Hutchinson.

Davoine, F. and Gaudillière, J.-M. (2004) *History Beyond Trauma*, New York: Other Press.

Elliott, H. (2011) 'Interviewing mothers: reflections on closeness and reflexivity in research encounters' *Studies in the Maternal*, Vol. 3, No. 1, www.mamsie.bbk.ac.uk, last accessed 23 November 2011.

Elliott, H, Ryan, J. and Hollway, H. (in press) 'Research encounters, reflexivity and supervision' *International Journal of Social Research Methodology* http://rsa.informaworld.com/10.1080/13645579.2011.610157, last accessed 23 November 2011.

Flax, J. (2010) *Resonances of Slavery in Race/Gender Relations: Shadow at the Heart of American Politics*, New York: Palgrave Macmillan.

Freeman, M. (2008) *Hindsight: The Promise and Peril of Looking Backward*, New York: Oxford University Press.

Gilroy, P. (2004) *Between Camps: Nations, Cultures and the Allure of Race*, London: Routledge.

Gramsci, A. (1971) 'The Study of Philosophy' in Hoare, Q. and Nowell-Smith, G. (1971) editors and translators, *Selections from the Prison Notebooks*, New York: International Publishers.

Hall, S. (1996) 'Minimal selves' in Baker, H.A., Diawara, M. and Lindeborg, R.H. (1996) editors, *Black British Cultural Studies: A Reader*, Chicago, IL: University of Chicago Press, (Originally published in 1987).

Haraway, D. (1991) 'Situated knowledges: the science question in feminism and the privilege of partial perspective' in Haraway, D. (1991) editor, *Simians, Cyborgs, and Women: the Reinvention of Nature*, New York: Routledge.

Jones, O. (2011) *Chavs: The Demonization of the Working Class*, London: Verso.

Lewis, G. (2009) 'Animating hatreds: research encounters, organisational secrets, emotional truths' in Gill, R. and Ryan-Flood, R. (2009) editors, *Secrecy and Silence in the Research Process: Feminist Reflections*, London: Psychology Press.

Massey, D. (1999) 'Imagining globalisation: power-geometries of time-space' in Brah, A., Hickman, M.J. and Mac an Ghaill, M. (1999) editors, *Future Worlds: Migration, Environment and Globalisation*, London: Macmillan.

Massey, D. (2005) *For Space*, London: Sage.

McLeod, J. and Thomson, R. (2009) *Researching Social Change*, London: Qualitative Approaches Sage.

Miles, R. and Brown, M. (2003) *Racism 2nd Edition*, London: Routledge.

Morrison, T. (1987) *Beloved*, USA: Alfred Knopf.

Mulinari, D. and Räthzel, N. (2007) 'Politicizing biographies: the forming of transnational subjectivities as insiders outside' *Feminist Review*, Issue 86: 89–112.

Rampton, B. and Harris, R. (2010) 'Change in urban classroom culture and interaction' in Littleton, K. and Howe, C. (2010) editors, *Educational Dialogues: Understanding and Promoting Productive Interaction*, London: Routledge.

Räthzel, N., Cohen, P., Back, L., Keith, M. and Hieronymus, A. (2008) *Finding the Way Home: Young People's Stories of Gender, Ethnicity, Class, and Places in Hamburg and London*, Göttingen: V&R Unipress.

Richards, M. (2011) 'Is it coz I is white?' [Report of an interview with David Starkey]. *The Voice*, 25–31 August 2011: 2.

Walkerdine, V, Olsvold, A. and Rudberg, M. (article submitted) 'History walked in the door: embodying history's secrets — towards an approach to researching intergenerational trauma'.

Westwood, S. (1990) 'Racism, black masculinity and the politics of space' in Hearn, J. and Morgan, D. (1990) editors, *Men, Masculinities and Social Theory*, London: Unwin Hyman.

Wetherell, M. and Potter, J. (1992) *Mapping the Language of Racism*, London: Sage.

doi:10.1057/fr.2011.63

100 | interruption, reproduction and genealogies of 'staying put' in diaspora space

Irene Gedalof

abstract

In her 1999 article 'The Scent of Memory', Avtar Brah maps the ways in which gendered, classed and racialised identities and subjectivities are produced in the diaspora space of Britain. 'The Scent of Memory' begins, repeatedly returns to and ends with the figure of a mother — Jean, a white English woman in the Southall of the 1970s and 1980s. One way of reading this article is as a series of interruptions, each of which allows us to see Jean differently, to replace her in what Brah has memorably termed the entanglement of genealogies of dispersion with those of staying put (Brah, 1996: 181). In this article, I stage my own set of speculative interruptions, through which recent feminist theorising of maternal subjectivities confronts the ways in which the maternal and the reproductive are conceptualised, metaphorised and mobilised in contemporary accounts of community cohesion, Britishness and belonging. At stake is our ability to challenge those still-dominant discourses that naturalise repetition and sameness as the necessary ground of belonging, obscuring and ignoring the gendered, racialised and other differences that mark Britishness, and which thereby reproduce the migrant and the minoritised as a problem for the stability of British identities. Following on from and extending Lisa Baraitser's claim that thinking about the relationship with the other 'might just as well start with the mother' (2009a: 153), I ask whether rethinking the reproductive can enable a more complex account of the ways in which 'the native' is transformed in diaspora spaces.

keywords

mothering; cultural reproduction; community cohesion; diaspora space; Britishness

(72–87) © 2012 Feminist Review. 0141-7789/12 www.feminist-review.com

> If ... we are serious about the ethical turn and that we want to account for human subjectivity through some understanding of how we come to be structured by our relation to others, then we could just as well start with the mother, whose structuring through a relation to her child poses all sorts of intractable problems, especially when posed in the feminine, when we begin to examine what it means to 'be for another'. (Baraitser, 2009a: 153)

In her 1999 article 'The Scent of Memory', Avtar Brah maps the ways in which gendered, classed and racialised identities and subjectivities are produced in the diaspora space of Britain. Taking as her focus the West London neighbourhood of Southall, she brings together personal narratives and the socio-economic and political contexts within which these narratives are located. Brah's remarkable article is distinctive not only for its original analysis, but also for its innovative structure and style – a 'meditation through a series of questions' (1999: 4). 'The Scent of Memory' begins, repeatedly returns to and ends with the figure of a mother – Jean, a white English woman in the Southall of the 1970s and 1980s – remembered by her son, Tim Lott in his autobiography, *The Scent of Dried Roses*. One way of reading this article is as a series of interruptions, each of which allows us to see Jean differently, to replace her in what Brah has memorably termed the entanglement of genealogies of dispersion with those of staying put (Brah, 1996: 181). Brah frames her article as a response to Donna Haraway's call for feminisms to consider the possibilities of 'post-humanist' figures that might exceed or disrupt the logic of 'the sacred image of the same' (Haraway, 1992: 87), and that through 'the self-critical practice of difference' (*ibid.*) might revision humanity as 'an intricate mosaic of *non-identical* kinship' (Brah, 1999: 6). In this article, I ask whether the mother might be thought of as one of these post-humanist figures.

Mothers, and the physical and cultural work of reproduction that they do, are still rarely thought about in these terms. More often, the figure of the mother in the history of Western thought stands as a metaphor for sameness. Physical reproduction – birth – is generally seen as the mere ground for the more important productive things that happen after we are born, and separation from the sameness of the mother is seen as crucial to developing as distinct individual selves. Following on from this way of thinking birth, cultural reproduction is also often conceptualised as mere repetition, the passing on of the same traditions, the same ways of behaving properly, of doing things, which bind an unmarked individual to a pre-existing community or culture. So, as many feminist theorists of the maternal have argued, the mother stands as an abject figure, as that which must be excluded and transcended, in order for the masculine subject to bring himself into being. The work of reproduction, necessary as it might be, remains encumbered with associations to stasis, sameness and resistance to change, and this manner of conceptualising reproduction continues to inflect the ways in which the work of making homes and reproducing structures of belonging is seen in the context of migration and the 'diversity' it brings (Gedalof, 2009). But might the mother — rethought, reframed, wrenched away from this logic of the same that ties reproduction to stasis — be more of a disruptive, 'post-humanist' figure for tracing an alternative narrative or genealogy of the work of 'staying put' than is usually thought?

In what follows, I stage my own set of speculative interruptions, through which recent feminist theorising of maternal subjectivities confronts the ways in which the maternal and the reproductive are conceptualised, metaphorised and mobilised in some contemporary accounts of Britishness and belonging. As Brah repeatedly comes back to Jean from different perspectives, to complicate the story of the mother remembered in her son's account, I want to complicate the memory of the mother that, I argue, still haunts these accounts of Britishness. At stake is our ability to challenge those still-dominant discourses that naturalise repetition and sameness as the necessary ground of belonging, obscuring and ignoring the gendered, racialised and other differences that mark Britishness, and which thereby reproduce the migrant and the minoritised as a problem for the stability of British identities. Following on from and extending Lisa Baraitser's claim that thinking about the relationship with the other 'might just as well start with the mother' (2009a: 153), I ask whether rethinking the reproductive can enable a more complex account of the ways in which 'the native' is transformed in diaspora spaces.

Britishness and the discomfort of strangers

> Real communities are bound by common experiences forged by friendship and conversation, knotted together by all the rituals of the neighbourhood, from the school run to the chat down the pub. And these bonds take time.
>
> So real integration takes time. That's why, when there have been significant numbers of new people arriving in neighbourhoods, perhaps not being able to speak the same language as those living there, on occasions not really wanting or even willing to integrate, that has created a kind of discomfort and disjointedness in some neighbourhoods. This has been the experience for many people in our country — and I believe it is untruthful and unfair not to speak about it and address it.[1]

In his recent speech on migration, David Cameron evokes many of the same sentiments Brah considers in 'The Scent of Memory', which have by now congealed into the familiar scenario of a settled population naturally unsettled by change. While much attention has been rightly paid to the ways in which 'the migrant' is produced in such discourse, what characteristics does this 'common sense' account ascribe to those who have stayed put? Popular political discourse on migration, diversity and the challenge to social or community cohesion

1 David Cameron, 2011, *The Guardian*, 14 April 2011, 'Immigrants should learn English — PM', http://www .guardian.co.uk/ politics/2011/apr/ 14/david-cameron -immigration- speech-full-text, last accessed 18th November 2011.

they are said to produce is constituted in part on the ground of a naturalised, taken-for-granted figure of the white Briton who is uncomfortable with change, who is naturally threatened by the interruption to a repetitive sameness that migration represents. This figure is sometimes explicitly represented by a mother. Most notoriously, Enoch Powell's 1968 'Rivers of Blood' speech took as one of its central images an elderly white woman whose sons had died for their country and whose 'quiet street' had been turned into a place of 'noise and confusion' by the arrival of immigrants (Webster, 1998). Here, Powell draws on the long-standing metaphorising of mother as nation, a naturalised object in need of defending by a masculinised subject-citizen, and a key part of the problematic gendering of the politics of nation that has been comprehensively critiqued by a range of feminist thinkers (see Kandiyoti, 1993 and Yuval-Davis, 1997 among many others).

Often, though, this characterisation of the 'native' extends beyond the explicit figure of a mother to an underlying representation of the work of reproducing structures of belonging as requiring familiarity and sameness. Gendered tropes of home, family and the domestic carry with them the weight of their naturalising baggage and are mobilised as necessarily signifying the comfort of the known, the stable and unchanging. Thirty-six years after Powell evoked his vision of the bereaved and assailed mother, David Goodhart, editor of the magazine *Prospect*, returned to this sense of a white British 'we' disrupted by change in his essay 'Too Diverse?', reprinted in *The Guardian* as 'The Discomfort of Strangers' (Goodhart, 2004). Goodhart starts from two sites that have been evoked repeatedly in the contemporary discourse of social and community cohesion that his essay helped to initiate — the domesticated space of 'the neighbourhood' and the naturalised space of the family:

> Britain in the 50s was a country stratified by class and region. But in most of its cities, suburbs, towns and villages there was a good chance of predicting the attitudes, even the behaviour, of the people living in your immediate neighbourhood. In many parts of Britain today that is no longer true. The country has long ceased to be Orwell's 'family'. (Goodhart, 2004)

In the case of both family and neighbourhood, he assumes that it is the recognition of sameness that forms the only secure ground for a sense of belonging together, and for the kind of relationality that would enable 'us' to share that sense of belonging and entitlement with others. In this, he takes his lead from the Conservative politician David Willetts who, he says, drew his attention to the 'progressive dilemma', in which the legitimacy of the welfare state principle of pooling and sharing resources is only sustained by the belief that its beneficiaries will be 'people like us'. In the context of contemporary migration, where 'more of our lives is spent among strangers' and 'we must not only live among stranger citizens but we must share with them', this legitimacy is strained:

> all such acts of sharing are more smoothly and generously negotiated if we can take for granted a limited set of common values and assumptions. But as Britain becomes more diverse that common culture is being eroded. (Goodhart, 2004)

For Goodhart, the once taken-for-granted 'glue of ethnicity' now is replaced by the 'glue of values' — meaning 'people who think and behave like us'. British values grow in part out of a specific history and geography, and there are problems if 'too many citizens no longer identify with that history' (ibid.). For Goodhart, the loss of this certainty places intolerable limits on the possibilities of 'solidarity with strangers'. Making more explicit the link between this vision of solidarity and the reproductive, among the list of basic norms that he argues a community must have in common is 'some agreement on the nature of marriage and the family'.

Under Labour, this narrative of the native unsettled by diversity and in need of reassurance through the articulation of common values or a common culture was repeatedly evoked, especially in the discourse of community cohesion, although it first appears in the elaboration of immigration and asylum policy, and also returns in the context of equalities policy. The 2001 White Paper on Immigration and Asylum, *Secure Borders, Safe Haven*, made clear a vision of the conditions under which the native could be expected to be open to difference:

> Countries offering refuge to those fleeing persecution and war, as well as accepting economic migration to meet their core economic and skills needs, *need to be confident in their identity and sense of belonging*, and trust their immigration and asylum systems to work fairly and effectively. Strong civic and community foundations are necessary if people are to have the confidence to welcome asylum seekers and migrants. ... *They must have a sense of their own community or civic identity* — a sense of shared understanding which can both animate and give moral content to the benefits and duties of citizenship to which new entrants aspire. *Only then* can integration with diversity be achieved. (Home Office, 2001: 9, emphasis added)

Labour thinking on immigration and asylum in the early 2000s also re-evoked a figure familiar from earlier debates on migration — the white working-class Briton whose stable sense of identity was being challenged by having to share the resources of social reproduction — health care, schools and housing — with those who don't 'think and behave like us'. As former Labour cabinet minister Stephen Byers put it, Labour needed to:

> ... reassure working-class voters that Labour understood their concerns about immigration. ... It is clearly the case that many of Labour's traditional supporters are those that fear immigration the most. They are concerned that their schools and health services are under increased pressure, *that in some way their national identity is*

2 'Cut health care for illegal migrants says Byers', *The Guardian*, 31 July 2003, emphasis added, http://www.guardian.co.uk/politics/2003/jul/31/immigration.immigration andpublicservices? INTCMP=SRCH, last accessed November 2011.

3 See Travis, A. (2009), 'Denham takes aim at white working-class resentment', *The Guardian*, http://www.guardian.co.uk/society/2009/oct/14/denham-white-working-class-resentment, last accessed November 2009.

4 *ibid*.

5 See Travis, A. (2008) 'White working class needs help in recession

under threat and that they have to pay for people who are simply exploiting the present system.[2]

This displacement of anxieties about change onto the racialised and classed figure of the white working class was particularly marked in the latter years of the Labour government policy discourse around both equality and community cohesion. We see its presence in the mobilising of a language of class 'trumping' gender, race and other equality strands in the effort to devise a 'new, more positive definition of equality' (Equalities Review, 2007, *A Fairer Future*, 2009) that would replace the 'narrow politics of identity' of the past. Days before BNP leader Nick Griffin's controversial appearance on the BBC's Question Time in October 2009, the then Communities Secretary, John Denham, announced a £12million programme to tackle resentment among white working-class communities across England and undercut right-wing extremism. While he insisted that it was not the role of the state to combat the BNP, he said the 'Connecting Communities' programme would address legitimate fears and concerns that, if neglected, could prove fertile territory for extremism. The areas named in the scheme, including then-BNP foothold Barking and Dagenham, were chosen under criteria including 'cohesion, crime and deprivation, perceived unfairness in the allocation of resources, and feedback from local people'.[3] Framing the issue as a question of fairness, and insisting that this was not a retreat from anti-racism, Denham nevertheless set up an opposition between class and race/ethnicity, with suggestions that the latter are characterised as being constrained in and reduced to a mode of identity politics, whose successes, together with the effects of the recession and recent migration, have now become a source of conflict and perceived unfairness:

> Denham said action to promote the leadership potential and capacity of black and Asian groups was necessary but could be seen by some as unfair. 'Class still matters in Britain and the politics of identity ignores it at its peril,' he told a London conference on community cohesion.
> The position and growing self-confidence of minority communities can be seen as a threat to communities under pressure.[4]

A year earlier, EHRC head Trevor Phillips had already raised the issue of reassuring the white working class when thinking about inequality and disadvantage. In an October 2008 *Guardian* article, Phillips is quoted as saying that in some parts of the country 'the colour of disadvantage isn't black or brown. It is white'. Phillips called for positive action to help underachieving white children in schools and higher education, identifying the poorer white working class as the true losers of the recession and said that if this was not addressed it could lead to an anti-migrant backlash.[5]

Others have shown how the 'community cohesion' discourse that developed through the Cantle Report on 'parallel lives' (2004), and the various reports of, and government response to the Commission on Integration and Cohesion in 2006–2008 work to produce the migrant as source of native unease (see Worley, 2005; Fortier, 2010). In these documents, despite their claims that cohesion is of concern to and should involve everyone, both settled and migrant, the work of cohesion is pitched very differently for each group. The migrant must actively integrate, resist self-segregation and isolation, be careful not to fall into the narrow attachments of identity politics, but the native's task is framed more passively, in that s/he must *be* reassured. As Fortier puts it, 'white unease' is recognised and given political value (2010: 25). So, in her speech at the launch of the Commission on Integration and Cohesion, speaking in much the same terms as David Cameron does today, the then Communities and Local Government Secretary Ruth Kelly said:

> And as this complex picture evolves, there are white Britons who do not feel comfortable with change. They see the shops and restaurants in their town centres changing. They see their neighbourhoods becoming more diverse. Detached from the benefits of those changes, they begin to believe the stories about ethnic minorities getting special treatment, and to develop a resentment, a sense of grievance.
>
> The issues become a catalyst for a debate about who we are and what we are as a country. About what it means to live in a town where the faces you see on the way to the supermarket have changed and may be constantly changing. (Kelly, 2006)

In this strand of the emerging narrative on cohesion and diversity, a pre-migration Britain is produced in which 'staying put' has meant that there is only continuity. Echoing Goodhart's framing of a past and a British identity defined by sameness, the Government's Response to the Commission on Integration and Cohesion (CIC) final report states:

> In the past, when notions of how to behave were shared across divides such as class and generations, there was less need to define what we meant by citizenship or to think about how different people could interact and adjust to each other. (Department for Communities and Local Government, 2008: 10–11)

In these accounts, the conflicts and contestations of gender, generation, class, sexuality, etc. would appear never to have troubled the work of belonging before the arrival of the migrant or the minoritised. While Goodhart at least acknowledged that 1950s Britain was a society riven by class difference, in the CIC report everyone in the British family knew how to behave; a glorious taken-for-granted sameness reigned in the home and the neighbourhood. 'Staying put' meant never having to confront or negotiate difference and this vision of the work of belonging is naturalised by its framing in the language of family. For Goodhart, 'Thinking about the conflict between solidarity and diversity is another way of asking a question as old as human society itself: who is my brother, with whom do I share mutual obligations?' (Goodhart, 2004). Goodhart's turn to fraternity ultimately leads him down a road of sameness, in which kinship is

says Phillips', *The Guardian*, http://www.guardian.co.uk/society/2008/oct/29/social-exclusion-race-immigration, last accessed November 2011.

always and only about the identical. But is there another family figure to start with, who might take us down a more promising road, where the constitutive role of difference isn't obscured in these ways?

interruption 1: starting with the mother

> An interruption is an insertion of a break between or among something that is otherwise continuous, which has ongoing movement or flow. To interrupt is to perform a stop in this flow, to punctuate the flow thereby creating a 'between' or 'among' in an otherwise undifferentiated continuum [...].
>
> Like its close allies, disruption and eruption, interruption reveals the taken for granted background of experience through its power to chop it up and intervene. Interruption segments, divides, dislodges, unbalances and disturbs the continuum. But in doing so, it creates a form in what is otherwise formless [...]
>
> [...] if the continuum is figured as the Same (that which is undifferentiated) then interruption is the appearance of difference that dislodges the Same from itself [...] So interruptions appear to have a productive force as well as a destabilizing one [...] the moment in which we are interrupted by the other, something happens to unbalance us and open up a set of new possibilities. (Baraitser, 2009a: 68–69)

In *Maternal Encounters*, Lisa Baraitser argues that, from the perspective of a subject who mothers, interruption is both productive and normal, that it marks and defines the everyday experiences and subjectivities of individual mothers. Mothers are being constantly interrupted by a child and responding to others' demands that interrupt their own. While this is not an argument she herself makes, I want to link her understanding of what we might call an individual reproductive subjectivity to the more collective work of reproducing social or cultural identities. What happens if we think about this kind of reproduction as being framed by interruption instead of repetition? What if the repetition that reproduction involves occurs on a ground of interruption, if indeed one of the key things that repeats is the process of being interrupted? What if the 'normal', the 'familiar', the everyday, is in fact the work of persisting in the face of, in tandem with, being interrupted, so that what is repeated is never in fact the same, because its conditions are always being changed, being interrupted?

What happens when we apply this way of rethinking reproduction to the work of reproducing belonging? The 'migrant' is a figure of interruption – something new and different arrives to make us stop and look around a space that has been invisible in its apparent repetitiveness, something that takes us outside of ourselves and could make us look at ourselves anew. This unsettles, but should we see that unsettledness as alien, as threatening to our selves, or could we recognise it as akin to the currently unvalued but ever-present repetitive interruptions, repetitions in interrupted spaces, interruptive repetitions that mark the work of mothering?

The figure of the mother — and with her, the space of home and reproduction — is so often evoked as the site of sameness in the face of change. Jean defined by one comment about a changing Southall that no longer feels like home. Powell's elderly white mother whose sons had died for their country and who is repelled by the noise and confusion on her once-quiet street. Goodhart's insistence that solidarity requires a common understanding of the nature of marriage and family. The migrant mother tied to her alien private sphere where she refuses to speak English and preserves outmoded traditions that mark her home as alien to an English space (Lewis, 2005; Gedalof, 2007). But if we refuse this way of framing the mother, if we see her as a figure of/in interruption herself, then we undercut this logic of sameness and trace her genealogy differently. She no longer becomes a resource for pitting the indigenous against the migrant, for opposing travelling to staying put; she becomes instead a figure of their entanglement.

> Perhaps what is required is a shift of perspective. Interruption is usually figured as the exception, a break in continuity that must be overcome, patched over, worked around, neutralized or denied. Interruption must be ironed out as it is what impedes us achieving our goals, stops us from getting wherever we are trying to get to, what keeps interfering with the forward thrust of our lives. But what emerges from the discussion so far is that interruption forms the ground of maternal experience against which all other maternal experiences are understood. (Baraitser, 2009a: 73)

Brah affects such a shift in perspective to end 'The Scent of Memory' with Jean holding out the possibility of a kind of kinship within, and not only across difference. She does this in part by refusing the terms of a narrative of Britishness that sees itself as emerging from a history sealed off from its imperial entanglements, refusing a narrative of Southall that covers over its past production and reproduction as the meeting point of multiple trajectories of moving and settling, by insisting, perhaps again with Haraway, that all origin stories begin, not in some lost, stable, known and knowable space, but always somewhere 'in the middle' (1991: 151).

There are perhaps some pressure points in contemporary community cohesion discourse that might also open some spaces for such alternative origin stories. One of these is the repeated and ultimately failed attempts to pin down what might be meant by the 'common culture' or 'common values' that so preoccupied mainstream political discourse during the Labour Government's engagement with diversity issues. Often, such attempts end in a highly restrictive image of a Britishness frozen in time, either like Goodhart's imagined uniformity of opinion on how to behave, or reduced to a set of stereotypes, generally anchored by

6 See EHRC head Trevor Phillips' now-notorious interview in *The Times* (2004) in which he called for an end to multiculturalism and argued that '[w]e need to assert that there is a core of Britishness. For instance, I hate the way this country has lost Shakespeare'.

warm beer and/or Shakespeare.[6] Attempts to avoid these restrictive terms swing to the other extreme of referencing values that are so generic to the contemporary 'West' as to lose any British specificity. The final report of the CIC, 'Our Shared Future' acknowledges this difficulty when it states:

> The point has also been made that care should be taken in using the term 'British values' — not because our national society has no values to which it is committed but, rather, because many of our broadly held values are common to people in other countries and calling them 'British values' feeds a 'them' and 'us' mentality where we imply that 'we British' have values which others simply don't share. (CIC, 2007: 65)

The CIC tries to open up its narrative of Britishness, first, by putting the emphasis on a 'shared future', as its title suggests, that is, on a sense of common belonging that is yet to be built in the context of diversity, but also by trying to include some strands of multi-vocality in the origin story. So, in outlining its plans for a proposed 'national futures campaign' it argues:

> The starting point for this must be the traditions and heritage of the country and its regions stretching back over hundreds of years — *with a recognition of the important role dissent and non-conformism have played in the past, alongside a binding national narrative.* It should incorporate events and projects designed to increase learning between different cultural communities and individuals within these, as well as between different nations of the UK and different regions of England. (CIC, 2007: 49, emphasis added)

Here at least is an acknowledgement that the origin story itself is constituted in part through its interruptions, including dissent, non-conformism and difference. A second possible break point in the discourse is the acknowledgment, in the CIC report as in Ruth Kelly's speech, that:

> evidence at a national level, via the regular Government Citizenship Survey, consistently shows that people who live in the most ethnically diverse areas are the ones that have the most positive perceptions of ethnic minorities. It seems that those who are the most frightened about change are those that have been least exposed to it. (Kelly, 2006)

This finding, which is consistently used to promote 'bridging' activities in the community cohesion project, sits at odds with the repeated refrain about people being unsettled *because* they see their neighbourhoods changing. But such a finding makes more sense when interruption is framed as normal, as part of the everyday work of reproduction.

In the community cohesion discourse, these break points are smoothed out by an over-riding logic that values 'bridging' over 'bonding' activities (see Fortier, 2010).[7] In the case of minority communities and migrants, as Fortier argues, this framing works to problematise 'bonding' activities as constrained in

7 'The social capital in a

the trap of identity politics, or the old-fashioned notion of 'single identities' (CIC, 2007: 34–35). In the case of 'settled' communities, I would argue, it turns attention away from re-examining just what it is that people might be doing to bond, and maybe discovering that ties of inter-relationality and belonging can entail more complicated negotiations of those everyday interruptions that require us to reproduce continuity. In consigning bonding to a space of repeating single, fixed, identities, the community cohesion discourse then also reinstates a public/private divide that reifies the private/reproductive as static and looks for dynamism only in the encounter between (still fixed) communities. But this way of thinking about bonding is not inevitable. If we revisit that 'primordial' bond, between mother and child, and see it particularly from the point of view of a subject who mothers, we might, with Baraitser, find resources for a different view. One in which the relationship with the 'unassimilable otherness' (Baraitser, 2009a: 8) that is the child can reveal 'the way otherness is always at work, structuring, infecting and prompting human subjectivity' (2009a: 28). Or in which 'the constant attack on narrative that the child performs — constant interruptions to thinking, sleeping, reflecting, moving and completing tasks' (2009a: 15) — invites us to see belonging structured, not by a seamless story of continuity and resolution, but by the interruptions that both require and enable repeatedly 'going over the same ground as a way of bringing something new into being' (2009a: 63). This is not to equate 'the migrant' with 'the child' or to suggest any simple equivalences between the work of otherness in producing individual subjectivities and its work in producing collective identities (see Brah, 1992). But it is to challenge, to try to cut the ground out from under, those moves that metaphorise the mother in order to make her a figure of necessary sameness, of repetitive stability, of seamless narrative and pristine origins, and that thereby try to make her a resource for anti-migrant discourses.

community is linked to the strength of its social networks between people. There are two types of social capital: bonding social capital is about networks of similar people such as family members and friends from similar backgrounds; and bridging social capital refers to relations between people from different backgrounds. Both forms of social capital benefit a community and its members, but only bridging capital is about people from different groups getting on (key to our measure of cohesion) — although we have found that bonding capital can give people the confidence they need in order to bridge' (CIC, 2007: 111).

interpellating a universal 'we': Britishness, tolerance and fair play

There is a second figure of the subject who stays put that emerges in the community cohesion discourse that I want to touch on — and interrupt — briefly. This is the Briton defined by his/her innate qualities of tolerance and fair play, who is represented, as Fortier has argued, as always inherently multicultural (2005: 560). In her examination of media reactions to the 2000 Parekh Report on the Future of Multicultural Britain, Fortier identifies the mobilising of:

> ... a conception of Britishness that centres on ideas of inherent diversity and mixity that dissolve differences. Mixing is a key principle of multicultural Britain, and is widely hailed as the antidote to segregation, differentialist politics, and the threats of racist violence and hate crimes. When couched in the language of kinship and bloodlines, the discourse

of mixing serves to trace the genealogy of the nation's inherent hybridity and to recast diversity as a timeless characteristic of Britishness. (2005: 560)

We can see this narrative make an appearance in the CIC report as well:

British society has for centuries experienced social change, and has welcomed the visitors and migrants that have come here. Our openness and tolerance is part of what has distinguished us as a country, and more recently our traditional characteristics of justice, liberty and fairness have been underpinned with strong laws to tackle discrimination, and to ensure equality across all groups. (CIC, 2007: 15)

Such an account of the genealogy of Britishness is of course breathtaking in the ways it obscures and disavows the violence of colonialism and its constitutive role in framing both British identity and immigration policy over the years (see Cheney, 1996; Hall, 1996). For Fortier, this appropriation of an always already diverse hybridity by the British 'we' also remains problematic because of the different ways in which it interpellates the unmarked white Briton and the still marked 'multicultural' subjects. The latter are invited to claim their Britishness by stressing their sameness to the unmarked norm:

Their skin is shed so they can reveal their true colour(s): displaying the right attitude and uttering and doing the right things — wave the Union Jack, join the British Army, praise family values, sanction the work ethic — thus making them eligible for incorporation within the 'welcoming' nation, who in turn can claim its own distinctiveness as a tolerant and inclusive society. (Fortier, 2005: 569)

Here the potential promise of a narrative that appears to embed difference into the structures of belonging and identity is undone, by insisting that both the particularistic ties of race, ethnicity, gender, etc., and the conflicts and contestations that these dividing practices bring with them be stripped away in the claims to belong to a universal 'we'. In this process, Fortier argues that the 'iconoclastic other within the new family portrait' (2005; 573) is foregrounded, not in order to defend cultural difference or to acknowledge the historical conditions of racialisation that produce otherness, but rather to restabilise the ability of an unmarked, white norm to claim the space of the universal through its intrinsic values of tolerance, fair play and integration.

The trope of the nation as family returns here to be mobilised in ways that insists on sameness — and so again we have a view of reproduction as tied to that sameness. A 'bloodline' in which we are all similarly different reinstates a genealogy from which specificities of positioning and power are erased. The 'iconoclastic other' is called out, but only to be reabsorbed into the general. In the space of public belonging enacted in this community cohesion discourse, it would appear that we can only be hailed in relation to the generic, so as to preserve that liberal myth of a universal public sphere stripped of particularistic ties.

interrruption 2: making things public

But what a sad, deprived and one-note space of the public this gives us. In 'Mothers who make things public' (2009b), Baraitser gives us a far messier, and therefore more engaging, image of the psychosocial work that goes on to make and re-make what counts as 'the public' and of the peculiar, ambivalent, maybe even anomalous place of the mother in such work. As Baraitser notes, philosophically and politically, the public is conceptualised as a gathering that produces the general, 'a peculiar collective whose parts are infinitely replaceable' (2009b: 12). In contrast, psychoanalytically, 'mothering in contemporary Western contexts is a practice that has the specific task of enabling the emergence of individuality from the generic' (*ibid.*). Drawing on Deleuze and Guattari's notion of the 'pack' or the 'swarm', an amorphous alliance that refuses to settle down within fixed binary structures, Baraitser asks what happens when mothers bring their work of reproducing specificity into the space of the public, where 'my child' is repeatedly chosen out of all the swarming children, and each mother is chosen as 'their mother' out of the swarm of other mothers. By bringing the work of reproducing particularistic ties into the space of the public, mothers deform the public's pretensions to the status of the generic, in which each part is replaceable by any other, or where the one can stand in for all others. Encumbered by the stuff of mothering — pushchair, bags full of nappies and wipes, changes of clothes, snacks and toys — spaces of/for the undifferentiated public reveal their exclusionary limits: the tight corners and angles on buses that make manoeuvring the buggy such a challenge; the wobbly table in the cafe that threatens to be overturned by the same overloaded buggy; the desolate open space that 'repudiates inhabitation' (*ibid.*: 19); the gallery or museum deformed by necessity into play area. At this very mundane, everyday level, mothering in public reveals how the universal and the generic have been appropriated by the particular expectations and interests of an unmarked some, to the detriment of others. At the same time, it remakes those spaces by insisting — at least temporarily — on bending them to the needs and desires of the particular. But mothering in public also reveals the work of making 'the public': each time a mother tells her child to stop standing on the bus seat, to wait in line and not mess with the barriers that keep the line in its place, to not talk quite so loud, 'they reveal the edge of what we think of as permissible "in public". They are the point that the child as non- (or not-yet) citizen is called on to behave as if it were a citizen, and in doing so creates "the public". And mothers are the conductors through which this "calling" passes' (*ibid.*: 20).

So powerful is the presumption that this reproductive work is and should be happening in private, and individually, that the collective public presence of mothers is rarely acknowledged. But Baraitser invites us to think about the effects of the everyday, amorphous gathering of mothers in public spaces.

When mothers 'mass' in this way, the entanglement of the general and the specific is revealed. A swarm of encumbered mothers repeatedly show up the edges of the generic and the general by their calling out to the particular, iconoclastic others who are their children. Where mothers mass, 'each mother herself emerges from the generic through her attempt at the virtuosic performance of motherhood, to make public this excess, which is itself the product of the ways individuality and particularity persist in the context of the generic' (2009b: 24). In opposition to the still-dominant vision of the public that appeals 'to a totalizing gesture that annihilates the fundamental equality and heterogeneity of an axiomatically indefinable social formation' (ibid.: 21), Baraitser sees her massing mothers as helping to produce some-thing more akin to Hardt and Negri's (2005) 'multitude', which, unlike unitary concepts such as the public or 'the people', resists being reduced to a single identity:

> The multitude is composed of innumerable internal differences that can never be reduced to a unity or a single identity — different cultures, races, ethnicities, genders, and sexual orientations; different forms of labor; different ways of living; different views of the world; and different desires. The multitude is a multiplicity of all these singular differences. [...] Thus the challenge posed by the multitude is for a social multiplicity to manage to communicate and act in common while remaining internally different. [...]
> The common we share, in fact, is not so much discovered as it is produced. (2005: xiv–xv)

Baraitser's account remains quite culturally homogeneous and needs to be further inflected and complicated by all the classed, raced and culturally specific ways in which this work of hailing entangles the generic and the particular to produce a 'common we share' that never settles down into a universal. Nor should this alternative way of conceptualising the public be seen as claiming some sort of utopian consciousness for mothers. Like the mothers Brah interviewed in Southall in the 1970s, mothering in public can also be a way of asking 'where have *they* come from' and why do they clutter up our pavements and our buses with their buggies, smelly food, loud voices, etc. — part of an ongoing contestation over which particularities will be admitted to the edges constituting the general, contestations within which mothers, like anyone else, can be complicit but which also has a particular valence when discursive constructions of mother as nation remain so powerful.

So starting with or returning to the mother carries with it all sorts of risks, especially when we take account of the ways in which feminised and familial metaphors have been used in colonial and postcolonial contexts to produce the others of a white, Western and masculinised subject. Maybe it would be better to just start somewhere else. And yet Brah starts with Jean and keeps coming back to her in order to find new ways of thinking difference. So, too, I want to argue, there might be ways to come back to the figure of the mother in order to dislodge her from the limited and limiting place she currently holds in dominant ways of thinking about identity and belonging that underpin contemporary community cohesion discourses and their vision of 'the native'. If we are looking for resources with which to trace genealogies of staying put otherwise, then revisiting the mother can be a fruitful place to start, if we rethink her as a figure for whom interruption is normal, and for whom the particular must always be entangled with any claims to a general 'we'.

acknowledgements

My thanks to all the members of the *Feminist Review* Collective for their comments on earlier versions of this paper, and in particular to Clare Hemmings and Avtar Brah for their close and critical reading of multiple drafts. My deepest appreciation, especially, to Avtar, for the intellectual inspiration she has provided over many years, in 'The Scent of Memory' and all her work.

author biography

Irene Gedalof is a senior lecturer at London Metropolitan University and a member of the *Feminist Review* Collective. Her research is concerned with questions of identity and cultural reproduction in the context of migration, and with the intersections of gender, race and ethnicity in Western and postcolonial feminist theory. She is the author of *Against Purity: Rethinking Identity with Indian and Western Feminisms* (Routledge, 1999) and of articles published in *Feminist Review, Camera Obscura, Journal of Ethnic and Migration Studies,* and *European Journal of Women's Studies*.

references

Baraitser, L. (2009a) *Maternal Encounters: The Ethics of Interruption*, New York and London: Routledge.

Baraitser, L. (2009b) 'Mothers who make things public' *Feminist Review*, Issue 93: 8–26.

Brah, A. (1992) 'Difference, diversity and differentiation' in Donald, J. and Rattansi, A. (1992) editors, *'Race', Culture and Difference*, London: Sage.

Brah, A. (1996) *Cartographies of Diaspora*, New York and London: Routledge.

Brah, A. (1999) 'The Scent of Memory' *Feminist Review*, Issue 61: 4–26.

Cantle, T. (2004) *The End of Parallel Lives? The Report of the Community Cohesion Panel*, Department of Communities and Local Government, July 2004.

Commission on Integration and Cohesion (2007) *Our Shared Future*, London: CIC.

Cheney, D. (1996) 'Those whom the Immigration Law has kept apart let no one join together: a view on immigration incantation' in Jarrett-Macauley, D. (1996) editor, *Reconstructing Womanhood, Reconstructing Feminism*, London and New York: Routledge, 58–84.

Department of Communities and Local Government (2008) *The Government's Response to the Final Report of the Commission in Integration and Cohesion*, London: DCLG.

Equalities Review (2007) *Fairness and Freedom: The Final Report of the Equalities Review*, London: Equalities Review.

Fortier, A.-M. (2005) 'Pride politics and multiculturalist citizenship' *Ethnic and Racial Studies*, Vol. 28, No. 3: 559–578.

Fortier, A.-M. (2010) 'Proximity by design? Affective citizenship and the management of unease' *Citizenship Studies*, Vol. 14, No. 1: 17–30.

Gedalof, I. (2007) 'Unhomely homes: women, family and belonging in UK discourses of migration and asylum' *Journal of Ethnic and Migration Studies*, Vol. 33, No. 1: 77–94.

Gedalof, I. (2009) 'Birth, belonging and migrant mothers: narratives of reproduction in feminist migration studies' *Feminist Review*, Issue 93: 81–100.

Goodhart, D. (2004) 'Too diverse?' *Prospect*, February 2004.

Hall, C. (1996) 'Histories, empire and the post-colonial moment' in Chambers, I. and Curti, L. (1996) editors, *The Post-colonial Question: Common Skies, Divided Horizons*, London and New York: Routledge.

Haraway, D. (1991) *Simians, Cyborgs and Women: The Reinvention of Nature*, London: Free Association Books.

Haraway, D. (1992) 'Ecce Homo, Ain't (Ar'n't) I a woman and inappropriate/d others: the human in a post-humanist landscape' in Butler, J. and Scott, J (1992) editors, *Feminists Theorise the Political*, New York and London: Routledge, 86–100.

Hardt, M. and Negri, A. (2005) *Multitude*, London: Penguin.

Home Office (2001) *Secure Borders, Safe Haven*, London: Home Office.

Kandiyoti, D. (1993) 'Identity and its discontents: woman and the nation' in Williams, P. and Chrisman, L. (1993) editors, *Colonial Discourse and Post-colonial Theory*, Hemel Hempstead: Harvester Wheatsheaf: 376–391.

Kelly, R. (2006) 'Speech Launching the Commission on Integration and Cohesion' *The Times Online*, accessed 20 April 2011.

Lewis, G. (2005) 'Welcome to the margins: diversity, tolerance, and policies of exclusion' *Ethnic and Racial Studies*, Vol. 28, No. 3: 536–558.

The Times (2004) 'I want an integrated society with a difference' Interview with Trevor Phillips, 3 April 2004.

Webster, W. (1998) *Imagining Home: Gender, 'Race' and National Identity 1945–1964*. London: UCL Press.

Worley, C. (2005) 'It's not about race. It's about the community': new labour and 'community cohesion' *Critical Social Policy*, Vol. 25, No. 4: 483–495.

Yuval-Davis, N. (1997) *Gender and Nation*, London: Sage.

doi:10.1057/fr.2011.61

100 | the sense of memory

Suki Ali

abstract

In recent years, there has been an increasing interest in the role of collective memory in ethno-national projects. In addition, there has been an expansion of research utilising memory work and auto/biographical methods, which have been particularly effective in the writing of feminists of colour. The paper is prompted by a return to Avtar Brah's 'The Scent of Memory' that it uses as a starting point to explore the relationships between competing accounts of 'private' memories of racialisation that come from mixed-race siblings growing up in a mainly white town. Drawing on interviews, the paper uses familial narratives and their individual telling, to show how sense is made of divergent experiences and memories of childhood and teenage in 1960s and 1970s Britain. The paper shows how narrative accounts are often negotiated through multiple senses, revealing them as both imagined and recalled, contested and negotiated. The paper considers the strengths and limitations of narrative analysis in understanding the relationship between individual and collective memories at both national and familial levels. It argues that the ways in which the social and personal memories are connected in the processes of subjectivation are unstable and opaque, and can only ever be partially known through the process of narrativisation.

keywords

memory; narrative; racialisation; mixed race; identity; auto/biography

(88—105) © 2012 Feminist Review. 0141-7789/12 www.feminist-review.com

Written in 1999, Avtar Brah's paper 'The Scent of Memory' is a response to a book written by Tim Lott about his mother Jean's suicide in 1988. Brah's own title, 'The Scent of Memory' plays on the title of Lott's book, 'The Scent of Dried Roses'. Despite the prominence of the word memory in the title, it appears only once in the paper, where Brah notes that the book is more about Lott's own memories of his mother than it is about her life. What are we to make of this? Brah wants to know how it is that this woman's life, with her account of a changing Southall, fits with her own memories and experiences from the mid-1970s, when she worked there as a young researcher interviewing white families. At the heart of her paper lies an investigation into a set of related questions about identity, place, history and narrative, centred upon issues of social difference such as race, class and gender, and how these inform understandings of life in Southall. In some ways then, her paper is not about memory at all in the way that some would understand it, it is about histories — the social histories of Britain and Southall recorded in conventional ways, and the personal histories narrated by Lott, Brah and her interviewees.

Brah's thoughtful acknowledgement of her own desire to 'know' Jean, but also to position her as some kind of window onto white working class Britishness is tinged with something else, something less easy to identify. Brah first encounters Lott's work on a Sunday morning, reading an article in *The Observer* newspaper. She recounts how touched she was by a line from Jean's suicide note in which she writes, 'This will be so bad for everybody but I hate Southall, I can see only decay. I feel alone'. Brah continues, 'But it was not just that. Which other, more intimate, chords had she touched in me'? (*ibid*.: 3). And it is through this evocation of the unknowable, inexplicable, the felt and sensed, which is by its very nature profoundly intimate, that we too are touched. We encounter the huge arc of histories that are bound to the lived experiences of Tim Lott and his mother, to Brah and her interviewees and by extension to us. I shared this moment of intimacy reading the paper, but more than that, I also shared a feeling of disjuncture, of being a stranger to the world described by both Lott and Brah. As a young child growing up in the 1960s and 1970s in a small, seaside town, my own experience of 'race relations' was quite different. In a mainly white town, the experience of otherness was distinct from the urban setting of a diverse capital city. In this paper, I take this moment of intimacy and connect it to others to explore further the question of 'the critical practice of difference' Brah refers to, by drawing upon a project which drew on auto/biographical and memory work. The original research was conducted over 15 years ago in 1995, and was prompted by a desire to explore the construction of 'mixed race' by using insights prompted from reading feminist autobiographical work on racialisation. Below, I return to the discussions I had with my two siblings and my mother, and draw upon new interviews with my sister, Lisa and brother, Nick.

The paper begins with a brief discussion of how Brah's methodological questions engage social and personal histories. It continues by using the auto/biographical research to explore the highly contingent nature of memories, and the difficult negotiation of a particular kind of familial collective memory that was contested and incomplete. The project revealed some strengths and limitations to the use of biographical methods and narrative analysis in trying to draw together psychic and social accounts of memory and history.

memory and meaning

Discussions about collective memory take many forms, and as ever, the term itself may mean different things depending on which 'field' one occupies. My own research has been guided by a concern with the way collectivities come to know themselves as such, and how the collectivisation of memories are positioned at the heart of national and ethnic projects. The kinds of questions that have framed my own work are: How is Britishness formed? What kinds of histories, memories and forgetting are authorised in accounts of Britain and Britishness? What kinds of groups and individuals can be incorporated into Britishness, and what is the consequence if their own memories and histories do not map on to the official versions? What violence is done, material and symbolic, in making and unmaking collectivities through memory and history? In approaching 'the collective' in this way, I follow a more cultural approach to memory work, and combine this with a commitment to centralising postcoloniality in discussions of national, ethnic and racial collectivity. Many accounts of the development of memory studies focus on 'periodisation' in European understandings of history (Radstone, 2000). However, postcolonial studies provide an alternative lens through which to think of the past in the present through subaltern studies (see e.g., Guha, 1982; Spivak, 1988) and the analysis of the problems with reclaiming or forming 'national culture', and the damage of colonialism to both group identities and individual subjectivities (e.g., Fanon, 1961, 1967). Avtar Brah's work shows us how to think through some of these postcolonial relationships between selves and others, and the creation of an 'us' and 'them' in social and personal histories in Britain. Early in her paper she asks, 'what do you think?', and it is the first of a series of questions that draw us into a meditation on how to develop different ways of thinking about forms of identification across difference (Brah, 1999: 4). Through her reading of Jean's story, we are shown the connections between strangers and ourselves, the linkages between histories of colonialism and the Southall of the 1970s. She begins by asking questions about not only *what* we think, but also *how* we think — how we know and make knowable — as she explores the possibilities of post-humanism and non-identical kinship (*ibid.*). Throughout the paper, we are invited to occupy the position of the other (as well as the Other) as she weaves her complex narratives of coexistence and codependency together. I have taken Brah's call to reflect on our own knowing to connect memory and subjectivity more broadly, and will go on to discuss this in relation to my research on mixed-race families and racialisation.

'I never really thought about it like that'

In the original research project, the initial impetus was not to explore memory at all, but rather to explore processes of racialisation and subjectivation. At the time, there was a dearth of writing on mixed race in the United Kingdom and even less on what it meant and how it might come to be an 'identity'. One provocation for the methodological choices was 'the auto/biographical moment' in UK feminist cultural studies of the 1980s and 1990s. Most of this work focused on its potential for challenging masculinist forms of autobiography, the importance of what might be learnt from personal, private histories in social and cultural research, and also the value of bringing social and cultural theory to bear upon the production of subjective narratives of self. This interdisciplinary work, challenged the form and function of autobiographical work and its relation to, for example, oral history, testimony and memorialising that can be represented through texts, spoken words, photographs and so on (see, for example, Cosslett *et al.*, 2000). However, it was the personalised and autobiographical writing of many black feminists and women of colour that provided the particular impetus for my project. Reading the work of, amongst others, Audre Lorde (1982, 1984), June Jordan (1989), Gloria Anzaldùa (1987) in the United States and Gail Lewis (1985) in the United Kingdom, provided profound moments of both recognition and differentiation across time and place on the meaning of subjectivation.[1] If Brah asks us about what we think, reading these women's words prompted *felt* responses of the kind Brah experienced for herself. The boldly personal forms of writing — critically self aware and analytically and politically sophisticated — provided powerful insights into the ways in which social and personal histories intertwine and inform each other.

My research borrowed loosely from 'memory-work' (Haug *et al.*, 1987) as it 'is a method and a practice of unearthing and making public untold stories, stories of "lives lived out on the borderlands, lives for which the central interpretive devices of culture don't quite work"' (Kuhn, 1995: 8). The interviews used family photographs and family stories, along with prompts and questions. They were taped and transcribed, and analysed using narrative analysis. In this approach to the biographical work, I drew on the notion of 'storied' selves; '... we organise our experience and our memory of human happenings mainly in the form of narrative — stories, excuses, myths, reasons for doing and not doing, and so on' (Bruner, 1991: 4). The links to poststructuralist theories of subjects formed through discourse are obvious (Davies and Harré, 1990). In addition, narrative approaches allow for the contradictory and conflicting nature of the storying of

1 I use the term 'subjectivation' as used in Butler's work on subjection, following Foucault, in which she suggests that 'No individual becomes a subject without first becoming subjected or undergoing "subjectivation"' (Butler, 1997: 11). This term is often used inter-changeably with 'subjectification'. The latter term appears in some places in the text, in keeping with its use by other authors cited.

selves (see e.g., Bruner, 1985; Reissman, 1993, 2002; Polkinghorne, 1995) and invoke 'the evolution of consciousness over time' (Thompson and Bauer 2002 in Phoenix, 2008). In my own research, what emerged from the memory work was a very varied set of narratives of and from the same family, the same town and the same relationships from my mother and siblings, who varied in age by 5 years.

Fifteen years later, I interviewed my brother and sister again, and what follows is a discussion of both of these processes, but with an emphasis on material from the second set of interviews. The research was auto/biographical in that I, the researcher, was one of the three siblings, and so was present at each of the interviews. In this sense, all of the interviews are a very obvious form of memory work in that the respondents all shared a familial history. In the first interview, the questions were asked in quite a formal way, and the answers given were followed up, although in quite an open-ended fashion. But after the 'interview' ended and even after the entire research process was complete, the discussions about what was said continued, with each of us talking about the process with the others informally and spontaneously. The research itself became an intervention into the family narratives, and in some ways became part of the new family stories being generated. However, what motivated the return to the project was not only the ways in which the process had changed both what and how the family 'remembered', it was also the moments of recognition and strangeness in rereading Brah's paper after some time. The 'little England' of our younger selves' memory is not the same kind of England as that of metropolitan London, yet its evocations are familiar, the sense of the time of unrest and upheaval is behind some of the local small town stories, and a general acceptance of casual racism widespread. It is these issues that will be explored further below.

'we were lucky really'

My siblings and I grew up in a small seaside town in the 1960s and early 1970s, my brother is 3 years older and my sister 2 years younger than I. Our mother, a white woman, raised us for the most part alone. Our father, Trinidadian Asian, moved away when we were small children, and we had little contact with him after that. My brother moved away to another town for college in his teenage years, I left for London aged 17 and my sister stayed on into her twenties. However, by young adulthood, all of us were living in London. For most of our childhood, we were the only mixed family in the area. One of our shared memories was of the exceptional nature of being brown in a mainly white town, and the noted arrival of other black and brown families to the area. The town was a typical seaside town in the South of England. It was well known for its old history — the battle between the Normans and Saxons, the Norman Conquest, put its name on the map of the official history of England.

Having been a fishing town, it relied heavily upon tourism, had little in the way of industry and was officially named a 'sink town' and 'depressed area'. As with many towns of its type, it had some areas of beautiful Regency property, an 'old town' with picturesque cottages and inns, and also run-down estates and areas of public housing.

One early common theme in the interviews was of what Jo Spence has called 'fractured class backgrounds' which produced 'cross-class' perspectives (Spence, 1991: 228, 230). Our maternal grandparents had both been poor and uneducated.[2] Our maternal grandfather worked from the age of 9 and became a successful small businessman. Like many of his generation, he became a Conservative voter and drummed into us the importance of education, which he said, '... no one can take away from you'. We all passed the 11 plus exam having had primary schooling paid for by him, and so were grammar school educated. We all expressed some conflict between working-class roots and middle-class cultural values, which were very hard to articulate, along with recognition of an ordinary kind of poverty that was evident in daily life. In the first interview N and L said:

2 We did not know any of my father's family and had a few close family members on my mother's maternal side with whom we had contact.

> L: I think ... I think I sort of almost thought we were middle class although I know now in reality we weren't [...] although I know financially we didn't have anything ... I never remember wanting for anything. (Interview 1995)

> N: Well, even though we were quite poor, I guess um ... in a lot of ways I considered myself ... well again if was *honest* probably *middle* class and even though Mum was very poor and obviously poor. (Interview 1995)[3]

3 From interviews conducted in 1995.

Interestingly, our mother and I felt that our family was working class. Much of the discussions centred on the tensions between the privilege of a good education and the daily concerns about buying food, paying bills and being clothed. The ambivalent feelings about this 'good childhood' with its obvious benefits, and the hardships, were experienced very differently by all three siblings. The youngest, L, remained focused on the positives — the proximity to a park, the beach — and said she didn't remember 'wanting for anything', whereas N remembered the 'food parcels' coming from the grandparents, and how his mother kept fixing her plastic flip-flops until they finally broke forever, and she cried in despair as they were her only shoes. As the middle sibling, I remembered some difficult aspects to our childhood; clothes that came second hand in plastic bags from friends and neighbours, pretending to be out when bill collectors came, and the fierce pride and shame that characterised the painful awareness of the social difference between us and our peers at our junior school. This then was a disjuncture between aspirations towards 'white' middle-class culture and relative economic poverty, but crucially was framed by the fact of the then rarity in that location of a white woman raising three brown children alone. The interplay of the cultural context of white privilege and everyday racisms were at the heart of the questioning and revisioning attempted in narrative form.

If it were clear during the 1950s that white women should preferably not marry black men, it was even clearer that they certainly should not divorce them. The perceived social and sexual deviance of interracial desire could only be ameliorated by the institution of marriage and a semblance of respectability. In the two quotes above, the struggle over sense making is evident — L clearly reassessed her understanding of poverty over time, as she looked back with adult sensibilities to childhood experiences. N makes the move of dissociating himself from his mother's obvious and evident poverty. In both narratives, the memories are evidently adjusted in relation to the interview. This kind of 'reality adjusting' fits well with the ideas outlined by many authors working in this field. Ann Phoenix (2008) takes up Judith Butler's (1997, 2004a, 2004b) work on subjectification to explore the narratives of adults who experienced serial migration from the Caribbean. The 'non-normative' family forms that the children experienced were narrated as adults using cultural conventions of happy families in ways that made their lives fit more easily into these 'normative', culturally sanctioned discourses to make, using Butler's terms, 'unbearable lives' become 'livable lives' (ibid.). Similarly, in both sets of interviews with my family, the adult interviewees also tried to adapt and reform complex and contradictory positionalities and memories from childhood and teenage. The meaning of class was contested repeatedly, and continued long after the interviews had ended. In fact, by the later interviews, L and N had revised their positions to emphasise working classness, whereas I began to acknowledge the middle-class aspirations and levels of privilege more. L particularly talked about her original optimistic responses to the questions, and how when she read the other interviews and discussed them with the family, she realised how out of sync she was with the others. Again, in some ways, we might see this as narrative revisioning and reality construction that relies on the accumulation of experience and, most importantly, the effects of memory work. However, due to the research being conducted within a family, there was no containment of these issues within a 'project'.

My sister reported that she experienced the first interviews as very enjoyable; that is surprising to me given I felt this to be a more formal encounter. She recalled searching through family photographs and how surprised and delighted she was at what she could remember about her childhood, which she said again she was 'very positive about'. She clearly expresses her own understanding of the social nature of the familial memory making, and the possibilities for revision and reworking, and how important it is to identity work.

> L: yeah I ... you know, irrespective of whether you have good memories or bad memories, it's where you've been, and what makes you who you are today. (Interview 2011).

Early feminist engagements with memory work have explicit views on the transformatory power of the processes of purposeful remembering and reworking of memory in ways that change perceptions of one's own positioning. This is a political act (Haug *et al.*, 1987), but can also have more therapeutic potentials (Spence, 1991). The extracts and discussion show that the process had prompted changes in perceptions of subjectivities, and this is explored further below. In addition, the interview transcripts and fieldnotes reveal a difficult side to the process in which the research became part of and influential upon the collective familial memories.

'the worst day of her life': forgetting the un-remembered

In looking at family snaps, it became evident that our visual narratives had a consensus to them, and similarly we had a set of 'family stories' that we could all recount as if by rote. One of these included the story of my grandmother arriving at my mother's wedding, having told her previously that she would not attend, clad head to toe in black complete with black hat and veil. Her mourning of the event and her visible protest was a tale so well told, that, when it came to the punch line — her reasoning for this act — my sister and I could repeat in unison that it was because it was '… the worst day of her life!'. We laughed. But then my sister revealed that my grandmother had left a half-written suicide note for my mother to see shortly before the wedding. I was shocked as I had, so I thought at the time, never heard that story before. In the second interview, I recounted this, and my sister, in turn was surprised that I hadn't known. With hindsight both of us could see how the 'family story' format, the comedic elements about our grandmother's histrionics, masked a deeper psychological hurt in the family. The social histories and cultural contexts that shaped the racism of my mother's generation had seeped into the familial relationships, but had been transformed into safe narratives of a much more superficial account of familial folly.

The story of the suicide note evoked a highly emotional response that echoed Brah's own account of reading about Jean's difficulty with the changing social landscape of Southall. My parents had been living in London in the 1950s and had experienced racist hostility to their relationship. What must it have been like to deal with that kind of aggression and disapprobation within the family, from her own mother, as well? The initial interview did not completely transform these painful memories through their speaking. Before talking to my sister for the second time, I reread her prior interview and realised I had forgotten, yet again, that she had told me that story, and how difficult I had found it. Yet my sister's memory of the interview and of the events and stories we discussed about our family and her life were almost exactly the same. It was striking how she had not changed what she understood to be her memories *per se*, even though she reassessed what interpretation she gave them.

I had always believed my brother found the initial process difficult on an emotional level. He was a willing participant, but at one point while discussing some family snaps, he broke down in tears. As someone who rarely showed grief or pain in this way, this was something of a shock. The interview was suspended while we talked a little about this. The photographs that provoked this response were ones of our father, sent to me by his partner, on my request, after his death. They showed our long absent father setting out on a fishing trip with some friends. N said that he found it difficult because he had to try to 'imagine' our father's life. In a sense, he could not locate himself and his memories in these pictures and this lack of structure or boundaries, and inability to imagine this familial connection prompted an emotional response that was out of character. When I reminded my brother that he had been so upset that we had had to halt the interview, he had also completely forgotten that. Despite the strong feelings it had evoked, he had been looking forward to the second session, and after it was completed, said he enjoyed it. During the discussion about the previous interview N said:

> N: yeah and it's whether you need to make sense of things anyway. I guess you only really do if you feel yourself conflicted or have issues with what happened. (S: yeah) Um which I am not sure I — well I probably did ... but then I don't feel the need to make sense of it ....

Yet later, he said he found himself:

> N: ... slowly just working it all out now, like an angry old man you know, whatever ... . (Interview 2011)

His narrative holds together as a story of a self, although one that has contradictions and paradoxes at its heart. There is both an acknowledgement and disavowal of the meaning of memories. However, this discussion of the process implies that we could all speak these memories into consciousness in order to gain some kind of 'mastery' over them, to make them 'bearable'. Yet what happens when we cannot put experiences into words, or bring memories to mind? What cannot be said, and how might this still be present and in some ways known to subjects?

'I don't really remember'

> A memory. The sun is going down. The group of children have been playing, in a disorganised way, some kind of game involving a couple of battered tennis racquets and a tennis ball. They are boys and girls, aged roughly between nine and twelve, about six or so of them who are part of a larger fluid 'gang' of friends and siblings. They are in the road, which is quiet

at this time of the evening, in this small, seaside town at the very beginning of the 1970s. Suddenly the mood changes. Two of the older boys' banter and scuffling has become more serious, 'Get out of here, go on get out, fuck off!'. He takes the racket and swings it hard, catching the other boy with a resounding thwack on the lower back and buttocks. It must have hurt as the wooden frame connected. 'Go on, fuck off out of here, we don't want your kind here!'. The other boy shrugs, half smiles and leaves, followed by his younger sister. This incident is disturbing to her, and she cannot say why. It is something more than the evident violence, the raised voices, all of which she finds more threatening than a childish fight might warrant. It is the expulsion of her brother from the group that is so upsetting. As she gets older, 'why don't you go back to where you came from' is repeated often, and she begins to understand why 'their kind', don't belong, and are not wanted. Within days the two boys are playing together again.

In his first interview, N repeatedly talked about how it was he didn't think he experienced much overt racism as a child. He said he began to become more aware of the way in which race entered into his relationships at secondary school. His insistence that his education made his racial difference manageable was a key theme of both discussions. He had been a popular-enough boy around the local area, and had a 'best friend' who lived a few streets away whom he mentioned a lot. But as the interview progressed, he began to say how hard it was to judge what people actually thought of him and whether racism was part of their judgement. He was never invited to his best friend's house, and at one point his best friend was not allowed to play with him. He didn't know why and said 'It's strange really, I can't put my finger on it'. This phrase stayed with me, and I asked him about it in the second interview. He used the phrase again, talking about how it was 'just a feeling really'. I told him the story above that was about his best friend attacking him, and he said, 'I don't remember that ... must be selective memory'. But he *did* remember something intangible that he felt about why he was not welcome. As we were not the only family to be poor, nor for that matter, to have a single mother raising us, less usual though that was at the time, he felt with hindsight that there was some kind of racism in the relationships between himself, his best friend Nick and Nick's mother. His senses played a key role in this — a vague unease, some glances, a feeling of discomfort, a memory that was felt rather than known. As he struggled with words, touch came to the fore in his inability to reach knowledge and to solidify the meaning of the connected impressions. His response, despite his inability to articulate it clearly, matched my own memory of the evening event — an embodied response to the violent expulsion of my brother from the group. I 'know' that this would not have made such an impression if this had been an isolated incident. But that 'outsider within' was a familiar feeling. Despite his inability to 'put his finger on it', N finally got to a place whereby in the second interview, he recalled he too was 'no angel' but seemed to be disproportionately punished by the community of friends and protective parents. His unconscious response, that evaded narration in a direct form, came to language by a series of revisions and returns. What he thought, what he knew, emerged from finding something from the embodied responses that remained some 40 years later.

N could not, in this instance, place himself within an existing discourse, and neither bring to mind nor to language the issues that made impressions upon him and shaped his own sense of self. This is then not the kind of 'reality adjustment' of the type that Ann Phoenix's work shows (Phoenix, 2008). In some ways, N did 'reclaim' a life to make it 'bearable' here, but he experienced and expressed it in unstable and contradictory ways. For him, insistence on privilege was not the reclamation of a normative discourse, as it did not ameliorate the poverty, or indefinable outsiderness. These experiences of everyday levels of racism were nothing like those encountered in the metropolitan centres, and the impressionistic accounts of alienation from my brother are contrasted by my sister's insistence that she too had not thought about racism in these terms. Of course, this disavowal of racial differentiation and its impact may be seen as a 'good' thing. But it was experienced as an erasure, most certainly at a later date. There was no single form for this but, over time, we had all made sense not only of the original memories in order to narrativise them, but we also promptly forgot some of this and then in some cases remembered it again.

making sense of memories

How are we to make sense of these tangled threads of self-making? One evident feature of the research was that it revealed the desire to make sense of the past, but this coexisted with a disavowal of a need to do so. What was most compelling to me in reviewing the original materials and the later discussions, was the way in which an analysis of the kinds of racism that was encountered in one context in England, was so far away from that described by Brah in her article. By 1976, a year which Brah focuses on in particular, we were all at secondary school and were becoming more aware of and more articulate about issues of race and racism in Britain. Yet neither N nor L linked these wider discourses to their own stories:

> N: I don't know when I realised that those sorts of things going on miles away actually affected me, not for an awful lot longer, later. (Interview 2011)

He described this as a form of 'naïveté'. The late 1960s and early 1970s in the south east seaside town seemed worlds away from the racial tensions of south London. While jobs and unemployment were high on the agenda for those outside of the tourist industry by the seaside, Brah describes the early 1970s in London as marked by several murders of young men, which resulted in Black and Asian people taking to the streets in a series of protests about overt and covert forms of racisms. The narratives of N, L and I are not recognisable as stories of 'big' traumas or deprivations in either the social or personal sense; there is no war, no rioting, no beatings, nor violent deaths. With the lack of media that we might take for granted today, it was possible for L to say she felt that we were growing up in a bubble and for N to say that he 'never thought about that stuff'. In addition, particular processes of racialisation and experiences of racism were profoundly marked by our mixedness. While we were, by virtue of being brown, 'Pakis', the embodied ambiguity of our racial identities was undoubtedly mediated by our white mother, and 'white cultural' values. Yet we were brown, and all of us could name how and when other brown and black people appeared in the neighbourhood or at school as this was so unusual. So, rather than a racism born of fears of 'swamping' as in the Southall that Brah and Jean inhabited, this was born of a much vaguer kind of exoticism and novelty. Our visible difference prompted different kinds of responses than it might have done in the urban environment, which was characterised by the fear and anger about larger numbers of foreign, visible, others that Brah describes. But what does the lack of awareness do to the way in which we might understand ourselves and others in processes of racialisation and subjectivation?

For one of us, L, there was an almost complete disavowal of any meaning to racial difference until young adulthood. L said she did not think of herself racially, and even though rationally she knew she was not white, she felt herself to be so. Again, the available discursive and symbolic positionings were at odds with her sense of her own embodiment. So while Avtar Brah can recognise that when her respondents are saying 'they' are a problem, she can understand that she was 'one of them', my sister could not connect these social processes with her experiences. She was not 'they'; 'they' were not *her*. When she was becoming more aware of her own positioning, she said she asked white people about how they thought of her, and reported that they often said 'I think of you as you'. Her otherness is made safe in a process of deracination. So while we may say that this is a form of subjectivation (there is either a 'you' that is being 'hailed' or a 'discourse' of 'you' that produces her subject position), the cultural position she occupies is still in some respects 'unintelligible'. She still could not quite recognise herself, and allowed others to recognise her as not white, or perhaps 'not quite white', with strong colonial overtones (Bhabha, 1994). The ability of the white observer to render 'colour' a 'detachable signifier' (Ahmed, 1997: 161) has a symbolic violence that has psychic consequences. It had a cost to L's own sense of self, leaving her with feelings of loss that she expressed as 'cultural'. She later tried to 'discover her cultural roots' and became very articulate about how her own racialisation was profoundly gendered and heterosexed. Here we can see that although there was a process of subjectivation, it was one that did not match the felt experiences, and bodily knowledge of the subjects. L could be 'white' culturally, and this made her British, but she knew this to be 'wrong' even though this was not something she could express at the time.

For N, making sense of his experiences, and his memories, was a process of what might be called, rationalisation:

> N: But my memory's probably flawed from a lot of those things ... and also I think you have to probably be aware of looking at things objectively at the time, you can't look at something *not* objectively and then suddenly become objective about it, or it's harder to. (Interview 2011)

He went on to disparage racist behaviour as often illogical, based upon imagined fears not on realities. N used education as a cover for difference and a way to claim social respect in later life. While consistently saying that he 'wasn't really aware of racism', he knew it through a recognition that occasionally the 'jungle bunny' taunts would seem to be used a bit too often, and with too much feeling. He seemed to accept that being called 'jungle bunny' was a part of life and that this kind of racism was just another variation of stupid childhood behaviour. He noted that he had spent a lot of time 'not thinking about anything really', being a wild teenager, and then pursuing a career. He repeatedly described himself as 'selfish', at one point saying he was too selfish to be politically aware.

In our later conversation, he speculated as to whether the focus on himself in both leisure and work, was in fact partly driven by a desire to escape from the kinds of issues we had been discussing. In many ways, N's account fits well with the idea that subject formation requires both mastery and submission, and mastery itself implies autonomy and the agency of the choosing subject. His narration of 'not thinking' was presented as choice. But as Davies suggests '... mastery requires [...] an imaginative capacity to form [oneself] out of the not-yet-known [...] The appropriate knowledge may lie outside one's grasp' (Davies, 2006: 433). For N, the notion of mastery, of making choices, is narrativised in both rebellion and conformity. He is both resisting and reworking available discourses on achievement and 'status', a term that was very important to him. He refused to see 'racism' even when it was clearly articulated. Although it could be argued that he 'ignored' certain events, he was also not fully aware of or able to know 'events' as 'events', and when asked about others' racial motivations, he repeatedly said 'it never occurred to me'. He does not only demonstrate agency in submission or mastery of discursive positionings. In some instances, he does not 'know' at all, and does not want to know, there is no 'imaginative leap' into a discursive space nor a desire for one.

For me, the knowledge that race mattered was evident and at times painfully experienced. Unlike my siblings, I felt the fact of brownness in a mainly white space quite acutely. Comments about appearance were frequent. While some were intended as compliments such as those about an acceptable brown skin tone, racism was often overt and hostile. The scrutiny became an unwelcome and inevitable feature of life as one of a few 'visible minorities' and I somehow knew this to be about 'race', even though I was not articulate on the subject then. As

Nirmal Puwar has argued, the 'somatic norms' in public space are dominated by a notion of neutrality, which is rather white, and male and the ability to master 'imperial/legitimate language' allows racialised others to become human. Yet, 'those who do not fit with their bodily hexis are never fully assimilated' (Puwar, 2004: 9). In his second interview, N noted he had little 'national pride' and speculated that this was due to his ethnicity:

> N: well just erm err the fact that perhaps you weren't made as welcome as ... (S mmm) ... yeah no that doesn't quite ring true 'cos I didn't quite feel ... unwelcome is the wrong word seeing as I was born and bred here but ... err ostracised ... I didn't actually feel ostracised ... (Interview 2011)

Again he could not verbalise what he felt, but could begin to articulate a sense of both outsiderness and insiderness to the national collective simultaneously. This kind of struggle shows how narrative analysis in memory work has to not only attend to these gaps between the social and personal, but also the multiple socials and personals which are unfolding. While it is usual to speak of 'intergenerational change' in family memories and social history work, we also need to be reminded of the way in which individuals of the same generation, in the same location, in the same family, can have very different accounts of 'the social' and 'the collective'. Our own stories were internally conflicted, and our own accounts of our own and each other's experiences varied hugely. While the revisioning that takes place in the narratives is of childhoods that are inevitably informed by ethnic, racial and national 'collectives' — Caribbean, Asian, Black, White, British and so on — this was not always in any immediate fashion, and often not conscious and agentic. So the ways in which cultural production of national and ethnic affiliations work in relation to racialisation require us to look very carefully at 'social context' and how the 'normative' works in practice.

who are you to me?

In the introduction to their influential book on cultural memory, Antze and Lambek comment:

> Beyond the insistent metaphorization of memory, we have been struck by the spread of talk about memory and especially by the interpenetration of individual and collective discourse: both how history borrows from psychotherapy and vice versa in their respective construals of their subjects, and how the memory of the individual — precisely that which is often taken to epitomise individuality — draws upon collective idioms and mechanisms.
> (Antze and Lambek, 1996: xiii)

While in broad agreement with this analysis, I would argue that 'drawing upon collective idioms and mechanisms' represents something of a simplification that suggests a process that is in some way transparent, open and available to all in equivalent ways. The differing accounts, and their differential revisions by family members show that the relationship of the individual to the 'collective' can be highly partial and very unstable. The narratives used by individuals are marked by gaps and erasures in relation to both the familial and the wider social context. Despite a strong sense of core family stories, all of us had not only different understandings of our class positionings in the past, but also revised them as a result of the research. Despite sharing family histories, our understandings of those too differed, and illustrated another layer in the complex processes of making 'bearable lives'. More importantly, while the work of subjectivation is in part managed through making sense of memory, it's also done through sensing memories and sense memories, which shape the present. These affective memories are powerfully felt and experienced, and shape selfhood and subjectivity in ways that confound explanation and narration. So while the work on cultural memory also alludes to the past in both literal and metaphorical accounts, psychoanalytic understandings of the way memory is always the present and past remade in the now, may be helpful in showing how differing positions can be held even where similarity would be expected, and where unexpected similarities and affinities show themselves across difference. This too helps us to engage with Brah's call to think.

In many accounts of subjectivation, the subject is produced through discursive positioning (or in Brah's piece, through interpellation). It is in the process of responding to discourse that subjects develop agency, and the processes of mastery and submission are tied together in ambivalence (Butler, 1997, 2004a, 2004b, Davies, 2006). Yet it is easy to slip into an analysis that implies an already knowing and already constituted subject who can respond to these calls. What space is there for the unconscious, the unknown, and the affective in these accounts? A narrative of subjectification that understands this as a form of 'evolution of consciousness', or that privileges the ego that forms the 'I', fails to account adequately for the role of the unconscious in these processes (see Campbell, 2004 on Butler). Holding on to this critique offers a conceptual explanation for some of the seemingly illogical, opaque and affective responses from my family. While it is possible to contain them in the discourse of narrative, some aspects of the unknowable self are lost in taking such a position. Indeed, Butler herself suggests that: 'There is that in me and of me for which I can give no account' (Butler, 2001: 27). It is important to acknowledge that some aspects of the self are not narratable and incorporate that into the important insights that narrative theory offers us. This is a different process than attending to silence and speculating upon what is not said. It was not possible to speculate on what the interviews revealed (or not) in the first instance, as the subjective accounts were not connected to known discourses, and only came partially to consciousness in the second interviews.

conclusions: thinking again

Brah's question 'What do you think?' opened up an invitation to which I felt compelled to respond. It asked for a reconsideration of the *what* and the *how* in thinking about subjectivation and racialisation, and the processes by which we are recognised by ourselves and others. Brah's critical practice of difference asks us to look to non-identical kinship and the recognition of difference as a way of forging connections. The kind of affiliation that Brah calls for is a form of social relationality, not mediated and understood through ties of blood or even culture. But it is also useful for understanding familial kinship as its emphasis on the social de-privileges and de-stabilises family as a discourse and metaphor. Looking in detail at the shifting narratives within the familial context over a period of 15 years has revealed the complexity of researching memory through narrative. This raises questions for future work that requires us to pay attention to the limits to narrative forms and to challenge 'the known' in the form of the conscious thought about our positionality. We must continue to develop our theoretical repertoires for understanding the relationships between the social and the psychic, the collective and the individual. So when Brah asks herself, who Jean was and how can she know her, she is in fact demonstrating the ways in which the formation of the self is relational, and 'you' are also forming of 'I'. It returns us to the ways in which 'I' am formed through and with the 'Other' and that this telling of stories of ourselves is, as Plummer (1995) has argued, a form of community making. The research process created us as siblings, but also remade us as subjects. During the process, and beyond the confines of the interviews, our family stories were expanded and revised, and our own understandings of our relations to each other and ourselves shifted, as well as solidified. These understandings were not confined to the familial arena, but also impacted upon our positionality as classed, raced and gendered beings, and thus our relations to wider collectives and communities.

To fully engage with the questions of gendered racialisation and subjectivation through memory work and narrative we must attempt ethically engaged, political accounts of self-making. The uses of auto/biographical methods and memory work have been important tools in anti-racist and postcolonial feminist research and writing. The call to speech and the requirement to listen are still two of the most powerful methods in this repertoire of sense making, and thus to the transformative practices of feminist praxis.

acknowledgements

I would like to thank the reviewers for their really helpful comments on the paper. I would also like to thank Carrie Friese, Sarah Franklin, and Ilina Singh for comments on an early draft.

author biography

Suki Ali is a senior lecturer in the Department of Sociology at the LSE. Her work engages with feminist postcolonial theory and her research interests include racialisation, embodiment, families and visual culture. She has published widely on these issues with particular emphasis on mixedness and mixing.

references

Ahmed, S. (1997) ''It's a Sun-tan isn't it?': autobiography as identificatory practice' in Mirza, H.S. (1997) editor, *Black British Feminisms: A Reader*, London and New York: Routledge.

Anzaldùa, G. (1987) *Borderlands/La Frontera: The New Mestiza*, San Fransisco: Spinsters/Aunt Lute Foundation.

Antze, P. and Lambek, M. (1996) editors, *Tense Past: Cultural Essays in Trauma and Memory*, London and New York: Routledge.

Bhabha, H. (1994) 'Of Mimicry and man: the ambivalence of colonial discourse' in Bhabha, H. (1994) editor, *The Location of Culture*, London and New York: Routledge.

Brah, A. (1999) 'The Scent of Memory: strangers, our own and others' *Feminist Review*, Issue 61: 4–26.

Bruner, J. (1985) *Actual Minds, Possible Worlds*, Cambridge: Harvard University Press.

Bruner, J. (1991) 'The narrative construction of reality' *Critical Inquiry*, Vol. 18, No. 1: 1–21.

Butler, J. (1997) *The Psychic Life of Power: Theories in Subjection*, Stanford: Stanford University Press.

Butler, J. (2001) 'Giving an account of oneself' *Diacritics*, Vol. 31, No. 4: 22–40.

Butler, J. (2004a) *Undoing Gender*, London and New York: Routledge.

Butler, J. (2004b) *Precarious Life: The Powers of Mourning and Violence*, London and New York: Verso.

Campbell, K. (2004) 'The plague of the subject: psychoanalysis and Judith Butler's psychic life of power' *International Journal of Sexuality and Gender Studies*, Vol. 6, No. 1/2: 35–48.

Cosslett, T., Lury, C. and Sommerfield, P. (2000) 'Introduction' in Cosslett, T., Lury, C. and Sommerfield, P. (2000) editors, *Feminism and Autobiography: Texts, Theories and Methods*, London and New York: Routledge.

Davies, B (2006) 'Subjectification: The Relevance of Butler's Analysis for Education' *British Journal of Sociology of Education*, Vol. 27, No. 4: 425–438, *Troubling Identities: Reflections on Judith Butler's Philosophy for the Sociology of Education*.

Davies, B. and Harré, R. (1990) 'Positioning: the discursive production of selves' *Journal for the Theory of Social Behaviour*, Vol. 20, No. 1: 44–63.

Fanon, F. (1967 [1961]) Constance Frarington, translator, *The Wretched of the Earth*, London: Penguin.

Fanon, F. (1967 [1952]) Charles Lam Markmann, translator, *Black Skins, White Masks*, New York: Grove Press.

Guha, R. (1982) editor, *Subaltern Studies: Writings on South Asian History and Society*, Vol. 1 Delhi: Oxford University Press.

Haug, F. *et al.* (1987) *Female Sexualisation: A Collective Work of Memory*, in Erica, C. (1987) translator, London: Verso.

Kuhn, A. (1995) *Family Secrets: Acts of Memory and Imagination*, London: Verso.

Jordan, J. (1989) *Moving Towards Home: Political Essays*, London: Verso.

Lewis, G. (1985) 'From deepest Kilburn' in Heron, L. (1985) editor, *Truth, Dare or Promise: Girls Growing Up in the Fifties*, London: Virago.

Lorde, A. (1982) *Zami: A New Spelling of My Name*, London: Sheba Feminist Press.

Lorde, A. (1984) *Sister Outsider: Essays and Speeches By Audre Lorde*, Berkeley, CA: The Crossing Press.

Phoenix, A. (2008) 'Claiming livable lives: adult subjectification and narratives of "non-normative" childhood experiences' in Kofoed, J. and Staunaes, D. editors, *Magtballader (Adjusting Reality)*, Copenhagen: Danmarks Paedagogiske Universitesforlag, 178–193.

Plummer, K. (1995) *Telling Sexual Stories: Power, Change and Social Worlds*, London and New York: Routledge.

Polkinghorne, D.E. (1995) 'Narrative configuration in qualitative analysis' in Hatch, J.A. and Wisniewski, R. (1995) editors, *Life History and Narrative*, London: Falmer Press.

Puwar, N. (2004) *Space Invaders: Race, Gender and Bodies Out of Place*, London and New York: Berg Publishers.

Radstone, S. (2000) 'Working with memory: an introduction' in Radstone, S. (2000) editor, *Memory and Methodology*, Oxford and New York: Berg.

Reissman, C.K. (1993) *Narrative Analysis*, London: Sage.

Riessman, C.K. (2002) 'Narrative analysis' in Huberman, A.M. and Miles, M.B. editors, *The Qualitative Researcher's Companion*, Thousand Oaks, CA: Sage.

Spence, J. (1991) 'Shame work: thoughts on family snaps and fractured identities' in Holland, P. and Spence, J. (1991) editors, *Family Snaps: The Meanings of Domestic Photography*, London: Virago.

Spivak, G.C. (1988) 'Can the subaltern speak?' in Nelson, C. and Grossberg, L. editors, *Marxism and the Interpretation of Culture*, Champaign, IL: University of Illinois Press.

doi:10.1057/fr.2011.71

working-class whiteness from within and without: an auto-ethnographic response to Avtar Brah's 'the scent of memory'

Lyn Thomas

abstract

Inspired by and responding to Avtar Brah's 'The Scent of Memory', this piece attempts to reinscribe race into an auto-ethnographic narrative where previously whiteness was unmarked. It explores the dynamics of gender, race and class through the author's personal history as a white English woman and class migrant, and through discussion of the broader political and historical context of that trajectory. The discussion includes analysis of the impact of British Conservative politician Enoch Powell's infamous 'rivers of blood' speech in 1968 on the author's white English working-class culture of origin in Wolverhampton, where Powell was a Member of Parliament. The article considers the speech's continuing ramifications in the twenty-first century and in more middle-class contexts, as evidenced by the recent evocation of the speech by historian David Starkey in discussion of the 'riots' of August 2011 in British cities. The personal history is reconstructed through a series of memory scenes that trace and retrace the author's experience and understanding of race and its intersections with class and gender; this is attempted in full cognisance of the constructed nature of memory, and of the performance of identity that autobiography entails. The piece draws on the work of the class migrant white French writer Annie Ernaux, with whom the author has been in dialogue since 1997.

keywords

race; class; whiteness; auto-ethnography; memory; Annie Ernaux

*fe*minist *r*eview *100* 2012

'The Scent of Memory' has accompanied me for a long time, asking questions I have, until now, not wanted to answer. Even now, how far I can answer them is unknown. The attempt involves both academic and personal writing, following what is now a long tradition of feminist boundary-crossing, between public and private, personal and political, academic and experiential knowledge (Heron, 1985; Steedman, 1986; Miller, 1991). It is the continuation of a process of auto-ethnography, begun in 1999 with the final chapter of my book on the French writer Annie Ernaux, where I thread a narrative of my own move from working-class to middle-class culture, via state-funded education, through my discussion of Ernaux's writing of a similar trajectory (Thomas, 1999). The missing dimension in this narrative of gender, class and education is race: in this article I will attempt to deconstruct the previously unmarked whiteness of the self narrated in my auto-ethnographies, exploring the absent scenes of learning (about) race.[1] My aim is not to create a more accurate or, in some way, complete or final version of self-narration, but to connect the personal story to a hitherto dis-avowed aspect of the social context of its construction, to anchor it historically in relation to colonialism and socially, to British 'diaspora space' of the 1950s, 60s, 70s and the present day (Brah, 1996).

1 The works of Ruth Frankenberg (1993) 'exploring whiteness through white women's life histories' (Frankenberg, 1993: 7) and of Vron Ware (1992) are clearly important precursors to my discussion.

This sketch of white self/selves is carried out in the spirit and inspiration of 'The Scent of Memory', where Avtar Brah reflects on the relationship of inner and outer, personal and social worlds in her thoughts on Jean Lott's suicide note and on her own responses to Jean, and to her white working-class interviewees in Southall in the 1970s. Brah's reflections are triggered by reading a review of Tim Lott's biography of his mother Jean who committed suicide in 1988. The words of Jean's suicide note 'I hate Southall, I can see only decay. I feel so alone' (Brah, 1999: 5) connect Brah to Jean's life through geographical location, and lead to a sustained meditation on the politics of race in that place, and on the possibility of making a connection with Jean, across difference. Towards the end of her discussion Brah comments:

> I have the fantasy that some disclosures — especially in relation to deep-seated feelings of such unmentionables as racism or homophobia — are shared as secrets within the intimate space of friendship, family, and 'community'. My study in Southall had offered me some glimpses but I did not have access to the 'intimate' history of such phenomena. (Brah, 1999: 24)

My intention here is to delve into my own 'intimate history', that of a white female subject constructed in the national space that Brah is discussing, and in a local area (Wolverhampton, in the West Midlands) that like Southall was transformed by postcolonial migration in the post-war period. At some points, I will discuss working-class cultures and histories in quite general terms, linking my own experience to significant economic and social changes in Britain in the twentieth and twenty-first centuries. However, it is important to note the specificity of the white English working class culture I am discussing here, which I refer to throughout as my culture of origin, and whose particular characteristics must be explored to avoid the homogenisation of the white working class that is currently a commonplace in dominant representations: 'stereotypes of "white trash" and "chavs" used simultaneously to describe and write off vast sections of Britain's population – often white, often living on council estates and nearly always poor' (Rogaly and Taylor, 2009: 3). These specificities of place, language and socio-economic realities that form my culture of origin will, to some extent, emerge through my discussion.

Avtar Brah describes how we are positioned in social space and material power relations by our 'interpellation' as classed, raced and gendered subjects. While deploying the Althusserian concept, she emphasises the negotiations and agency involved in this process, where we are neither completely determined nor completely free; she also points to the dynamic between the psychic and the social, the conscious and unconscious. Similarly, whiteness is conceptualised here as 'a process, not a "thing", as plural rather than singular in nature' (Frankenberg, 1997: 1). Within Brah's framework, I will consider my trajectory through modes of whiteness, and the connections between this trajectory and the stories Avtar Brah tells of her white working-class interviewees in Southall, of South Asian migrants settling in Southall in the post-war period, of Jean, and of Brah's own memories of the violent and everyday racisms of the 1970s. As I add a further layer of narrative to these intersecting stories, I will highlight the crossing points, of history and geographical location, where new insights can, perhaps, emerge. In 'The Scent of Memory' Brah seeks, through the figure of Jean, 'a window on the whiteness' from which she is excluded by her own positioning as a racialised subject. In looking at whiteness from within, I am also seeking a window, and perhaps, a way out.

Brah provides a further framing dimension for this discussion through her deployment of the Urdu terms *ghair, ajnabi, apna/apni*. Simple translation of these terms would be misleading, as Brah explains:

> An 'ajnabi' is a stranger; a newcomer whom one does not yet know but who holds the promise of friendship, love, intimacy. The 'ajnabi' may have different ways of doing things but is not alien. She could be(come) 'apna'; that is 'one of our own'. The idea of 'ghair' is much more difficult to translate for its point of departure is intimacy; it walks the tightrope between insider/outsider. The difference of the 'ghair' cannot be fully captured by the dichotomy of Self and Other; nor is it an essentialist category. Yet, it is a form of irreducible, opaque difference. (Brah, 1999: 19)

Brah emphasises the possibility of movement between categories, of transformation. A woman who treats others as *ghair* because of their skin colour may change her positionality when given access to anti-racist projects and discourses, and 'the "ghairness" may be transformed' (Brah, 1999: 20). These terms are resonant for my discussion of race and racism in my own history, not the least because of the transformational possibilities Brah emphasises. They also resonate in the intersecting story of class and class mobility in my narrative. Without knowledge of Urdu, my deployment of these terms must be approximate and tentative; I am also mindful of the dangers of colonising appropriations, the need to recognise the boundaries of space and time between differently constituted subjects. As Iris Marion Young puts it: 'Whilst people may be in touch and their communication may construct relationships of similarity or solidarity between them, their positions are nevertheless irreducible and irreversible' (Young, 1997: 50). Ethical communication, therefore, is always based on 'asymmetrical reciprocity' resulting from the differences of history and perspective between subjects, but also from the fact that the opening of a communication is always a gift: 'the trust to communicate cannot await the other person's promise to reciprocate, or the conversation will never begin' (Young, 1997: 50). 'The Scent of Memory' would seem to be exactly this kind of gift, in that it very explicitly opens possible communications and dialogues. My response then is an offering in response to this gift, and an effort to communicate and translate across cultures, to learn the meaning of the Urdu terms, and use them, while recognising and cherishing the differences of culture, history and positionality that they embody.

Brah's explanations in English are very close to the distance within intimacy that I am trying to describe here in relation to my class migrant position, a distance that is 'irreducible' and 'opaque', heavy with affect of various kinds, with anger, grief, resentment and loss. As a middle-class woman with economic, social and cultural capitals that most of my family cannot imagine, let alone possess, I am, at times, a class enemy, something akin to *ghair* to my own *apne*, my family and acquaintances in my culture of origin. In her book on her mother's life, Annie Ernaux describes how her mother feels when she comes to live with Ernaux and her bourgeois husband:

> Living with her children was about discovering a world she was proud of (to her family she would say: they are very well set up!). It was also: not drying teacloths on the radiator in the hall, taking care of things (records, cut-glass vases), paying attention to hygiene (not wiping the children's noses with her own handkerchief), discovering that we paid no attention to things that were important to her [...].[2] It was living in a world that welcomed her on the one hand and excluded her on the other. One day, in anger: 'I don't fit into the picture'. [...]. It took me a long time to realise that my mother felt ill at ease in my house in exactly the same way I had as a teenager when I met people who were 'better than us'. (Ernaux, 1988: 77)

2 [...] denotes section of text omitted. All translations of Ernaux's texts are the author's own.

Ernaux, in this moment, becomes foreign, perhaps *ghair*, to her own mother because of classed differences of practice and values. Race is one of the areas where such differences can emerge, and where the feelings of anger and loss of those 'left behind' in the culture of origin, and of the class migrant herself, can be stirred. I will return to this theme later in my text.

This discussion takes place in a broader social context where, all too often, white middle-class people throw up their hands in horror at 'white working-class racism', while their own racisms remain unexamined. An instance of this occurred in 2007, when *Celebrity Big Brother*[3] generated protests on Indian streets and the intervention of politicians in Britain and India. The 'race row', as it became known, was about the racist bullying of Bollywood star Shilpa Shetty by other housemates, notably Jade Goody, who had shot to fame in 2002, after coming fourth in the *Big Brother* series of that year and becoming infamous because of her (white working-class) 'ignorance'. In 2007, there was a public reaction to the scenes of *Celebrity Big Brother*, where Shetty was called 'Shilpa Poppadom' by Jade, and subjected to rage and rejection. Forty thousand viewers complained to the media 'watchdog' OFCOM, some switched off, finding the programme too painful to watch, but many switched on: the programme's flagging ratings received a welcome boost and the audience share rose to five million. The then Chancellor of the Exchequer, Gordon Brown, and the Minister for Culture, Media and Sport both intervened to condemn the behaviour of Jade and her group. On BBC2's *Newsnight* the presenter Jeremy Paxman declared that white British people should not be associated with the behaviour of 'these stupid women', redefining them, in Brah's terms, as *ghair*. Without, in any way, condoning Jade and her friends' behaviour, we can observe that she became a vehicle for white middle-class people in powerful positions to seize the moral high ground, and distance themselves from any implication in the raced hierarchies of British society. Paxman's comments, particularly, indicate how some middle-class white performances of anti-racism can all too easily be accompanied by the reinforcement of gender and class hierarchies.

As a recent Runnymede report — 'Who cares about the white working class?' — points out, critiques of multiculturalism by middle-class actors such as journalists and politicians often deploy a similarly instrumental representation of 'the white British working-class' as the victims of the policy, oppressed and silenced in their own country. In this way, working-class people are simultaneously viewed as perpetrators of racism, and as victims of 'anti-white discrimination' in public discourse. A further layer of contradiction is added by the persistent distinction between the respectable working classes and those who would have been termed the 'undeserving poor' in the nineteenth century, and in the twenty-first have become the feckless and feral 'underclass' (Gavron, 2009; Skeggs, 2009). Bonnett (1998) argues that in the nineteenth century the working classes who previously had been negatively racialised 'became white' as a result of the need to suture them into the white nation and imperialist project; he suggests that in the post-welfare age of the late twentieth and twenty-first centuries, the 'whiteness' of some working-class people is again called into

3 Endemol for Channel 4 (2001–2010), for Channel 5 (2011–).

question. Similarly, in a discussion of class and race in a London Further Education college, Preston argues that:

> There is a distinction between a respectable, cosmopolitan, middle class whiteness (Skeggs 2002), and one which is insular, disordered and with low economic and educational aspirations. [...] this manifestation can be best understood in terms of the historical process of racialisation of the white working class, and other racial groups. (Preston, 2007: 43)

In these diverse representations, white working-class cultures become one of several 'abjects' of contemporary British society; on the one hand encouraged by some middle-class commentators and public discourses to attribute the inequalities they endure to immigration, and on the other, constructed as outside polite society, precisely because of such attitudes, in combination with the classed, raced and gendered tropes of unwillingness to work, dirt and fecundity. My own position as a white British class migrant in relation to these representations and realities of race and class is complex, reflecting a dual location within my culture of origin, and distanced from it, by education and the struggle to 'get away'. This dual positioning 'within and without' is inevitably a thread running through this article.

The context of this discussion, like the inequalities resulting from raced hierarchies, is material as well as discursive. The contrast between the friendly, but less affluent North and the wealthy coldness of the South is one of the tropes of British national identity, and the Midlands are considered like the North to be at the 'friendly but poor' end of this pole. While a recent report found that the inequalities of wealth between North and South were less great than popularly imagined when differences of cost of living are taken into account, the West Midlands nonetheless emerges as a region that has done particularly badly under New Labour, with both the lowest median income and the lowest rate of income growth since 1996–1997 (IFS report, 2010).[4] The roots of these inequalities are, of course, deeper than recent government policy (though this has certainly played and plays its part). The 'Black Country'[5] was defined as the industrial hub of Britain and in my childhood, in the 1950s and 60s, steel and ironworks still dominated working lives. My Aunty Clara would say with pride 'where there's muck there's money', looking out at the grim landscape surrounding her terraced house. The decline of the manufacturing industry has had and continues to have a profound social, cultural and economic impact on the region; as Lupton and Power comment on areas such as the West Midlands:

> Industrial collapse left a legacy of high worklessness, poverty and declining social conditions. The physical environment of industrial areas was blighted by contaminated land, obsolete infrastructure and the debris of two centuries of rapid growth and exploitation of natural local resources. (Lupton and Power, 2004: 14)

The contrast between the certainties and pride expressed by my Aunt, the description of a region in terms of blight, debris and obsolescence and the lived

4 IFS report (2010) http://www.ifs.org .uk/pr/hbai2010 .pdf, last accessed 12 September 2011.

5 The term refers to an area north and west of Birmingham and refers to the black dirt and dust resulting from coal mining and heavy industry that was supposed to cover the area. The name seems to exemplify the racialisation of the white working class; in one anecdote, while travelling through the area by train, Queen Victoria asked for the window experience of such places is one of the significant aspects of my 'culture of origin' that I aim to explore here. Despite a core of Labour wards in the urban areas of Birmingham and Wolverhampton, the West Midlands is arguably more conservative politically than some other sites of post-industrial decline such as the coal-mining areas of Wales and the North of England, or urban Scotland; in general elections it is seen as 'one of the traditional swing regions' (Baston, 2010). A tradition of small workshops, artisanal labour and family firms may in part explain how in the political life of the region, trade unionism and the labour movement are counter-balanced by more conservative tendencies.[6] Both of these threads are present in my parents' stories of their working lives, where the names of small firms and of 'the bosses' loom large, and jobs seem to be given almost as a personal favour by magnanimous factory owners. Resignation rather than resistance is certainly a feature of my culture of origin; two of my aunts, for instance, made and sold fur coats in a shop in Wolverhampton for a pittance in the 1960s and 70s. They never complained about the low wages, the dual task of making the product and managing the shop, or the lack of even the most basic facilities in their place of work (they were obliged to use the public lavatories in the town centre). The damage wrought by neoliberal policies and global recession has done nothing to alter this culture of resignation, the sense that things are getting worse, and inevitably so.

A significant aspect of the decline of industrial Britain in the late twentieth century is not only loss of employment, but also the fragmentation of white masculine identities. My own father moved from skilled manual work into (aptly named) 'white-collar' employment, but the importance of learning and having 'a trade', of a world of 'blokes' and 'mates' remained part of his culture, and of the culture that surrounded me as I grew up. Phil Cohen analyses the 'compensatory desire for a unitary and ideally productive body-of-labor [...] freed once and for all from the dead hand of alienation' experienced by those who are subjected to the alienating mental and physical régime of manual work, in factories and down mines (Cohen, 1997: 247). Cohen emphasises the 'almost exclusive masculinism of this project' (ibid.). Although my father and other men in our street worked long hours in factories, they were 'breadwinners', supporting wives (trapped in the domestic world of post-war white British femininity) and children. Ordinary white 'blokes' could thus construct a positive identity, reinforced by the habitus of masculine labour, as Cohen describes: 'a narcissistic connection between labor and the white body is facilitated as a means of denying the symbolic wounds and real injuries of growing up working-class' (Cohen, 1997: 252). The other body of labour, alienated, degraded, subject to control, could be projected onto those 'whose faces do not fit into the immediate work habitus (i.e. "wrong" age, race, gender, or ethnicity)' (Cohen, 1997: 248).

Cohen goes on to describe how under post-Fordism this Bourdieuian harmony, which 'continuously transforms necessities into strategies, constraints into

blinds to be lowered, so that she would not have to gaze on the grimy landscape and its inhabitants.

6 I am indebted to my friend and colleague Helen Crowley, and to Richard and Rob Osborne who also grew up in a white working-class family in the West Midlands for these insights.

preferences' (Bourdieu, 1984: 175), is disrupted; the jobs on which it was based have disappeared and appenticeships are a thing of the past. The jobs now may be cleaner (service industries rather than factories), but the body is still subjected to discipline and, furthermore, is often selected for its 'presentability'. Faceless globalised bureaucracies can at any moment close down the employment source, devastating a local economy and the lives that depend on it. Cohen argues that the emergence of 'skinhead youth international' is symptomatic of the losses these changes have brought for working-class men (1997: 255). In my culture of origin, the impacts of these changes are less violent, but no less significant. The young men of my circle of acquaintance do not enjoy job security, do not all, even, have jobs; and yet they still aspire to the identity and habitus of the working-class 'breadwinner', and survive because of the networks of 'mates' who can be called on to mend a car or plaster a wall. The habitus underlying these networks, perhaps because it lacks the material base which daily presence in pattern shop or foundry provided for my father, is experienced as fragile and 'threatened', and the threat is sometimes perceived in terms of race, of whiteness surrounded or overwhelmed.

My father's trajectory in the war and post-war period points to the material structures of inequality between white and black British at this time. He enjoyed not only a secure identity as a skilled worker, but also the possibility of social advancement. After the war, my father left the army and returned to work in a factory in Crewe as a pattern-maker. On being put on a four day week, he returned to his home town Wolverhampton, and found a job in a pattern shop there. After a further redundancy he became a sales representative, and eventually a technical sales representative with an engineering firm. The move into 'white-collar' employment that he had been able to make in the army as a member of the Royal Signals Corps was thus replicated in civilian life. His role in the foundry was to assist in detecting and correcting errors in the iron castings that the firm made. These castings were made by a largely Indian workforce. My father speaks of having an 'excellent' relationship with these workers, some of whom he refers to as 'good blokes', a phrase that may be translatable as *ajnabi*, perhaps even *apne*. He recounts being invited to an evening of Indian music and dance, and being one of two white men present: 'of all the management people who were invited, only two turned up'. After the concert, they all went for a meal in an Indian restaurant:

> Harjit came up to us and said you're not going home yet, we've booked a table in a restaurant, so I said but Harjit I can't eat spicy food. He said don't worry, we'll have something made specially for you. All the Indians had a normal Indian soup and I had a soup that was specially made for me. (Interview with Arthur Thomas, aged 88, December 2010)

Despite this moment of conviviality, the picture that emerges from my father's account is of a deep cultural and social divide between the white management and Indian workers, who are homogenised as 'Indian' and whose regional, ethnic and religious affiliations and backgrounds remain unknown to their white co-workers and managers. Some white working-class men were able to capitalise their skills and their whiteness, to move out of manual labour (and particularly the physically tough work of the blast furnace) and into middle management, sales or administration. My father is not a manager, but his identification is clearly with the white management of the foundry. My own social mobility, predicated on my father's, thus has its roots in these colonial structures.

This moment of conviviality between Indian British and white British working men is perhaps an early instance of what Paul Gilroy describes as 'the spontaneous tolerance and openness evident in the underworld of Britain's convivial culture' (Gilroy, 2004: 144). However, it goes against the grain; as Cohen argues 'any kind of transracial working-class alliance based on recognising the real historical individuality of black labor' (1997: 252) cannot be permitted. The educational structures that would have allowed my father to learn that historical specificity are not in place. He can learn French and German in evening classes, but not Punjabi, Urdu or the colonial history that has brought the men alongside whom he works daily, to these shores. If the inadequacies of the education system and limited access to it are one way in which such alliances are denied, another is the mobilisation of race for political advantage, an interpellation of the strongest and crudest kind. On 20 April 1968, Enoch Powell made the infamous 'rivers of blood' speech that was to enter national and local mythology either as a deplorable public vindication of racism or as a brave defence of Britain/England, depending on the socio-political mesh through which the speech was interpreted. Brah refers several times to Powell as a formative element of the political context of the murders motivated by 'racial' difference and the political conflict and confrontation on the streets between the National Front and Asians in Southall in the 1970s. Powell's speech also vehicles the 'defensive Englishness' (Brah, 1999: 18) that Brah finds in the talk of the 'ordinary' people she interviewed. In Powell's speech, England and Englishness are under threat. It is a particularly resonant interpellation in the geographical area where Powell was, as a local Member of Parliament, a well-known and popular figure even before he made the speech.

A central figure in the speech is a white woman, about whom he has received a letter from a constituent:

> Eight years ago in a respectable street in Wolverhampton a house was sold to a Negro. Now only one white (a woman old-age pensioner) lives there. This is her story. She lost her husband and both her sons in the war. So she turned her seven-roomed house, her only asset, into a boarding house. She worked hard and did well, paid off her mortgage and began to put something by for her old age. Then the immigrants moved in. With growing fear, she saw one house after another taken over. The quiet street became a place of noise and confusion. Regretfully, her white tenants moved out. [...]

She is becoming afraid to go out. Windows are broken. She finds excreta pushed through her letter box. When she goes to the shops, she is followed by children, charming, wide-grinning piccaninnies. They cannot speak English, but one word they know. 'Racialist,' they chant. When the new Race Relations Bill is passed, this woman is convinced she will go to prison. And is she so wrong? I begin to wonder.[7]

7 http://www .telegraph.co.uk/ comment/3643823/ Enoch-Powells-Rivers-of-Blood-speech.html, last accessed 25 November 2011.

8 'The woman who never was', broadcast BBC Radio 4, Monday January 22, 2007, http://www .bbc.co.uk/radio4/ history/document/ document_ 20070122.shtml, last accessed 25 November 2011.

Powell's speech mobilises the familiar representation of woman as symbol of nation, and the powerful trope of defiled white womanhood in racist discourse (Ware, 1992). The immigrants from India and the Caribbean who were indeed transforming Wolverhampton's streets and cultures in the 1950s and 60s are associated in the speech with dirt, noise and disorder, threatening not only white femininity, but also the respectable white working class who had won the war and 'done well' through hard work. In 2007, a Radio 4 documentary[8] – 'The woman who never was' – attempted to establish whether Powell had invented the woman, concluding that he had not, and with the help of a historian, Simon Burgess, identifying her as Druscilla Cotterill. Interviews with Druscilla Cotterill's former neighbours, 'the immigrants who moved in' paint a complex and contradictory picture, where Mrs Cotterill is at times a well-loved figure who stayed in the street till her death in 1978, at others a bit moody and unpredictable. These oral histories depict a woman who would look after her neighbours' children or join them for a drink, and who was often seen staggering back from the pub; she does not resemble the lonely and isolated figure cowering behind her locked door of Powell's speech. The 'excrement' episode is both categorically denied and attributed to another house and to other motivations – 'nothing to do with race'. Like Jean Lott, Powell's beleaguered war widow and her response to the people arriving from former colonies remain mysterious, unknown; she is portrayed as *apni* by her neighbours, while in Powell's speech, they are *ghair* to her.

The 'truth' of the story is, of course, impossible to trace; its national impact, on the other hand, is well known, and split on class lines. The Conservative party under the leadership of Heath struggled to dissociate itself from the taint of Powell's racist language, and he was immediately dismissed from the Shadow cabinet. In Wolverhampton and in London, however, there were demonstrations in support of Powell and dockers went on strike. In the spirit of 'The Scent of Memory' I want to look at less public manifestations, at the ripples the speech created when it fell like a stone into the white English working-class culture I grew up in, and at the construction of race in that culture more broadly. I will do this through a series of interconnected memory scenes. In this process, I am conscious of the constructed and complex nature of memory 'always already secondary revision' (Kuhn, 2000: 186). The scenes I offer here are amalgamations of sense memories and narratives that I (and sometimes my parents) have made over the years; they are inflected by visual images of the periods, especially family photographs, and thus connect with feminist memory work around photographs by Kuhn herself, Jo Spence (Spence, 1986; Kuhn, 1995), and by Annie

Ernaux, who in her auto-ethnographic writing projects makes frequent use of descriptions of family photographs (Ernaux, 2008). At once personal and historically specific, family photographs epitomise memory's ability, as Kuhn argues, to connect with 'the intersubjective domain of shared meanings, shared feelings, shared memories' (2000: 191). I hope that the scenes I describe here, 'snapshots' seen through the lens of race, have a similar capacity. Kuhn describes the memory text as characteristically 'collagist, fragmentary, timeless, even musical'; her phrase accurately describes the nature of these scenes, which, in being juxtaposed and linked thematically, create a new memory collage. In making this collage, I am evoking and working with emotions such as shame and loss; but it is also a *mise-en-scène*, of classed whitenesses. The middle-classness, which in 1999 I described in terms of the masquerade (Rivière, 1929), is ever more entrenched, and yet in the unearthing of some of these scenes the desire to be accepted into the new milieu, to perform class appropriately there (and the attendant fear of failure) is recounted and comes again into play in the act of writing. Perhaps what Kuhn calls 'a desire to forestall death', expressed through the telling and retelling of memory stories, is also significant here (Kuhn, 2000: 193), for the scenes reconstruct the life of my small family of three, a life whose days must inevitably be numbered since my parents are 84 and 89 years old. Ernaux's writing projects are underpinned by her desire to save her culture of origin and everyday life from oblivion. In her diary of her mother's decline and death from Alzheimer's, the illness itself a kind of double oblivion, Ernaux comments:

> What I am writing is not literature. I see the difference between this and the other books I have done, or rather, I don't, because I don't know how to write anything that isn't about this, this desire to save, to understand, but to save first of all. (Ernaux, 1988: 103)

I share with Ernaux this desire to save from oblivion a culture of origin that does not habitually find literary expression; here that project must attempt to include hitherto disavowed aspects of the inheritance.

The first scene is my memory of entering what I now know, thanks to Avtar Brah's work, as 'diaspora space' (Brah, 1996). As African Caribbean and Indian people moved into the centre of Wolverhampton in the 1950s and 60s, the phenomenon of 'white flight' occurred, and new estates were built on the edge of the town. My parents bought a house on one of these estates in 1955. They were moving, not from the town centre, but from Crewe, for work. 'White flight' does not form part of their narrations of this daring move into home ownership, but through their move, my parents are becoming more respectable, whiter than their own parents, who, on my mother's side, went to the pub every night, had a 'flutter' on the horses, kept pigeons in the garden, and bowls of dripping in the pantry. Between our estate, the perfect vision of 1950s white Britain, and the town centre were the areas of settlement of the new migrants. The drivers and conductors of the buses that navigated these spaces and transported me and my parents into town were usually black or Asian. As the bus got nearer to town, the diversity of its occupants increased. These were, in my memory, warm, convivial spaces, where there were jokes, and where children and babies were smiled at and admired. It was also on the bus that I first noticed differences of skin colour and of styles of dress, and would stare in fascination until my mother told me off. My desiring gaze focused on the colour and textures of women's dress and on the contact between white and black hands as money and tickets were exchanged. These memories have the quality of an almost pre-verbal existence, but I could speak, and did, apparently, in a loud voice, asking, to my mother's intense embarrassment, 'are they made of chocolate?'. Where had I acquired, at so young an age, the notion that a different skin colour might indicate a deeper difference between human beings? The association of black people with a fairy-tale world where houses are made of sweets and people of chocolate perhaps stems from the 'golliwogs' I saw daily on jam jars, the 'golliwog' toys that white children played with in the 1950s, or the popular 'Black and White Minstrel Show', first broadcast in June 1958.[9] The question posed by a white child on first meeting African Caribbean and Asian British people is spoken from a subject position that even at that age assumes its own normativity, its power to define, to be the subject of the gaze. I entered the diaspora space of the bus, where bodies are pressed together, and gazes traverse the compressed space, joyfully, confidently. This is in sharp contrast to bell hooks' account of a parallel but diametrically opposed journey through the white areas of the southern American town where she grew up. She is the object of the white gaze, averting her own eyes in terror: 'I remember the fear, being scared to walk to Baba's, our grandmother's house, because we would have to pass that terrifying whiteness — those white faces on the porches staring us down with hate' (hooks, 1997: 175).

The next scene is around the time of Powell's speech. By now adolescent, I attend an all white, comprehensive school, staffed by teachers who felt they were educational pioneers (the headmaster, Sir Godfrey Cretney, was knighted by Harold Wilson for services to education). The 'memory scene', however, is at home, in the garden of our 1950s semi-detached house. I am listening to our neighbour telling my mother stories about Asian people living in nearby Whitmore Reans (the area of town we travelled and travel through on the bus). Over the garden fence, I hear the stories of smells and dirt that Avtar Brah's interviewees also evoke. Houses overflow with people, gardens with dirt, rubbish, even excrement, as 'they' do not know how to use lavatories. I half hear the stories that are spoken *sotto voce*, like the tales of difficult labours or heavy periods overheard during childhood. Initiated earlier into a culture of suffering women's bodies, whose unclean manifestations must be hidden from the male gaze, replaced by a simulacrum of powdered and lipsticked über-femininity, I am now interpellated as a white female subject, invited to construct myself as the binary opposite of the frightening dirt, chaos and smells of 'blackness'. The women's

9 We did not yet have television, but I may have heard talk, or seen still images.

talk mobilises them as the guardians of the white enclave of the suburb; their daily labour to keep all surfaces in the new semis gleaming, to scrub clean their husbands' foundry-black collars and to dress their little girls in spotless dresses, white socks and shoes becomes more than a struggle for respectability: it acquires a symbolic dimension as respectability, cleanliness and whiteness merge. This Wolverhampton suburb is constructed, like Southall, 'in terms of a vulnerable feminised space' through a discourse that 'displaces female anxiety about male aggression onto a fear of colonialism's Other' (Brah, 1999: 10).

Initially this interpellation is irresistible. In July 1968, at fifteen, I spend three weeks in a French family. On one hot afternoon I sit behind the shutters with my French 'mother' and 'grandmother' talking in my still halting French about the 'problem of immigration'. My language is not Powellite, but the 'defensive Englishness' of his speech is the subtext of my account. Politicians in London, I tell them, do not understand. All of this is well received. One year later I return to the same family. Another year of liberal humanist education has generated resistance to that earlier interpellation; I am ashamed of what I said the previous year, and hope they have forgotten.

The next scene takes place in an Oxford women's college in 1972. I am beginning to make friends with the only African student in my year, probably in the whole college. She is public school educated, like most of my fellow students. She and I and another white friend are one day talking about black women trying to bleach their skins white. I mutter something about the sadness of this self-loathing, and the need for self-acceptance, and it is misheard as 'Even if you're black you need to accept who you are'. Both my new friends roar with laughter. I realise I have said something racist and am filled with shame. The shame of class is compounded by the association of my working-class culture of origin with racism. This scene is one of many experiences at Oxford of not 'fitting into the picture', not understanding the codes, or deploying the kind of cultural know-ledge that is absorbed without effort in middle-class milieus, the 'total, early, imperceptible learning, performed in the family from the earliest days of life' that studying hard cannot replicate, and which generates the 'paradoxical rela-tionship to culture made up of self-confidence amid (relative) ignorance and of casualness amid familiarity, which bourgeois families hand down to their offspring as if it were an heirloom' (Bourdieu, 1984: 66). In this way, my white middle-class peers at Oxford would approach the world with complete confi-dence; 'self-confidence amid (relative) ignorance' would have allowed them to breeze through the difficult moment of confrontation with race, to avoid, perhaps, the awkward turn of phrase that had plunged me into an abyss of shame.[10] The certainty of one's place in the world leads also to the kind of bluff of innocence in the face of raced (or classed or gendered) inequalites that white middle-class media and political commentators regularly perform, for instance in the 'race row' of 2007.

10 Bourdieu here is not just explaining his survey results; his comments, like mine, are drawn from experience,

albeit, in his case, only reluctantly and recently acknowledged (Bourdieu, 2007): that of a scholarship student from a small village in the South-West of France, who finds himself in the gallic equivalent of Oxbridge, the *École Normale Supérieure*, at twenty.

The final scene is the most difficult to describe, and can only be given as a sketch, an outline. It brings us back to the present, to April 2011, and to the kind of intimate space Brah refers to: a living room in Wolverhampton. I am talking about my new cats, who probably have the same black father. The inevitable joke 'there are plenty of black fathers round here' is made. Laughter. Then it all pours out: the sense of being surrounded by alien cultures, of once respectable areas of the town being ruined, of something being taken from 'us' by 'them'. Finally, Powell is referred to, how he had to have police protection after making that speech, how 'everything he said has come true'. The family visitors leave, and I (having remained silent in their presence) make an angry speech to my parents.

I care about those who expressed these sentiments as deeply as I reject the sentiments themselves. They are, to me, *apne*, even if in that moment they became *ghair*. As I write the scene, I betray them; I am reminded of the quotation from Genet, which stands as epigraph to Ernaux's book about her father *A Man's Place*: 'écrire est le dernier recours quand on a trahi (writing is the only recourse for those who have betrayed' (Ernaux, 1984). My first task is to try to under-stand; the second, far more difficult, somehow, to educate, without patronising or alienating or upsetting the delicate balance of intimacies in a context where all too easily I can become the 'class enemy' from the South, with her posh accent and money to burn on foreign holidays and fancy food. The racialising discourses that traverse my white working-class culture of origin, where Powell still casts his shadow, are, as I have argued, intensified by the loss of a certain secure sense of self, which white working-class men, at least, enjoyed. The memory scenes reveal, however, that the notion of a golden age of secure employment, now lost, is a construction rather than a reality; my father's early working life and upward trajectory, for instance, are marked by crises, redundancies and periods of unemployment, while my grandparents had none of the consumer goods now taken as the norm in all but the very poorest homes in Britain, and lived on bargains such as cracked eggs and broken biscuits from the market. Despite this, when the stories of being 'taken over', of the association of decline with the presence of black and Asian people in Britain, emerge, they are tinged with nostalgia for a white working-class culture that is perceived as a lost utopia compared to the contemporary struggle for survival; the postcolonial melancholia discussed by Paul Gilroy (2004) is also a thread in these patch-worked opinions. Some white femininities still seem, in this location, to be struggling to claim respectability through an identification with 'order' and respectability, keeping 'difference' outside the polished and preened home and suburb. However, at the same time, these discourses are not consistent; my father will repeat the British National Party mantra 'England for the English', and in the next breath explain how he made space in his front garden for mourners to park their cars when the Sikh family up the road suffered a bereavement. In these contradictions a space opens up, and I am able to interject 'So you don't really believe in England for the English do you?'; in this perfect illustration of the dialectic between postcolonial melancholia and everyday conviviality discussed by Gilroy (2004), my father concedes the point, and moves, as in the past, to a more open position.

Perhaps the sense of being embattled and beleaguered, which sometimes translates into the expression of racist views, is as much the result of the loss of a positive cultural identity as of material insecurity. The internalisation of the scorn and derision heaped on white working-class people through terms such as 'chav', through negative representations in popular culture, and through the political mobilisation of discourses of the 'feral underclass' (Bonnett, 1998; Preston, 2007; Wood and Skeggs, 2008) may result in a defensive strategy, where a form of distinction is claimed/reclaimed by differentiating oneself from people of colour. Combating these pejorative and stigmatising representations and at the same time fighting what Paul Gilroy has called 'the conditions in which ignorance can thrive' seem to be important interventions for academics and educators to make in the current conjuncture.[11] The crucial knowledge that 'we are here because you were there' (Mercer, 1994: 7) is what is missing from the Powellite discourses, along with the cultural openness and confidence that education and travel bring. However, education is clearly not always transformative; it can function, as Bourdieu (1984) argues, to reinforce or even *make* the unequal hierarchies characteristic of 'meritocratic' capitalism. The recent intervention by historian David Starkey on BBC2's *Newsnight* after the scenes of violence on British streets in August 2011 underlines the limitations of education in élite institutions and the important point that racism is not 'the property of a particular social class' (Rogaly and Taylor, 2009: 198). On this occasion, Starkey brought Powellite discourses back into the political mainstream, directly quoting Powell's most flamboyant metaphors of rivers and blood and adding his own 'flames lambent' wrapping around Tottenham and Clapham. Starkey's analysis of the 'riots' consistently associated 'blackness' with violence, and in a feat of combined racism and classism claimed 'the chavs' have 'become black', that is, violent and unruly (Quinn, 2011). In the face of this kind of 'academic analysis', the value of education of the kind offered by London Metropolitan University, where I have been employed for the past twenty-two years, and of others like it, cannot be underestimated, since it is education in and through 'diaspora space' *par excellence*. It has been, and remains, an education to work or study there, despite the lack of value and material resources attributed to it by successive governments. Tragically, as I write, Caribbean studies, history and philosophy are being erased from the curriculum; languages, women's studies and Irish studies were earlier casualties of market-led education.

But perhaps education in the spaces of intimacy is also possible and important, and perhaps shame can be part of that process, 'a potential, a change agent for the self' rather than simply a negative emotion (Munt, 2007: 8). In my analysis of

11 Paul Gilroy, lecture at the Faculty of Social Sciences, London Metropolitan University, 4 April 2011.

12 A peace rally was held on 14 August 2011 in Summerfield Park, Winson Green Birmingham; it was attended by 5,000 people and addressed by Tariq Jahan: 'Blacks, Asians, whites, we all live in the same community, Why do we have to kill one another?' http://www.mirror.co.uk/news/top-stories/2011/08/15/brian-reade-birmingham-peace-rally-s-message-of-hope-115875-23345495/#ixzz1XIOLwBBO, last accessed 17 August 2011.

my own trajectory, it is clear that shame has played its part, alongside education, in bringing out into the open the 'racist secrets' of my past. It is clear also that this kind of shame, with the potential for greater self-awareness, is present in the narratives of others in my culture of origin, in my mother's embarassment at my loud question in the bus, or even in the neighbour's hushed tones. The work of transforming shame into a positive force, of bringing the secrets into the open, and analysing their constituent parts so that all can become aware of the ideological weight that they carry is delicate but necessary relational work in the intimate spaces of working-class whiteness. In this spirit, I will end this article by quoting the parent who has been least visible in the piece so far, my mother. Soon after the death of three young British Asian men in the violence in Birmingham in August 2011, she commented on the tragic loss of these 'lovely lads', a phrase that carries the notion of 'our own' conveyed by *apne* and that certainly bears no relation to *ghair*. After the peace rally held in Birmingham a few days after their deaths,[12] echoing the words of Tariq Jahan, the father of the one of the victims, my mother commented: 'perhaps now we can all live in peace together'. My mother's words do not represent a closure, any more than that peace rally could resolve the tensions and complexities of Britain's postcolonial multiculture, but they do represent a step across the garden fence into public space, an opening and openness to the imagining of new and more inclusive forms of conviviality.

acknowledgements

The article is dedicated to my parents, Betty and Arthur Thomas.

I would like to thank the *Feminist Review* Collective past and present for the education, friendship and support that has made it possible to write this article. In particular I would like to thank Avtar Brah, Helen Crowley, Clare Hemmings, Nirmal Puwar and Irene Gedalof for comments and discussion. I am indebted to Avtar for writing the piece that triggered it all; like many others, I have been inspired and comforted by her generosity and serenity of spirit.

author biography

Lyn Thomas is Professor of Cultural Studies and Deputy Director of the Institute for the Study of European Transformations at London Metropolitan University, where she has taught French, film and media since 1989. Her writings include *Annie Ernaux, An Introduction to the Writer and Her Audience* (Berg, 1999), *Fans, Feminisms and 'Quality' Media* (Routledge, 2002) and *Annie Ernaux, à la première personne* (Stock, 2005). She has edited a collection on *Religion, Consumerism and Sustainability: Paradise Lost?* (Palgrave, 2010), and co-edited *The Theory and Politics of Consuming Differently* with Kate Soper and Martin Ryle (Palgrave, 2008). In 2011, she co-authored a research report: *Suspect Communities?*

Counter-terrorism policy, the press and the impact on Irish and Muslim communities in Britain, with Mary Hickman, Sara Silvestri and Henri Nickels. She was a member of the *Feminist Review* Editorial Collective from 1998–2011.

references

Baston, L. (2010) 'West midlands general election guide' *The Guardian*, 26 March, http://www.guardian.co.uk/politics/2010/mar/26/west-midlands-generalelection-guide, last accessed 12 September 2011.

Bonnett, A. (1998) 'How the British working class became white: the symbolic (re)formation of racialized capitalism' *Journal of Historical Sociology*, Vol. 11, No. 3: 316–340.

Bourdieu, P. (1984) *Distinction: A Social Critique of the Judgement of Taste*, trans Nice, R. London: Routledge and Kegan Paul.

Bourdieu, P. (2007) *Sketch for a Self-analysis*, trans Nice, R. Cambridge: Polity Press.

Brah, A. (1996) *Cartographies of Diaspora: Contesting Identities*, London and New York: Routledge.

Brah, A (1999) 'The Scent of Memory: strangers, our own, and others' *Feminist Review*, Issue 61: 4–26.

Cohen, P. (1997) 'Laboring under whiteness' in Frankenberg, R. (1997) editor, *Displacing Whiteness: Essays in Social and Cultural Criticism*, Durham and London: Duke University Press.

Ernaux, A. (1984) *La Place*, Paris: Gallimard, trans Leslie, T. (1991) *Positions*, London: Quartet Books, and (1992) *A Man's Place*, New York: Seven Stories Press.

Ernaux, A. (1988) *Une Femme*, Paris: Gallimard, trans Leslie, T. (1990) *A Woman's Story*, London: Quartet Books, and New York: Seven Stories Press.

Ernaux, A. (2008) *Les Années*, Paris: Gallimard.

Frankenberg, R. (1993) *White Women, Race Matters: The Social Construction of Whiteness*, London and Minneapolis: University of Minnesota Press and Routledge.

Frankenberg, R. (1997) editor, *Displacing Whiteness: Essays in Social-Cultural Criticism*, Durham and London: Duke University Press.

Gavron, K. (2009) 'Foreword' in Sveinsson, K.P. (2009) editor, *Who Cares about the White Working Class?* London: The Runnymede Trust.

Gilroy, P. (2004) *After Empire: Melanchloia or Convivial Culture?* London and New York: Routledge.

Heron, L. (1985) *Truth, Dare or Promise: Girls Growing Up in the 1950s*, London: Virago.

hooks, b. (1997) 'Representing whiteness in the black imagination' in Frankenberg R. editor, *Displacing Whiteness: Essays in Social and Cultural Criticism*, Durham and London: Duke University Press.

Kuhn, A. (1995) *Family Secrets: Acts of Memory and Imagination*, London and New York: Verso.

Kuhn, A. (2000) 'A journey through memory' in Radstone, S. (2000) editor, *Memory and Methodology*, Berg: Oxford and New York, 179–196.

Lupton, R. and Power, A. (2004) *The Growth and Decline of Cities and Regions*, London: CASE, LSE, http://sticerd.lse.ac.uk/dps/case/cbcb/census1.pdf, last accessed 12 September 2011.

Mercer, K. (1994) *Welcome to the Jungle: New Positions in Black Cultural Studies*, London: Routledge.

Miller, N.K. (1991) *Getting Personal: Feminist Occasions and Other Autobiographical Acts*, New York and London: Routledge.

Munt, S. (2007) *Queer Attachments: The Cultural Politics of Shame*, Aldershot and Burlington, VT: Ashgate.

Preston, J. (2007) 'How the white working class became "Chav": the making of whiteness in an Essex FE College' in Preston, J. (2007) editor, *Whiteness and Class in Education*, London: Springer.

Quinn, B. (2011) 'David Starkey claims "the whites have become black"' *The Guardian*, 13 August 2011, http://www.guardian.co.uk/uk/2011/aug/13/david-starkey-claims-whites-black, last accessed 17 August 2011.

Rivière, J. (1986; first published 1929) 'Womanliness as masquerade' in Burgin, V., Donald, J. and Kaplan, C. (1986) editors, *Formations of Fantasy*, London: Methuen.

Rogaly, B. and Taylor, B. (2009) *Moving Histories of Class and Community: Identity, Place and Belonging in Contemporary England*, Basingstoke and New York: Palgrave.

Skeggs, B. (2009) 'Haunted by the spectre of judgement: respectability, value and affect in class relations' in Sveinsson, K.P. (2009) editor, *Who Cares about the White Working Class?*, London: The Runnymede Trust.

Spence, J. (1986) *Putting Myself in the Picture: A Political, Personal, and Photographic Autobiography*, London: Camden Press.

Steedman, C. (1986) *Landscape for a Good Woman: A Story of Two Lives*, London: Virago.

Thomas, L. (1999) *Annie Ernaux: An Introduction to the Writer and Her Audience*, Oxford and New York: Berg.

Ware, V. (1992) *Beyond the Pale: White Women, Racism and History*, London and New York: Verso.

Wood, H. and Skeggs, B. (2008) 'Spectacular morality: "reality" television, individualisation and the remaking of the working class' in Hesmondhalgh, D. and Toynbee, J. (2008) editors, *The Media and Social Theory*, London and New York: Routledge.

Young, I.M. (1997) *Intersecting Voices: Dilemmas of Gender, Political Philosophy and Policy*, Princeton, NJ: Princeton University Press.

doi:10.1057/fr.2011.62

100 | mediations on making *Aaj Kaal*

Nirmal Puwar

abstract

This article excavates a discussion on the mediations that informed the making of the film *Aaj Kaal* by Asian elders, in a project directed by Avtar Brah and coordinated by Jasbir Panesar with the film trainer Vipin Kumar. It brings this largely unknown and inventive film to the foreground of current developments in participative media research practices. The discussion explores the coming together of the ethnographic imagination and performative pedagogies during the course of an adult education community project centred on South Asian elders making a film. Collaborative dialogic encounters illuminate post-war British front rooms, the seaside and public spheres from what is usually an unlikely vantage point of view in public accounts.

keywords

method; pedagogy; participatory; ethnography; South Asian; Southall

(124–141) © 2012 Feminist Review. 0141-7789/12 www.feminist-review.com

introduction

The opening scene of the film *Aaj Kaal* (1990, translated *Today, Yesterday and Tomorrow*) fills the screen with the words:

> This film was made by the users of the MILAP DAY CENTRE in Southall, Middlesex — A Day Centre for the Elderly.

Over the last 10 years, there has been a proliferation of social research using new media technologies, harnessing a range of materials and devices, including photography, video, maps and blog diaries (Pink, 2001; Blunt *et al.*, 2003; Rose, 2005; Blunt and Dowling, 2006; Kuhn and McAllister, 2006; Back, 2007; Rose, 2010). Alongside the use of visual, audio and digital technologies, there is a steady emergence of curatorial practices within the social sciences (Latour, 2007; Puwar and Sharma, 2012). Slowly, disciplines are making way for new modes for producing and communicating research, beyond the flat page of the academic journal article or book. The dominance of the written script in academia is gradually (and not without resistance) being accompanied by exhibitions and events, including theatrical pieces, music performances or audio and visual installations. Today, these practices are often presented as encompassing entirely 'new' directions. Suffice to say, these practices do not come from nowhere, they emerge from somewhere. Although it is not always easy to ascertain the creative aspects of social research in methods books, it is important to register that there have been significant antecedents to the more experimental approaches currently being generated.

Some years before the recent proliferation of imaginative ways of conducting social research, over 20 years ago, Avtar Brah led a project, which involved the making of *Aaj Kaal*. The film was ahead of its time, notably because it was made by South Asian elders, with the researcher Jasbir Panesar and the film teacher Vipin Kumar at the Milap Day Centre in Southall, West London. There is much to learn in developing our methodological practices by turning our attention to the making of the film *Aaj Kaal*. The project was led by reflexive pedagogic and participative processes of learning with the elders who attended the Centre. It is much more common to film elders but not to teach elders to *make* a film. Participant cooperation and responsibility within a non-competitive environment were central to the methodology developed in this cross-sector pedagogic collaboration. To date, the film has been overlooked in academic discussions. Notably, Brah directed the project some years before the publication of her renowned book *Cartographies of Diaspora* (1996), yet discussion of the film does not feature here or in any of her other published works. This is not surprising given that the film was part of a community adult education project, rather than a research project. Today, the writing would be expected to sit alongside a 'package' of work that entails the made product, as well as the written text. For example, Bruno Latour co-edited a 500 page, part catalogue and part academic treatise, book for the exhibition *Making Things Public* (2005); signalling a specific scale and set of cultural imperatives.

A different set of mediations underlined the journey of Brah's project, which located writing academic text at the bottom of her list of priorities. It has to be stressed that Brah, Panesar and Kumar saw themselves as being in the middle of a pedagogic practice, rather than a research project. I have deciphered these mediations from private and public conversations I conducted with Brah and Panesar, as well as from the project report, photographic documentation and the film, which they generously made available to me. In this article, I turn to these mediations in order to appreciate the context of the project and the key considerations that made the film *Aaj Kaal*. Infused theoretically, these practical and political mediations remain important for the ways in which we might endeavour to develop cross platform collaborative projects today.

participative methods

The use of media technologies has been especially attractive to social researchers engaged in participative methods. Media devices have often enabled the active involvement of participants in collecting and crafting their stories for researchers and wider publics. A different set of eyes, hands and ears, to those of prying academics have, at least in theory, the potential to participate in what is found, told and shown. Lest we get carried away by the so-called democracy of participation lent by media technologies, it is always important to bear in mind that the close up view can at the same time intensify the symbolic violence of research encounters. The use of intimate (self) observations, which media devices can facilitate, does not mitigate against the underlying technology of surveillance, which any research can very easily unthinkingly enact.

Aaj Kaal was produced in a reflexive and careful manner, in the context of an adult education project; the field in which Avtar Brah grounded her academic life. So first and foremost the film was an exercise in participative pedagogy. Paulo Freire (1972) was a key influence, not least because Brah taught in the Centre of Extra-Mural Studies at Birkbeck College. The emphasis on dialogue and the dialogic in his work, on the link between praxis as well as community education and the importance of lived experiences for developing a mutual humanity between teachers and students were influential. This is in contrast to what Freire termed as the 'banking' notion of education, whereby it is assumed that teachers deposit education in to the receptors (students). Notwithstanding inherited and circulating power dynamics in learning situations, the accent is placed on developing a shared space of active and inventive co-learning. These general principles have had a huge influence on teaching practices, as well as the coupling of teaching and research methods. Being a community education initiative rather than a research project, if we reflect on how Brah's team developed learning situations, we can see how their exploratory open-ended learning experiments became sites and spaces for dialogue between researchers and elders about diaspora, gender, home, war, violence, discrimination, political and cultural exchange. All of which are persistent themes in Brah's oeuvre of works (1987, 1989, 1994, 2002). While she did not directly publish out of *Aaj Kaal*, there is no doubt that her previous research informed the pedagogic projects she embarked on (Brah and Hoy, 1987) and these in turn inflected her writings, especially those on Southall (Brah, 1978, 1999).

Today, it has become commonplace to grant cameras to those who participate in research and to then use the images collected to elucidate stories from unforeseen angles. The process of active engaged self-presentation is attractive, because it does, to some extent, offer a method for sharing the field of vision and the space of authorship while providing educational learning strategies. This research learning strategy is one that is becoming customary, especially for research with young people. For instance, in one of the earlier projects of this kind, back in the nineties, young people were given photography and film training as a way of delivering accounts and depictions of risk and safety in the making of the geo-political landscape of the city (Back *et al.*, 1996; Rathzel and Cohen, 2008). The fact that Brah and Panesar worked on an educational basis specifically with Asian elders, in Punjabi, in a community day centre, brings a different orientation to participative media methods. The deployment of multi-media methods in research on the elderly has become a growing area of interest. What is less conventional is the central placement of Asian elders in the United Kingdom, who spoke little English, as the central *makers* of a film. While Asian elders feature in research-based films, often in a testimonial mode, they are less likely to have been granted the training and encouragement of learning some of the basic skills for actually crafting a film amongst each other.

pedagogic practices

Increasingly projects facilitate adults (especially refugees) to partake in photography projects where they themselves take photos of life in exile. The ethics of this partaking are no less complicated than when researchers take the photographs themselves.

At a moment when sociology could easily slip into building forms of visual sociology involving quick short-term fieldwork contact, which is problematic on ethical grounds (Patai, 1991; Gatenby and Humphries, 2000), it is important to remember that the temporality of research also has consequences for the quality of what we know. The long duration of the filming process undertaken by Brah and Panesar was central to the trust and rapport that was built up between the facilitators and the elders, including between the elders themselves. Clearly, this project experience was deliberately in contrast to the snap, grab and snatch practices, which we are in danger of producing if the ethics of our research encounters are overlooked. In fact, visual practices complicate the ethical issues of research even further, of which there has been considerable discussion in different disciplines, including documentary film practice (Katz and Katz, 1988).[1] Moreover, the contemporary climate of speeded up academic productivity, fuelled by an auditing culture of measure and value (Evans, 2004), is generating conditions of academic labour production pressured by fast (almost just in time) output targets of publishing and impact. The 'edu-factory' we are becoming due to the longstanding auditing culture, as well as the transformation of universities from public to private, market-led institutions, will undoubtedly have consequences for the shape and conduct of the craft of research.[2] Projects are likely to be constrained by the need to meet targets for publication and impact, working in the United Kingdom to the changing measures of research assessment exercises.

A very different academic and social sector environment had informed Brah and Panesar's project at the Milap Day Centre. Certainly, at the time it was not common for researchers to use media in the way they did, as an educational and oral history tool. But at the same time, they were assisted first by the fact that there was a move towards combining media skills with voluntary and activist work, which built on a tradition of film collectives and cooperatives, including feminist groups.[3] In addition, in the eighties there was a growing movement of 'black' film workshops and initiatives, such as the Sankofa and the Black Audio Film Collective and Retake (Mercer, 1989). These initiatives were a resource in the community available for projects to collaborate with, as Brah and Panesar's project did. Second, the project emerged out of the interrelation between educational community work and the work of oral histories. The Oral History Workshop movement led in the United Kingdom by Raphael Samuel (1976) combined adult education with the collection of oral histories. The British Empire formed a part of the oral history workshops. But this research was not embedded with considerations of diaspora, migration, colonial and postcolonial lives, which have been the cornerstone of Brah's teaching and scholarship. Indeed the oral history tradition developed in different formations across the globe. Subaltern Studies in India, for instance, focused on the 'small voice in history' as opposed to Indian national elites (Guha, 1996). In the Italian context, oral historians were very much situated within social and political movements (see Instituto De Martino); here feminist analysis led the way in treating oral histories as live narratives (Passerini, 1987).

Amidst the crisis of representation in the practice of ethnography (Clifford and Marcus, 1986; Clifford, 1988), in the 1980s the emphasis shifted from realist ways of handling fieldwork to working with them as stories, narratives and accounts that fashioned an ethnographic imagination not only by the researcher, but also

1 Thynne, L. (2011) 'Ethics, politics and representation' in *Child of Mine*, *Jump Cut: A Review of Contemporary Media*, No. 53, Summer, http://www.ejumpcut.org/trialsite/ThynneEthics/text.html, last accessed 21 October 2011.

2 see http://www.edu-factory.org/wp/edu-factory-journa-issue-1/ accessed 29 November 2011.

3 This for instance in London (UK) involved *The Berwick Street Collective*, which produced the well known *The Night Cleaners* (1975), as well as *Circles* and *Cinema of Women* and what then merged into *Cinenova* in 1991.

by the participants themselves. In a corollary move, the dialogic turn in cultural theory in the 1980s had very productive manifestations for methods, including oral history. Alessandro Portelli (1991, 1997), for instance, raised the importance of looking at myth, lies and fantasy within oral stories; foregrounding the 'art of dialogue' in telling and listening. Thus the imagination is seen to be in play in the very way in which stories are told and life is lived (Willis, 2000). Moreover, Norman Denzin has noted that there are near invisible boundaries separating everyday theatrical performances from formal theatre, dance, music, MTV, video and film. Across time, collaborations with practitioners working with different media have merged testimonies with music, film and theatre. There has been the generation of what Denzin (1993, 1996) has termed as 'performance texts', where the dramaturgical, narration and multiple perspectives are theatrically performed. Trinh T. Minh-ha's film *Surname Viet Given Name Nam* (1989) is, for instance, located by Denzin as a performance text. Performance Ethnography (2003) is, for Denzin, hinged on co-participation in pedagogic practices to develop a multi-voiced braided performative telling of the world. *Aaj Kaal* can be located as one such production.

group dynamics

Brah and Panesar came to the project as community activists committed to adult education initiatives. They sought to extend the work of the Centre of Extra-Mural Studies to multi-lingual learners in Southall. Both of them had by this time been active in the voluntary sector and in campaigns for justice and welfare in Southall. Brah had, for instance, in the late seventies been one of the founding members of Southall Black Sisters (1990). While she conducted her fieldwork in the locality for her doctorate in the 1970s, her thesis was not only analytical, but also informed by her everyday entanglements with political life in the area. In addition to her activism and voluntary work in Southall, Panesar also grew up in the area. Together, both of them had an extensive network of contacts to embed an educational project. In the cluster of groups that came together to deliver the project, the Dominion Community Centre in Southall provided the technical equipment. The project was itself located within a series of adult community education partnership initiatives, led by Brah and Panesar, between the Centre for Extra-Mural Studies, Birkbeck College, Ealing Council and a number of voluntary groups. The film project with the Asian elders was thus one of several courses coordinated by Brah and Panesar extending university adult education to multi-lingual ethnic communities in Southall through media and language studies. The specific focus was on the unemployed (young and elder). All projects were deployed with acute attention to previous histories of educational inequalities, as well as the gendered dynamics of learning.

Elders at the Milap Day Centre had requested that they were interested in learning video skills in order to film important occasions in their life.

Figure 1 On the set
Source: Photograph provided by Jasbir Panesar

Unanticipated, the initiative grew to become much more than the acquisition of technical film skills. The process first involved a 3-day workshop tailored to the needs of the facilitators, the project worker and a representative from a local community video activist group (the Creative Media Group). These workshops were delivered by consultants from Real Time, a video collective. After this initial work, Vipan Kumar ran regular weekly sessions (in Punjabi) over a 2-month period with the elders themselves, slowly expanding their skills from using the camera to techniques of interviewing, planning, story boarding, scripting and directing. It is important to keep in mind that it was through being in a learning environment to acquire these skills that the reels of film footage emerged (Figure 1).

In terms of group dynamics, Brah and Panesar were very conscious to facilitate a non-competitive, non-intimidating environment with different members cooperating and taking responsibility. Right at the start, a contract had been agreed, which granted control over the content and direction of the film to the elders, rather than the academic project leaders. While the facilitators prompted discussions and helped to steer conversations on topics that were of interest to the elders, the decisions over which topics to focus on and film further were led by the participants. During the course of filming a continuous process of watching, feedback discussions and re-shooting scenes emerged among the group.

There were challenges too, both technical and social. For instance, irregular attendance patterns, due to health and life-cycle issues, made it difficult at the start of the process for a core group to emerge, not least because people had to be constantly updated on training sessions they had missed. While the group was open to both men and women, it became a predominantly female group with three of the women who consistently attended becoming experienced and confident guides in the group. To ensure as full participation as possible, there was an emphasis placed on developing listening skills. The facilitators encouraged the quieter ones to speak and operate the camera. Hence, all participants were prompted to take turns on the equipment and to have an input on what to film. Panesar (1990: 156) has noted: 'This stopped people dominating while more confident people were put to good use in showing new people how to use the equipment and encouraging them to take part in the discussion'. Practising the art of interviewing and being interviewed, as well as the 'art of listening' (as Panesar (1990) termed it in the report), were key to how the elders learned to use a video camera and film each other.

For those who were not literate or not confident with writing the storyboard, the facilitators wrote down their ideas for them. They did not want the scribe to limit the participation and imaginative flair of the elders. In order to use the camera as a device to generate dialogue rather than intimidate, Panesar mentions:

> ... the elderly members [...] were given the flexibility to give alternative names to the various parts of the video equipment so they would be able to relate to the functions of the equipment more rapidly. The camera lens, for example, was re-named 'Dhoorbin' [binoculars] by the group. (1990:146)

Notably, the facilitators were not placed as outside professionals but rather as participants who were themselves for the first time learning the skills of working with the equipment. Moreover, in the dialogic nature of the exchange, the elders saw the facilitators as learners of the oral histories they were articulating. While the focus of this article is on the film *Aaj Kaal*, the group actually made two films. One film was directly on the Milap Day Centre, which had been set up in the 1950s to overcome the difficulties faced by the South Asian elderly in Southall, in terms of providing welfare advice and a social centre. The second film became *Aaj Kaal*. Inter-generational relations with siblings, racism, marriage and issues of caste, as well as interfaith co-existence were all discussed in the raw footage of the latter.

So while the project started as an educational project, whereby the elders would learn the skills of video making, through the very practice of learning the focus shifted to making film for an audience. During the course of making the two films, the participants decided that they would like to make *Aaj Kaal* public, available for educational purposes in local authorities, schools and universities. The researchers took on the responsibility of making this practically possible by raising additional funding and bringing in extra professionals. For the participants, the film would provide a public record of the living memories of Asian elders who had lived in the United Kingdom for over 30 years.

public conversations

In the introduction to the film, a member of the group states:

> We often don't get the opportunity to speak and tell our opinions on television.

Who is granted the visible public presence of speaking from a locality is a highly contested process. In Southall, this has over time become a charged issue, not least because several prominent Asian figures in the media have been forged here; and this is a process that does not happen without tension and conflict. For musicians, producers, filmmakers and other workers in the cultural sector, visibility is part of their Public Relations (PR). Having a claim over the stories told of Southall is also a part of PR. The contest over community representation involves claiming the authority to speak on behalf of Southall, thus granting visibility to particular networks over others, especially over those who are seen as competitors or who are simply judged to be less worthy and distinguished. When researchers enter the terrain they can unknowingly become hijacked and steered towards granting visibility to specific personnel and networks. Often men, and some women, already in the public eye, young and old (e.g., Kuljit Bhamra and Gurinder Chadha) can become mediators and gatekeepers of the local story to cultural institutions. For this reason alone, *Aaj Kaal* is significant, in that it reshuffles who tells the story, as well as how it is told, through a uniquely participative and performative process, led by female Asian elders.

The kind of telling that ensues in the film is not one that simply unfolds a realist form of storying. Referring to the elders, Panesar (1990: 158) mentions that the film '… contains their views, their perceptions and their life experiences told in their own way'. Thus, it is important to register that this is a chronicle of *how* the elders have chosen to tell these stories, through the performative art of dialogue (Portelli, 1991; Denzin, 1993; Willis, 2000), as instituted through the film practices in which they participated. There is a great sense of ownership that comes across in the way in which the film unfolds. A dramaturgy is in evidence in the very curatorship of the film. Elderly women take a prominent role in the making of the film, they move with the microphone that accompanies the camera, moving from one setting in Milap Day Centre to another, inviting people to respond to their questions. As they span the space, they cover different aspects of the social life of the centre. They move between mixed spaces, as well as all-male and all-female zones in the site.

Most of the film is conducted in Punjabi (with English subtitles). Sound, music and gestures are central to the affective qualities of the film. What is presented to us is a 'sensuous' ethnography (Stoller, 1997). There is a good dose of humour in the film, often delivered in the interactional gestures between users of the centre. For example, surrounded by five women, with one holding a long handle

Figure 2 The Kapta scene
Source: Aaj Kaal (1990)

boom mic, an elderly man delivers a *kapta* (verse); an art of communication that is/used to be frequently performed, usually by men, at in/formal social gatherings. He speaks of the longing for love and the arrival of a heroine as they (the men in the centre) are still in the joy of life, even as some of them are, as he states, in our eighties and 'with our white beards' (Figure 2). Unfortunately, none of the names of the elders are stated in the film neither in a spoken form, or as titles and credits.

We hear of the stories that these participants have carried with them across continents, including visceral descriptions of dismembered bodies witnessed during the Partition of British India as part of the Indian Independence Act, 1947. The rape of women and their suicides during this period of violence are documented here by one of the elderly women with an in-depth texture of feeling. The temporality of the moment is delivered in an embodied re-membering. The gendered pain, shame and ostracisation of the women is relayed in the mode of being a serious news reporter and witness to a suffering that still remains publicly unspoken and continues to be borne by the women who endured the injustices of war in the production of nations, maps and boundaries. Standing tall and straight faced, the story is told by one older woman with a sombre authority. As the ways of telling shift between different time periods and spaces, we also hear of the interfaith lives shared in pre-Partition India, as well as the global diaspora in East Africa. The colonial ties of Empire, World War II and industry inflect the tales of British lives. The struggles of settlement in the United Kingdom, including housing and education, as well as discrimination in workplaces which deskilled people, are recalled by different characters (men and women) in ways that carry their bodily signatures. The habitus of trade, accent, political skill and modes of public address form the basis of the impressions the tellers leave on the screen. It is important to bear in mind that even when the men are speaking it is the women who are doing the filming. The mode of address, especially from the women, is often directed with a sense of assurance to the viewer. In between the close-up shots of individuals and the wider angles of groups sitting together, we see glimpses of their own group dynamics from gestural communications during the course of making the film. Prompts to speak or even to keep out of particular frames, as well as the choreography involved in setting their bodies in formation for the camera become especially visible from the in and out shots. The hands and eyes (glances) are particularly important for directing what is in or out, as well as for the generation of togetherness between the tellers.

Some stories of locations are told more often than others. In the plotting of the post-war political history of Southall clashes with far-right movements in the late seventies and early eighties have been important elements to how territories were changed, claimed and defined. This includes the high-profile case from 1979 of the killing of Blair Peach by police at an anti-fascist march against racists in Southall. There has been considerable documentation in academic literature, film and political chronicles of these key moments involved in the racialised political challenge to exist and belong in the United Kingdom (CARF, 1981; Baumann, 1996; Brah, 1996; Axel, 2001; Kaur, 2003). However, these accounts are rarely publicly recounted by an Asian elderly woman, as is the case in *Aaj Kaal*. With a sense of assurance and defiance, a sharply focused mature woman with white hair speaks a story with a combination of wit and witness of the skinhead gatherings, the police protection of the far right as they descended on Southall as a mar-kedly Asian area, as well as the anti-vigilante action of young men who fought against the racist onslaught on their location.

A considerable amount has been written on public spheres, formal, subaltern and transnational (Fraser, 1990, 2007). Rarely has the attention turned to the kind of meeting places that are fostered by diasporic Asian elders who have gathered in parks to play cards or in front rooms to have an all-female singing and dance session. Thus, the orbit and imagination of public spheres has eclipsed these largely informal groups. In race, diaspora and identity studies there has, until very recently, been an overwhelming focus on the youth, and their hybrid cultural formations and music genres, rather than those produced by the elders. In the film, we see how each of these social scenes is offered a place to thrive in Milap Day Centre. Like a number of Asian Day Centres that were formed across the United Kingdom in the post-war years, we discover how Milap Day Centre is a meeting place that has become central to the lives of these elders. Some of these types of centres are now becoming a yesterday, effected by a generation that passes away, as well as government cuts that cannot register the necessity of

Figure 3 Seaside trip
Source: Aaj Kaal (1990)

these social support venues to the vitality of old age. In the film, there is a very clear sense for how the Centre is a part of the public sphere of these elders; a site where they can seek legal and welfare advice, as well as share a meal, garnering a social life together, away from immediate family, with whom relations can be full of complications. Time out with alternative company includes outings (Figure 3).

Footage from a trip to the seaside shows the men riding donkeys and women getting a feel for the seawaters on their feet as they stand on the sea bed with their *salwars* rolled up to their calves. These scenes of the British seaside do not feature in Martin Parr's famous photographs of the British working class seaside. For the official record, it is important to state that the lives of Asian elders in Southall and at British seasides were granted a filmic life in *Aaj Kaal* before *Bhaji on the Beach* (1993, Director: Chadha) or *Acting Our Age* (1991, Director: Chadha), which echoed (for professional broadcast production) the images of *Aaj Kaal*.[4] Such are the politics and economy of representing Southall. Needless to say that the attention to ethics, pedagogy and co-participation (in *Aaj Kaal*) are absent from Chadha's productions, which have been scripted, produced and directed within an entirely different political and cultural economy.

4 Once the participants had decided to make the film public, funding was obtained by Panesar through a small grant from REPLAN/NIACE, to provide English translations and to conduct editing and dubbing. After a consultative meeting with the group members, Panesar

social scenes

The Milap Centre is not a dreary mind-numbing place where elders are simply parked in chairs. There is a good deal of combustion and action. While the men may gather to play cards, the levels of social engagement between the women heighten as they swing from sitting around, chatting, exchanging humorous banter while knitting, to occasionally holding impromptu singing and dancing sessions among themselves. The finale of the film is one such scene, which is no doubt staged for or rather provoked by the filming process. Together the women in the film reinvent female 'social scenes' (Blum, 2003; Puwar, 2007) that have taken place at social gatherings, especially at times of celebration, such as weddings and parties. In the United Kingdom, such scenes, as meeting places and forms of cultural encounter, were usually enacted in British front rooms in the post-war period, with the men told by the women to stay out of these all-female spaces or, in fact they may already have been away at the pub, as was often the case for this generation. Sanguine, contemplative and risqué words were used in the *bolian* (oral verses and couplets) that South Asian women have carried and reinvented across space and time, in their diasporic journeys of migration.[5] Sometimes they are simply sung together while sitting down together. At other times they become a part of a *gidda*. For *gidda*, girls and women usually form a circle. All of them clap their hands and sing *bolian*, while two or three of them come to the centre and perform a dance together. *Gidda* is an expressive dance formation that has enabled Punjabi women to air their joys, frustrations and sorrows. It is full of gendered mimicry and risqué words and moves. *Gidda* sessions could last for hours. When in full swing they involved using objects and clothing, often found close at hand, to improvise male bodily comportments or drunken states of trance. So towards the end of *Aaj Kaal* we are given a glimpse of these scenes. An elderly woman kicks off a *gidda* session with great vigour by singing and swinging her right arm in a communal and strident mood to the air. Soon she is twisting her hands in the air and stepping to a rhythm and thud in the feet that provide the percussion bass, while the rest of the group clap and sing the chorus. As she takes the singing lead both she and her partner (a slightly younger woman) set the tempo of the room, dancing their bodies in circling moves around each other. Their gestures and voices fill the architectural volume of the room. The elder leader of the session brings a definite signature to her style, as she both claims and opens up the space with her expansive moves and auditory tones. While the songs change and the topics they cover alter, the women pressure and gesture to each other to take the floor and hold the fort next (Figure 4).

In the United Kingdom, as this generation have passed away and there have been huge changes in the entertainment industry of private functions, impromptu *gidda* sessions are less likely to break out today. The DJ system and the *dhol* player (usually both male) have for instance come to dominate song and dance at large parties. Rather tellingly, *gidda* groups, consisting of five or six women in 'traditional' village dress are now available to hire. As the oral tradition of the *bolian* is now less likely to be practised on a regular basis, there is limited

and the Milap Day Centre staff, three Asian women were contracted from UMBI Films to carry this work out, including Gurinder Chadha.

5 In earlier periods when transnational and communication travel was limited for most migrants to letters and telegrams, due to cost and technological developments, audiotapes of *bolian* were recorded at home among female relatives. These were usually sent as parcels among relatives when weddings and other special occasions could not be attended easily across continents.

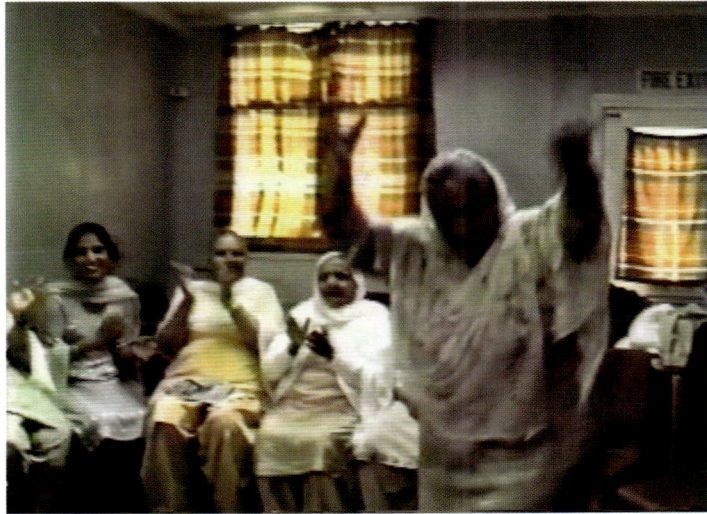

Figure 4 Gidda at the Centre
Source: *Aaj Kaal* (1990)

knowledge of the lyrics in everyday culture in the United Kingdom. For earlier generations, as we see in the film, the *gidda* sessions were central to how they settled and made Britain a home for themselves, in an admixture of pleasure, performance and gendered territory. It is in these private zones that they made their public lives together. These modes of coming together provide one layer, so far largely unregistered, of migration and settlement in the making of the post-war British front room. Territories are not only made in the political battles on the streets, they are also generated in the social and cultural gatherings in homes, which function as semi-public spaces. *Gidda* instituted a performative shaping of architecture, with gendered *bolian* comprising the affective properties of taking occupation and home-making together.

Aaj Kaal was launched at a public event held in the Dominion Centre in Southall (Figure 5). Over one hundred people attended, mainly women. The event celebrated the achievements of the elders who participated in the film. They were publicly introduced and granted a certificate for their achievements from the Centre for Extra-Mural Studies, Birkbeck College, University of London. There was a public screening and food was served. The occasion honoured and valued the efforts of the elders during the course of the project, as well as granting visibility to the importance of the Milap Day Centre to their social and cultural welfare. At this celebratory occasion an impromptu *gidda* session also set into full swing. The launch as an event was a culmination that marked how the project was driven by community practice work rather than academic value. Hence, it is not surprising that Brah and Panesar were focused on the educational

Figure 5 Avtar giving education certificates at the launch in the Dominion Centre
Source: Photograph provided by Jasbir Panesar

developments of the elders, rather than on writing academic articles from the project.[6]

conclusion

It is important to keep in mind that the film-based educational project was actually initiated by Brah many years before she wrote the article 'The Scent of Memory: strangers, our own, and others', which has inspired the Issue 100 of *Feminist Review*, of which this article is a part. My article has been an exercise in memory work in a number of different respects. It has engaged in the excavation work to remember the making of *Aaj Kaal*. As we embark on a raft of multimedia-based research (pedagogic) practices, we have much to learn from the theoretical, political and practical mediations which informed this project. The film is a powerful historical register and methodological tool in the further development of dialogic participative methods and modes of engagement using media practices.

As I have watched the film again and again, I have been conscious that probably all of the (unnamed) elders who feature in and made the film have passed away. *Aaj Kaal* offers an ethnographic imagination that allows us to contemplate and savour the somatic enactment of the vivacity, endurance, pain and humour of this first generation of South Asian British women and men.

coda

This article is dedicated to my eldest brother (Harbans Singh) and my mother Kartar Kaur, who attended a Day Centre in Coventry (the Asian Gosford Centre)

6 Although it has to be said that a report they wrote at the end of the project has enough material in it to pull a book together (see *Darkmatter*, forthcoming).

for over 15 years and started doing so in 1994 when she had to endure the unbearable pain of losing her eldest child Harbans Singh, my brother, aged only 46 when he passed away. At a time of immense loss and vulnerability, the Centre's elder Asian participants and staff became stabilisers for her.

I wrote this article while she recovered from a broken hip after a fall in the Centre in July 2011. Soon after, due to cuts and other reasons, the centre closed down. At the age of 91 she is still adept at keeping in step to the *gidda* with her zimmer frame in tow, as she did at her 90th birthday celebration party in the Summer of 2010.

acknowledgements

I would like to thank the generous time and support provided by both Avtar Brah and Jasbir Panesar during the course of writing this article. Avtar has been a warm sharp mentor and (wise) friend in my life and academic work. I am pleased to have found the time to partake in this celebration hundredth Issue of *Feminist Review* in her honour and as my last writing 'act' before I leave the fold of the *Feminist Review* Collective into which she very carefully and gently brought me over 10 years ago. Lizzie Thynne and Irene Gedalof have granted this article a close reading and encouraged me to reflect on several dimensions again. Thank you.

author biography

Nirmal Puwar is a Senior Lecturer in Sociology, at Goldsmiths, University of London. She is Director of the Methods Lab (http://www.gold.ac.uk/methods-lab/). Her first book was *Space Invaders*: *race, gender and bodies out of place* (Berg, 2003). Currently, she is writing a new book on 'The Impossibility of Obama' (Bloomsbury Academic, 2013). She has co-edited a number of collections including: *South Asian Women in the Diaspora* (2003); *Post-Colonial Bourdieu* (Sociological Review, 2009); *Intimacy in Research* (History of the Human Sciences, 2008); *Noise of the Past* (Senses and Society, 2011); *Live Methods* (Sociological Review, 2012) and ten issues of *Feminist Review*.

references

Axel, B.K. (2001) *The Nation's Tortured Body: Violence, Representation and the Formation of a Sikh Diaspora*, (Chap. 19) Durham and London: Duke University Press.

Back, L. (2007) *The Art of Listening*, Oxford: Berg Publishers.

Back, L., Cohen, P. and Keith, M. (1996) *Finding the Way Home*, Working Paper 1, Issues of Theory and method, Centre for New Ethnicities research, University of East London.

Baumann, G. (1996) *Contesting Culture: Discourses of Identity in Multi-Ethnic*, London: Cambridge University Press.

Blum, A. (2003) *The Imaginative Structure of the City*, Montreal: McGill-Queens University Press.

Blunt, A. and Dowling, R. (2006) *Home*, London: Routledge.

Blunt, A., Gruffudd, P., May, J., Ogborn, M. and Pinder, D. (2003) editors *Cultural Geography in Practice*, London: Arnold.

Brah, A. (1978) 'South Asian teenagers in Southall: perceptions of marriage, family, and ethnic identity' *New Community*, Vol. V1, No. 3: 197–206.

Brah, A. (1987) 'Women of South Asian origin in Britain: issues and concerns' *South Asia Research*, Vol. 7, No. 1: 39–54, (Re-printed in Braham, P., Rattansi, A. and Skellington, R. (1992) (editors), *Racism and Anti-Racism: Inequalities, Opportunities and Policies*, Sage).

Brah, A. (1989) 'Black struggles, equality and education' *Critical Social Policy*, Vol. 9, No. 25: 83–89.

Brah, A. (1994) 'Time, place and others: discourses of 'race', nation and ethnicity' *Sociology*, Vol. 28, No. 3: 805–813.

Brah, A. (1996) *Cartographies of a Diaspora: Contesting Identities*, London: Routledge.

Brah, A. (1999) 'The Scent of Memory: strangers, our own, and others' *Feminist Review*, Vol. 61: 4–26.

Brah, A. (2002) 'Global mobilities, local predicaments: globalisation and the critical imagination' *Feminist Review*, Vol. 70: 30–45.

Brah, A. and Hoy, J. (1987) 'Politics of urban experience: teaching extra-mural courses' *Multicultural Teaching*, Vol. 6, No. 1: 22–27.

CARF (1981) *Southall: The Birth of a Black Community*, London: Institute of Race Relations.

Clifford, J. (1988) *The Predicament of Culture: Twentieth Century Ethnography, Literature and Art*, Cambridge, MA: Harvard University Press.

Clifford, J. and Marcus, G. (1986) *Writing Culture: The Poetics and Politics of Ethnography*, Berkeley: University of California Press.

Denzin, N. (1993) *Performance Ethnography: Critical Pedagogy and the Politics of Culture*, London: Sage Publications.

Denzin, N. (1996) *Interpretative Ethnography: Ethnographic Practices for the 21st Century*, London: Sage Publications.

Denzin, N. (2003) *Performance Ethnography: Critical Pedagogy and the Politics of Culture*, London: Sage Publications.

Evans, M. (2004) *Killing Thinking: The Death of the Universities*, London: Continuum.

Fraser, N. (1990) 'Rethinking the public sphere: a contribution to the critique of actually existing democracy' *Social Text*, (Duke University Press) Vol. 25, No. 26: 56–80.

Fraser, N. (2007) 'Transnationalizing the public sphere: on the legitimacy and efficacy of public opinion in a Post-Westphalian World' *Theory Culture & Society*, Vol. 24, No. 4: 7–30.

Freire, P. (1972) *Pedagogy of the Oppressed*, Harmondsworth: Penguin.

Gatenby, B. and Humphries, M. (2000) 'Feminist participatory action research: methodological and ethical issues' *Women's Studies International Forum*, Vol. 23, No. 1: 89–105.

Guha, R. (1996) 'The small voice of history' in Amin, S. and Chakrabarty, D. (1996) editors, *Subaltern Studies*, No. 9, Delhi: Oxford University Press, 1–12.

Katz, J.S. and Katz, J.M. (1988) 'Ethics and the perception of ethics in autobiographical film' in Gross, L., Katz, J.S. and Ruby, J. (1988) editors, *Image Ethics: The Moral Rights of Subjects in Photography, Film and Television*, New York and Oxford: Open University Press, 119–134.

Kaur, R. (2003) 'Westenders: women, whiteness and sexuality in Southall' in Andall, J. (2003) editor, *Gender and Ethnicity in Contemporary Europe*, Oxford: Berg.

Kuhn, A. and McAllister, K. (2006) *Locating Memory: Photographic Acts*, Oxford and New York: Berghahn Books.

Latour, B. (2007) 'Interview with Bruno Latour: making the 'Res Public' by Tomás Sánchez Criado, Ephemera' *Theory & Politics in Organization*, Vol. 7, No. 2: 364–371.

Latour, B. and Weibal, P. (2005) editors *Making Things Public: Atmospheres of Democracy*, Cambridge, MA: MIT Press.

Mercer, K. (1988) *Black Film, British Cinema*, in Mercer, K. (1989) editor, Black Film/British Cinema, Documents 7 British Film Institute Production Special.

Panesar, J. (1990) Unpublished Project Report on Adult Education with the Unemployed in Southall, Project Directed by Avtar Brah, Centre for Extra-Mural Studies, Birkbeck College, University of London. Funded by REPLAN/NIACE.

Passerini, L. (1987) *Fascism in Popular Memory: The Cultural Experience of the Turin Working Class*, Cambridge: Cambridge University Press.

Patai, D. (1991) 'US academics and third world women: is *ethical research* possible?' in Gluck, S.B. and Patai, D. (1991) editors, *Women's Words: The Feminist Practice of Oral History*, London: Routledge.

Pink, S. (2001) *Doing Visual Ethnography*, London: Sage Publications.

Portelli, A. (1991) 'On methodology' in *The Death of Luigi Trastulli, and Other Stories: Form and Meaning in Oral History*, Albany: State University of New York Press, 27–42.

Portelli, A. (1997) 'There's always goin' be a line: history-telling as a multivocal art' in *The Battle of Valle Giulia. Oral History and the Art of Dialogue*, Madison: Wisconsin University Press, 24–39.

Puwar, N. (2007) 'Social cinema scenes' *Space and Culture*, Vol. 10, No. 2: 253–270.

Puwar, N. and Sharma, S. (2012) 'Curating sociology: sociological mutations' in Puwar, N. and Back, L. (2012) editors, *Sociological Review*, Special Issue on 'Live Methods'. Malden, MA: Wiley and Blackwell.

Rathzel, N. and Cohen, P. (2008) 'Finding the way home: young people's stories of gender, ethnicity, class, and places in Hamburg and London' Transkulturelle Perspektiven, Vol. 7. V & R Unipress.

Rose, G. (2005) *Visual Methodologies: An Introduction to Interpreting Visual Materials*, 2nd edition London: Sage Publications.

Rose, G. (2010) *Doing Family Photography: The Domestic, The Public and The Politics of Sentiment*, Surrey: Ashgate.

Samuel, R. (1976) 'Local history and oral history' *History Workshop Journal*, No. 1: 191–208.

Southall Black Sisters (1990) *Against the Grain: A Celebration of Survival and Struggle*, Middlesex, SBS.

Stoller, P. (1997) *Sensuous Ethnography*, Philadelphia: University of Pennsylvania Press.

Willis, P. (2000) *The Ethnographic Imagination*, Cambridge: Polity.

Filmography

Aaj Kaal (1990) Extra-Mural Studies, Birkbeck College, University of London, 20 minutes. To view the film online see: http://darkmatter101.org/site/2011/11/29/aaj-kaal/.

Surname Viet Given Name Nam (1989) Associate producer Jean-Paul Bourdier, Directed by Trinh T. Minh-ha, 108 minutes.

Night Cleaners (1975) Berwick Street Collective.

Acting our Age (1991) Directed by Gurinder Chadha.

Bhaji on the Beach (1993) Directed by Gurinder Chadha.

doi:10.1057/fr.2011.70

the sound of memory: interview with singer, Mohinder Kaur Bhamra

Navtej Purewal

Navtej Purewal (NP) interviews the singer Mohinder Kaur Bhamra (MB), a prominent voice of South Asian Punjabi music since the 1960s in the UK. For those unfamiliar with her music, she signifies an era of early South Asian settlement when communities were up against not only racism and racialisation in London and other cities in England, but also the changing patterns of shift work and migration to family, community and culture. She performed and recorded albums in the genre of Punjabi *geet* (folk music) in which she voiced many of the desires, concerns and changes of those times amidst immense social and cultural change. Born in Uganda, spending her childhood and teenage years across Uganda, India and Kenya and subsequently settling in London in the early 1960s, she talks about her experiences of making music while charting out new terrain during an era when public musical performance was not easily associated with South Asian Punjabi women. Mohinder Bhamra was a pioneer in the establishment of what is today a vibrant music industry in the UK. Starting with informal private gatherings, she quickly established herself as an icon of her times through her knowledge and style of singing Punjabi folk music, which resonated through its popular appeal and innovation. She carved a path for future generations of South Asian creative performance in the UK through her visibility, style, social themes of her lyrics and her symbol as a prominent South Asian female voice of the diaspora (Figure 1).

a note in the form of an introduction

Mohinder Bhamra is my maternal aunt (*Masi*). She and my mother are among four sisters within a larger extended family in which social relations are mainly maintained by family and which today spans three continents. My personal introduction to music was through these women, which includes not only my mother but all three of her sisters, as music is an integral part of

(142–153) © 2012 Feminist Review. 0141-7789/12 www.feminist-review.com

Figure 1 Mohinder K. Bhamra
Source: The Southall Story, www.TheSouthallStory.com

our family and women's social and collective experience. Music has travelled wherever our family have travelled and settled, and the sharing of this music between women and across generations of women has been an important source of cultural expression. As a child, I admit that I never thoroughly understood the lyrics of my Aunt's songs, but enjoyed the music all the same for its sound and indeed the associations it had for me with my relatives in London whose prominent presence within the blooming British Asian music industry was always a source of admiration for me. It was only later, after becoming interested in understanding the dynamics of diaspora, gender, history and culture that I understood how potent and meaningful many of her songs are, particularly when situated within Southall and the UK South Asian diaspora experience. The covers of her albums of the 1970s and 1980s showed an image of a woman with a sense of self-confidence to be aspired to. Possibly more importantly, however, was the symbol that she presented for me as a woman singing not just wedding songs, which are more conventionally viewed as 'women's music', but also popular songs composed and written about the themes and sentiments appealing to the audiences to whom she and her sons were performing. Her music to me, over the years, has come to represent a voice of compassion towards women's experiences of migration to England, social change, love and estrangement, and human emotions. This is markedly distinct from wider contemporary trends within Punjabi popular music towards hypermasculinity and fetishisation of women as sexual objects. Conscious of her role as an artist and having her own personal challenges in taking the public stage, Mohinder Bhamra has insisted throughout her career on maintaining the dignity of her voice, reflective of her understanding of the affect of performance and lyrical content in the politics and making of community.

Her music has resounded for decades in homes, on the radio, and at family and public functions as Southall has evolved and become a hub not only of the UK South Asian community, but also of South Asian cultural production globally. These two arenas of 'community' and cultural production tend to be associated with male power and authority in which women feature as symbolic showpieces or markers of 'culture' rather than as voices or agents. Even today, her performances represent a women-centred musical gathering that commands attention through cutting and often playfully humorous lyrics, rather than attracting it. Interestingly, her career burgeoned during the era of economic restructuring in England, when both South Asian men and women had a presence in the factories and foundries of London and the Midlands. It is no wonder that her career continued to develop after the economic downturn of the late 1970s and accelerated thereafter as her music appealed to audiences for the ways in which it spoke to their histories, struggles, memories and times. She embodies so many aspects of Avtar Brah's (1999) counter to the homogenous, racialised, 'English' discourse of Southall from it being a place of 'indifference and unfamiliarity' to a site and community of connectedness, familiarity and empathy.

In this interview, Mohinder Bhamra reflects upon a number of significant themes. First, she speaks of accepted conventions around girls 'proper' behaviour and her determination from a young age to challenge them while setting an example for others to not blindly accept rigid thinking in the name of culture. In this respect, she tells of her childhood and how music was not always viewed as permissible for girls to participate in publicly by elders in the family and the community in India and East Africa during the 1940s and 1950s as she grew up. Her perseverance to pursue her passion of singing can be seen in how she negotiated pressures to behave within social mores while continuing to sing opportunistically when chances arose — a defiant strategy of feminist engagement through the vehicle of women's and folk music. Second, she reflects on her experiences of migration, marriage and early settlement in London as a time of experimentation, musical discovery and formation of new communities through the sounds of music, whether at gurdwaras, public functions, private parties or weddings. Her rise to fame within a few years of arriving in London in the early 1960s shows how migration opened up possibilities for her to renegotiate gender dynamics within her personal life through increased autonomy and engagement with the public life of Southall. Her memories of migrating to England reflect upon the essence of the times from the 1960s and 1970s, when her music played to the experiences of struggle and settlement of South Asian communities. Finally, she reflects upon how she tread many fine lines in becoming one of the first public South Asian female singers in Britain. She forged a path as a female performer to maintain respectability in the public eye of the community while challenging stereotypes that were being internally imposed and perpetuated by women to remain seen but not heard. The content and lyrics have thus been as significant as the sound of her music in how they relate and speak to listening audiences.

In a sense, this interview has been in-the-making ever since I can remember. Mohinder Bhamra has shared numerous aspects of this history over the past few decades with me, whenever I have visited her in her home in Southall, during our countless conversations over cups of tea, during late night chats or in the kitchen while preparing food. The process of putting this interview together forced me to put to paper those aspects of this 'women's story' that are often left in the kitchen, never making it to the table, as it were. The fraught status of the female artist highlights this in so many ways. Up against gender roles at home, and duties and expectations as mothers, daughters, daughters-in-law and wives, female artists are often projected in the public eye either as an anomaly or as sensationalised figures removed from the social realities of the audiences observing and consuming them. That this interview was done in the quintessential women's space of the home and kitchen, of which Mohinder Bhamra is such a skilful master, is revealing of it also being a site of autonomous recollection, remembrance and retelling. As both a space of cooking and creativity, it is liminally removed from the gaze of men's interpretation, interruption and ownership. Although her three sons and husband have been prominent in the performance and production of her music, her musical journey has been one that has constantly been up against gender norms and values of the times which she, in most senses, had to tread alone. Having only sons, I feel I have been privy to many of her reflections in this respect.

Though Mohinder Bhamra's life story is, in part, about her interest and career in music, it is also about the visions of community and family that women of her generation shaped in the process of making spaces for themselves in Southall's early South Asian community. This interview could be seen as an attempt to 'write back' to Avtar Brah's (1999) invitation to engage with the notion of Southall as a place of dynamic, changing social topography. The 'scent', or here more aptly 'sound', of memory that Mohinder Bhamra represents of Southall sings of a place in which South Asian women have been agents of change in writing themselves into the history of Southall through their evolving modes of relating, identifying and connecting both individually and collectively. I suppose, in doing this interview, I too feel a part of that collectively owned history.

interview

NP: *Where do you think your interest in music first began?*

MB: I first became interested in music when I was quite young, maybe about four or five years old. My father had a bello-piano, the kind that has keys but also has foot pedals. I used to watch him playing that. He would play the organ along to any song he would sing. I would join in and we would sing songs. On my own I would then sing short songs too like '*Sunha de sunha de Krishna, tu bansari di taan sunha de Krishna*' (transl. 'Play me a tune from your flute, Krishna'). As I was only singing along, it was only later that I realised I'd actually sung something.

... When I was in 5th grade and went to a government school in Ludhiana, I would get the girls together during break or lunch time and set the *dholki* (two-sided drum) on the table and we would all sing together – from Lata Mangeshkar film songs like *Jhoome jhoome dil mera chanda ki chaand* to *tappe* and *boliyaan*. We would use our scarves to cover our heads or faces and play-act the songs. We had just a bit of time during lunch with all of us girls together, but we made good use of it in whatever way we could. The teachers came to know that I sang and from the school environment I received a lot of encouragement and began to have an idea that people enjoyed listening to me. The teachers specially asked me to sing the national anthem *Jan man gan* when Pundit Jawaharlal Nehru and his sister Vijay Lakshmi came to watch our school games. I sang it as they both entered. That's it. That's how I was encouraged early on in school and how I started singing in the public.

NP: *What are your memories of your childhood in India and East Africa of the 1940s and 1950s?*

MB: I was born in Uganda and was about 5 or 6 when my family moved to India. When I was around 13 or 14 we moved back to Africa to Kenya. While studying at a government school in Ludhiana I decided that I would do the *Gyani* (Sikh theology and classical music) course as well. So in the evenings I used to go to attend classes at Guru Angad Dev Punjab College for the *Gyani* course. I sat most of the exams before we left for Africa but still had the final year 6 papers left to complete. But when I got to Kenya, the elders started saying 'it's time to get married, time to get married'. Where does that leave studying after that? Nowhere really. And when I got to Kenya the school there said that they'd put me in year 7 because they said that the level of my government school education in India was lower than that in Kenya. I said 'I'm not going to sit in a lower year!' so I stayed home, did the household chores, would go to *gurdwara* (Sikh temple) to do *kirtan* (spiritual hymns) while completing the *Gyani* course from Africa. I eventually sent the papers to India from there and passed.

NP: *When did you have opportunities to sing and do music in East Africa?*

MB: Every week we went to *gurdwara*. First we would go to one *gurdwara* and then another *gurdwara* would invite us to perform there, and so on. We (my sisters, cousins and I) first sang in *gurdwara*s in Kisumu and then after getting married in Nairobi.

NP: *What was the atmosphere like in Kenya in terms of music?*

MB: There wasn't as much live music in those days as you might think. It was mainly songs on the radio from India that people listened to. There weren't music groups, as such. *Raag* (classical scales) was sung by people who were knowledgeable about music and who sang at the *gurdwara*. The *raagi* or *gyaani* (priest) who I learned from (Gyaani Bhola Singh) used to come home to teach me the harmonium, and I learned the basic scales (*sa, re, ga, ma, pa dha, ni sa*) from him as well a few *shabads* (sacred hymns). Then I thought 'if I can do this with a *shabad*, then why not with popular songs?'. So then in the evenings I would practice old popular tunes on the harmonium. From there, I just started playing .... So in Africa I didn't really perform *geet* (popular folk songs) like I did when I came to England.

NP: *Do you mean there were fewer opportunities to sing in Africa?*

MB: There *were* opportunities, but it was never really allowed to be developed because of the mindset. If you were to do it, then family members would say in a derogatory way 'who do they think they are, minstrels?'. The general attitude was that *geet* shouldn't be performed by girls but *kirtan* was seen as acceptable. It didn't look good to people if we went somewhere and sang *geet*. So there wasn't that much freedom to sing at home or outside of the home.

NP: *Even at weddings?*

MB: Definitely not. I only remember a few times when my sisters and I did sing all together at family weddings, with me hitting the *dholki* (small two-sided drum) with the spoon to keep the beat. We just sang one or two *geet*, but that's about it. But when I moved to England in 1961 and a few years later had begun to perform at programmes, my elders (who were still in Kenya) heard that I was performing and had to accept it.

NP: *How did you begin to perform in England so soon after migrating from Kenya?*

MB: After I arrived in 1961 I started to get bored. My husband was studying for his exams and I would go to the local park to pass the time with the children. So one day I said to him to take me to the *gurdwara*. We started going regularly to Stepney Green *gurdwara* where I was always asked to perform *kirtan*. It was either Shepherd's Bush *gurdwara* or Stepney Green *gurdwara*. But it all started at Stepney Green. I have photos of that time when I was not only singing *shabad*s but sometimes also playing the *dholki* (Figure 2).

NP: *How were religious services and kirtan done during that time?*

Figure 2 Stepney Green *Gurdwara* 1963
Source: The Southall Story, www.TheSouthallStory.com

MB: There weren't resident priests from India in those days like there are today. People from the congregation who had some of knowledge and understanding would perform *kirtan* in the *gurdwara*s ... so when my turn would come, I would play the *dholki* as well as sing. If someone else would sing, then I would accompany them on the *dholki* ... after the service was completed, the organisers would say to me 'sister, you must come next week again and sing'. I was the only woman performing *kirtan* during those early years ... the congregation conducted the entire service. *Kirtan* would be performed by one person, the *ardas* (final prayer of blessing) by someone else ... I was often asked to do the *ardas* as there was often no one else to do it. Those times were like that. But we all managed and enjoyed taking part in it all.

NP: *So you were living in a close-knit community in the 1960s?*

MB: No, initially we lived in North London. At that time in those areas there were not that many Asians. We lived in Finsbury Park, Muswell Hill, Palmers Green and then eventually we came to Southall. A friend of ours, the late Tarsem Purewal (who founded the Southall-based Punjabi newspaper *Des Pardes*), came to visit us in North London. I remember him saying to us, 'where do you people live? Why do you live so far away?'. He meant that Southall was where the community was concentrated ... the public is the one who listens to you, so if the public likes you then it's important to listen to the public. That means you have to live within the public to be a part of it. By 1962 I started going to *gurdwara* very regularly, performing *kirtan* so the public I was performing to was either in the *gurdwara* or in private parties.

NP: *So then you moved to Southall?*

MB: Yes. When we moved to Southall people quickly came to know, and I started to get very busy. If there was ever a holiday to be celebrated- Vaisakhi, Diwali, Republic Day, Independence Day, Udham Singh's commemoration, Indian Worker's Association (IWA) events — I would perform.

NP: *And private parties too?*

MB: From 1963 onwards I began to perform at private parties. At that time, there weren't that many of 'our people' in London, meaning Asians — Sikhs, Muslims, Hindus ... private parties would be mixed, where there would be everyone sitting together. It was a really good atmosphere. That time really ignited my desire to pursue my interest in music ... there would be *ghazal* (light classical music) evenings where I would sing popular *ghazals* which most people were familiar with. We used to feel like we were just sitting at home. Someone would sing a folk song, another person would sing a *ghazal* ... many of the Muslims in those gatherings were avid listeners and really liked the fact that I sang both *ghazals* and *geet*. I started getting invitations to their parties and functions too.

NP: *How did you make the transition from kirtan to popular Punjabi music?*

MB: I did the first wedding in 1966. I was especially asked to do that wedding by Tarsem Purewal who had heard me sing in one of those *ghazal* evenings. He said 'I'm going to get married and I don't want a priest to do the ceremony. I want you to sing the marriage rites'. That was the first one. From 1967 onwards we began to receive many invitations to perform at weddings. I could perform not only the religious ceremony but also the cultural programme. After doing one, we would be invited to do others. We never took money for those performances in those days. People invited me because they wanted to hear me ... we never thought of taking money for those bookings. An invitation would come and we would go to perform (Figure 3).

NP: *In those days how did you manage performing regularly while managing family responsibilities?*

MB: My second son Satpaul was born in November 1961 and the following February I performed [laugh]. Because he was so small, I just took him along with me even as an infant. And that's how my eldest son Kuljit became so familiar with the *tabla* from a young age, by being at those gatherings and seeing how people enjoyed listening to him play. Eventually, my youngest son Ambi learned to play the accordian. That's how things start, I suppose, by listening, watching and performing from a young age ... as babies, I remember my younger two sons with me as I sang. As they all three grew up, my sons accompanied me on the *tabla*, mandolin and accordian, so they were all part of the programmes and would be with me throughout the performance. Of course there was housework to do, but I would do it all as quickly as possible and get free to go to the evening programmes. Because I had support from my immediate family, it was a pleasure

Figure 3 A wedding ceremony at Shepherd's Bush *Gurdwara* 1977
Source: The Southall Story, www.TheSouthallStory.com

to do those programmes. My husband, who worked as a structural engineer, would give his evenings and weekends to the music even though he himself wasn't a musician. I know that I was able to pursue my music largely because of his support ... without that, it would have been impossible.

Since I didn't work outside of the home ... Well, for a little while I did work: at a crochet knit company for six months, at the BOC mailing office and then during the Christmas period at a sausage factory sticking labels onto packets of sausages but had to quit because the ink irritated by eyes! But that was just a temporary job anyway.

NP: *Several of your recorded songs are about women's concerns and desires but also about harsh realities of life ... Is there any song which you feel captures this most?*

MB: *Ni aae na valayat kuriye* (transl. 'Girl, don't come to England').[1] The lyrics were written by Mohinder Singh Khaira, a well known writer from Coventry. We used to see him at weddings when we performed, and we came to know that he wrote songs. As we developed the arrangement of the song and performed it in different places, I saw how popular that song had become because it really resonated with the audiences of the 1970s. The chorus of that song goes: 'If you have any desires to keep the veil (*ghund*), don't come to England. Here you have to work hard, look after children after doing shift work, etc.' People used to make special requests for us to sing that song and a few others like that because of the nature of that whole subject ... .

1 *The Ultimate Collection – Mohinder Kaur Bhamra, Keda Records.*

During that era, people appreciated the content of lyrics. They really listened to the meaning of the lyrics. They had lived through hard times of migrating and settling in England, working extremely hard, and appreciated songs like that which were created out of the poetry based on the sentiments and experiences of the community. Mohinder S. Khaira was one writer who wrote like that but there were several others who wrote lyrics for me with content relating to the issues and sentiments of those times.

NP: *What do you think about the content of popular Punjabi music being produced today?*

MB: These days people dance to the beat. It's true that people of the older generation know Punjabi and understand everything and enjoy the lyrics. But today there is less emphasis on lyrics and more on the beat. To me, the aim of a song should be to put across the meaning and the message to the listener. A song should be timeless and maintain its message over time ... Of course, there are Gurdas Mann and Hans Raj Hans who have recorded some excellent songs with deep meanings and with clean, decent lyrics which live on ...

One writer presented me with lyrics, and he insisted I sing the last verse exactly as he had written it: 'it's just you and me and no one else'. I said 'I don't feel right singing that.' He said 'it has to be sung that way, otherwise just leave it.' So I left it ... .

Writers should think that if they've written a good song that they should use their real name so that people know who they are. Many writers use pseudonyms so we don't even know who they are. They get the fame when the song becomes a hit but there is no connection between the person who writes and the lyrics being sung. These things bother me. And the indecent lyrics that many writers compose ... this further encourages that trend.

NP: *But your songs, while most are about women's experiences, feelings and desires, manage to keep away from those types of lyrics.*

MB: Like another one of Khaira's songs *Raataan chad de ve* (transl. 'Stop working the nightshift, my dear') which is about a woman who is complaining to her husband that she has to spend her nights alone as he works the night shift .... When people first caught onto this song they remembered the hard times they had seen, the loneliness of the new routines of working and life in England. The man then replies 'don't be silly, don't we need money to live on?' showing the real practicalities of life ... .

There are excellent artists these days, but indecent lyrics have taken over ... and the trend to show scantily dressed women ... So the lyrics of the *geet* are hardly noticeable, but what you see is the woman. She is there to be looked at in order to sell the song. That's another thing that bothers me.

... No one can say to me that I did anything without decency by being a performer. I used to perform with several male artists — Daljit Sagoo, Charanjit Pammipuri and Avtar Kang. I mean, all of them sang with us at weddings for 2—2.5 hours and we'd all go home to our respective homes after the programmes. I had my family, they had their own families. So it never occurred to us we were doing anything improper. We had respect for the music. We presented the music respectfully, and we were recognised for that ultimately too. Sometimes the public make requests for songs like *Nain preeto de* (transl. 'Preeto's eyes') which are popular but which lack the kind of meaning I aspire to sing. One day I was sitting down and thinking about it and thought 'I'm not very fond of that song, actually. It's lyrics aren't worthy and I think that I just shouldn't sing it'. I decided that from that moment onward that the next time someone requested it I would say that I don't know it ... but sometimes we sing songs just because they have a good tune without thinking about the lyrics. That's ok too. But to knowingly sing improper, derogatory lyrics is wrong ... like many of the songs we hear being produced in India today ... it shouldn't be that a song is playing and it's not suitable for children to listen to.

NP: *What kind of image is being projected about women through contemporary Punjabi music? How have you managed to maintain your own your image while being in the public eye?*

MB: That image largely depends on women ... to what extent they want to reveal themselves. Because in the end, everything is in women's hands ... they can make or break it for themselves. But a woman needs to know where to stand and how to act ... but for me the most crucial issue was my own family. My elders used to say, 'ok, she lives in England and sings and her husband is with her, but still it doesn't look good'. So when they were visiting England in the 1970s I took them along to a performance in a local college that I was invited to perform at. They were reluctant to go but went along to watch me, despite feeling embarrassed. Afterwards, they said to me, 'was *that* all it's about?'. They were surprised at how civilised and cultured the event was .... In their minds, they had had an image from India of women singing and there being lecherous, gawking men hanging all around (Figure 4).

NP: *How do you feel when you look back at your life and your career as a singer now?*

MB: Whatever I am, I am. If I had done music full-time, maybe I could have done more with my career and have been even better. But I have enjoyed looking after the household, gardening, cooking, raising children and then grandchildren. So that's how I've spent my life. I have no regrets and feel that I can proudly say that I fulfilled my desires and ambitions to pursue what I enjoy doing most — music.

Figure 4   Wedding party in 1980 with Charanjit Bawa and sons Kuljit and Satpaul
Source: The Southall Story, www.TheSouthallStory.com

author biography

Navtej Purewal is lecturer in Sociology, School of Social Sciences, University of Manchester, Oxford Road, Manchester M13-9PL, UK.

reference

Brah, A. (1999) 'The Scent of Memory: strangers, our own and others' *Feminist Review*, Issue 61: 4–26.

doi:10.1057/fr.2011.59

open space

100 | an autochthonic scent of memory?

Nira Yuval-Davis

In her article 'The Scent of Memory' Avtar Brah explores some of the issues that arise out of the way a son, Tim Lott, discusses the suicide of his mother in Southall in his book, *The Scent of Dried Roses*.

Brah refuses to 'know' Jean, the mother, and to assume the nature of her relationships with and views of other people in Southall of the 1970s and 1980s and what was exactly implied in Jean's suicide note when she stated that she hated Southall, where she had lived all her life. Brah leaves open the question of whether Jean saw only threat in the Black and Asian immigrants that settled in Southall or/and also developed bonds of affection with the children of these communities who studied in the Southall school in which she had worked as a dinner lady. And yet, relying on interviews she carried out with people of similar social locations to that of Jean in Southall around the same time, Brah meditates on the racialised situated gaze — and existential anxiety — that people like Jean had been feeling in Southall after it became a vibrant multi-racial borough (what Jean described in her suicide note as 'decay').

The title of Brah's article has been inspired by the title of Lott's book, but it is also a very apt one, as memories are embodied and senses of smell and touch, as well as vision and sound, play extremely important roles in triggering performative signifiers of belonging. My own 'Scent of Memory' of Avtar (or Taro — as she is known to her friends and family) Brah and of our first meeting is definitely embodied. It involves not only scent, but also taste — when she taught me how to eat Indian food and why one needs curry to 'wet' any grilled or tandoori 'dry' food. The scent, actually, was that of snow — we met in Aberdeen, at the British Sociological Association (BSA) Conference in 1974 — the first on 'sexual divisions of labour', organised by the wonderful — now both gone — Sheila Allen and Diana Leonard. Although, like all BSA Conferences, it took place during the Easter vacation, it snowed for the first — and only — time that year, during the conference. Taro and I were drawn to each other during that conference for reasons that probably became more articulated to both of us over the years. As virtually the only 'visible other' women at that conference, both PhD students, both newly arrived from

(154–160) © 2012 Feminist Review. 0141-7789/12 www.feminist-review.com

studies in the USA, our situated gazes took both delight at the complex, dynamic, Marxist and feminist sociological perspectives that dominated the conference, as well as dismay that ethnic and racial divisions, so central to our autonomously budding intersectional theoretical frameworks, were not just ignored but invisible at that conference. In that sense, some of the questions Taro contemplates in her 'Scent of Memory' article were already present for us at that forum of our initial encounter.

It is the question of emotional attachments, as well as the contesting political projects of belonging, that constructs differential meanings of embodied signifiers of belonging, which are at the heart of the meditation/exploration in Brah's article.

Stuart Hall (2000) has posited 'the multi-cultural question' as the most important question of our time: the possibility of people who, coming from different backgrounds, origins, cultures and religions, can learn to live with each other without assimilation on the one hand and without fixating and naturalising the differences between them on the other. In other words, the extent to which boundaries as borders can encompass, rather than challenge — or be challenged by — boundaries of competing collective identities.

Paul Gilroy (2004) posited pluralist conviviality and post-imperial melancholia as the two existential alternatives in which British people have been experiencing multi-cultural coexistence. Jean's suicide hints of such melancholia. And while we cannot 'know' Jean, it is important to explore what is the political, if not the emotional, project of belonging, which constructs the particular common sense of such melancholia. Given the recent rise of the English Defence League (EDL) and of similar organisations in the rest of the West (e.g., Norway — although there is no space here to discuss Breivik's particular project), understanding these political projects is of primary importance.

To do this, I would like to introduce the term 'autochthony', which Peter Geschiere (2009) defines as 'the global return to the local'. 'Old racism' basically constructed 'the Other' as essentially racially different, while what is generally known as the 'new racism' constructed her/him as essentially culturally different. However, while autochthony is a racist discourse that uses origin, culture and religion as signifiers of immutable boundaries like other forms of racism, its focus is spatial/territorial, a mode of what Manuel Castells (1997) called 'defensive identity communities', except that these days it often applies to majoritarian as well as minoritarian community discourses.

Part of neoliberal governmentality is to remove from most people the expectation, let alone the guarantee, of long-term employment in the same place, or even in the same kind of work, of regular holidays and sufficient funds to live on in their pension. Other elements of the 'risk society' (Beck, 1992) follow, including in relation to housing and place of living, networks of friends and even membership in a family unit. All these push people into memberships in Castellian 'defensive identity movements'. These anxieties by majoritarian members of the society are also important, however, for policy makers who often attempt to use the deprivation of migrants' and refugees' rights as an easy way to appease these anxieties (Fekete, 2009; Squire, 2009) and to reinforce a weakening sense of national 'cohesion'. The basic underlying political issue here, however, is the boundaries of belonging that are assumed in the collective 'we' and the extent to which the construction of 'us' versus 'them' in this debate continues to be naturalised. This is the context in which the rise of extreme right autochthonic movements needs to be analysed.

The UN, in its declaration of the rights of indigenous people, has accepted autochthony as the French equivalent of indigeneity.[1] However, given the way the term is often used in Francophone languages but also, for example, in Dutch, where the people are divided into 'autochthones' (those who belong) and allochthones (those who do not), I was persuaded to follow Geschiere's differentiation between the two. Indigeneity remains the discourse of marginal racialised people in settler societies claiming rights, while autochthony is the term to be used in relation to the discourse of privileged hegemonic majorities defending access to what they perceive as threatened privileges and resources. However, I would argue that these two constructions interpenetrate each other and cannot be totally differentiated in many historical locations.

1 http://www.unhcr.org/cgi-bin/texis/vtx/refworld/rwmain/opendocpdf.pdf?reldoc=y&docid=471355bc2, last accessed April 2011.

As is the case with other political projects of belonging that construct notions of 'custom and tradition' and claim that their version is the only true version, autochthonic political projects of belonging claim to be eternal and pre-modern; nevertheless, they are as selective and contemporary as other political projects of belonging, which celebrate pluralism and conviviality of difference. Autochthonic political projects of belonging, however, are not only far from celebrating the conviviality of difference, but, as carriers of the claim of being 'autochthone' − 'of this soil', those who really belong − they are not prepared to tolerate the 'others'. They see in them a threat (which kind of threat or combination of threats changes in different locations − cultural, political, economic, genetic) and construct the relationship with them as a 'zero-sum' game − it's either 'us' or 'them'.

Geschiere (*ibid.*: 21−22) rightly claims that 'autochthony' can be seen as a new phase of ethnicity, although in some sense it even surpasses ethnicity (see also Yuval-Davis, 2011a, 2011b). While ethnicity is highly constructed, relationally and situationally circumscribed, there are limits to these reconstructions in terms of name and history. Autochthony is a much more 'empty' category and thus more elastic. It states no more than 'I was here before you' and, as such, can be applied in any situation and constantly redefined and applied to different groupings in different ways. As Nadia Fadil, at a recent IRR Conference on

2 See http://
www.epim.info/
wp-content/
uploads/2011/03/
Islamophobia-and-
progressive-values-
irr-2011.pdf, last
accessed April 2011.

Islamophobia,[2] mentioned, in Belgium people of western origin like white Americans are not usually identified as allochthones.

On the other hand, a few years ago, my local neighbourhood theatre in London, the Arcola ran a play called 'Crime and Punishment in Dalston'. Based on the dialogues the playwright (Farr, 2002) heard when he worked with local youth, it explores the enmity between Afro-Caribbeans and Turkish and Kurdish refugee communities in Dalston, in which the Afro-Caribbeans constructed themselves as the local autochthones. I heard a similar discourse from some of my local black students when I was teaching the sociology of racism. The repudiation — accompanied by various 'descriptions' of the refugees as dirty, lazy, those who have come to take our housing and our jobs — was of a very similar character to what the white working class used in order to repudiate these blacks and their families 15 or 20 years earlier, and which Brah encountered from her interviewees. This is, of course, not a unique phenomenon, and the growth in gang warfare among different groupings of youth from both majority and various minority groupings in most global cities can be seen as one form of expression of such autochthonic politics of belonging, although often these gangs are far from being ethnically homogeneous.

While the spatial/territorial notion of autochthonic politics of exclusion and belonging is very important when we come to understand specific local geographies of fear, it is crucial when we attempt to understand the specificity of contemporary extreme right politics in Europe and elsewhere, which continuously argue that they are not racist, although they are very much against all those who 'do not belong'. The British National Party (BNP), for example, who used to be identified with older versions of racism, have come to describe themselves in their constitution as the party of 'the indigenous people' of Britain who just happen to be White, getting their so-called scientific backing from the 2010 book by Arthur Kemp — *Four Flags: the indigenous people of great Britain*, claiming that the genetic purity of the indigenous British people is higher than anywhere else in Europe — disregarding that other similar parties in Europe make similar claims concerning their people.

3 http://
theenglishde
fenceleagueextra
.blogspot.com
/2010/11/jewish-
gay-join-us-
english-extremists
.html, last accessed
April 2011.

4 http://
vladtepesblog
.com/?p=21251,
last accessed April
2011.

On the other hand, in some cases, such as the EDL, the organisations have both Jewish and Gay sections[3] and include also Sikh, Hindu and Afro-Caribbean members, something unimaginable in the older kind of extreme right organisations with neo-Nazi ideologies. For them, the line that separates autochthones from allochthones is different. As Trevor Kelway, EDL spokesman, claimed: 'An all-White group doesn't look good. They can join the EDL as long as they accept the English way of life .... Those with multi-identities do not belong here. Stop the Islamisation of Europe!'.[4] Interestingly, as we can see, the changes in the construction of the boundaries of belonging are not just ethnic and cultural but also sexual. Tolerance towards homosexuality has shifted, in a relatively short time, from an unacceptable signifier of ultra liberal people that the Extreme Right despised, into a signifier of a liberal western culture that differentiates between the pre-modern racialised 'Other' and the enlightened West. The 'pioneer' of this change was the gay leader of the Dutch rightist party Pim Fortuyn who was murdered in 2002. Another significant development is that these days, three of the leaders of this kind of extreme right party in Europe are women, signifying a wider change of gender politics among the ranks of these parties.

Autochthonic politics of belonging can take very different forms in different countries and neighbourhoods, while they can also be reconfigured constantly in the same places. Nevertheless, like any other forms of racialisation and other boundary constructions, their discourses always appear to express self-evident or even 'natural' emotions and desires: the protection of ancestral heritage, the fear of being contaminated by foreign influences and so on, although, as Geschiere (2009) points out, they often hide very different notions of ancestry and contamination.

Of course, autochthonic politics are not the only available contemporary political discourse of belonging (Yuval-Davis, 2011b). Avtar Brah (1996) herself has been influential in developing a counter political project to autochthony, which she calls 'diaspora space', which is an inclusive political project of belonging. In the comment she inserts in 'The Scent of Memory' when quoting Anne Michaels' *Fugitive Pieces*, she insists that her call for empathy and responsibility to the past should include 'all our pasts, I hope, for this is crucial if we are not to collapse into ethnic cleansings of all kinds' (Brah, 1999: 24).

'Diaspora spaces' are not only inclusive and convivial, but normatively they also decentre the hegemonic majority and construct non-hierarchical, non-racialised legitimate attachments and belonging for all those who inhabit a particular space/place/society. Diaspora space does not obliterate or homogenise intersectional differences, but encompasses them with equal respect and consideration. Although Brah, in her work, explored differentiated racialisations, her notion of the 'diaspora space' follows Patricia Hill-Collins' (1990) resistance to 'hierarchies of oppression' and allows for a dialogical standpoint epistemology in which 'the truth' can only be approximated by a dialogue that is informed by the participation of people from differentiated intersectional social positionings and standpoints (see also Stoetzler and Yuval-Davis, 2002).

However, it is important to emphasise that while such diasporic spaces are conducive for developing convivial multi-cultural spaces of belonging, they should not be confused with political alliances based on 'transversal dialogues' (Yuval-Davis, 1994, 2006; Cockburn and Hunter, 1999; Reilly, 2008).

In 'transversal dialogues' as in the case of 'diaspora spaces', differential positioning and attachments are recognised and respected while being decentred. However, transversal dialogues are more bounded, as the different participants share a normative value system. This allows them to transcend boundaries and borders and to establish a long-term alliance of support and cooperation that goes beyond a coexistence that can break up in times of scarcity and other forms of social, political or economic crisis. Taro Brah and I have been conducting such a transversal dialogue for more than 35 years, as well as sharing affectionate bonds of friendship. We do not always agree, but we also trust and share the underlying values that shape our specific positions regarding specific questions from our different intersectional locations. I look forward to another such 35 years at least ....

author biography

Nira Yuval-Davis is the Director of the Research Centre on Migration, Refugees and Belonging (CMRB: http://www.uel.ac.uk/cmrb/index.htm) at the University of East London. She has been the President of the Research Committee 05 (on Racism, Nationalism and Ethnic Relations) of the International Sociological Association, a member of the Sociology sub-panel of the Research Excellence Framework (REF), a founder member of Women Against Fundamentalism and the international research network Women in Militarized Conflict Zones and an editor of the book series 'the Politics of Intersectionality' (Palgrave Macmillan). Among her major books: *Racialized Boundaries* (Routledge, 1992); *Gender and Nation* (Sage, 1997) and *The Politics of Belonging: Intersectional Contestations* (Sage, 2011).

references

Beck, U. (1992) *Risk Society: Towards a New Modernity*, London: Sage.

Brah, A. (1996) *Cartographies of Diaspora*, London: Routledge.

Brah, A. (1999) 'The Scent of Memory: strangers, our own and others' *Feminist Review*, Issue 61: 4–26.

Castells, M. (1997) *The Power of Identity*, Oxford: Blackwell.

Cockburn, C. and Hunter, L. (1999) 'Special Issue on Transversal Politics' editors, *Soundings*, Vol. 12, Summer.

Farr, D. (2002) *Crime and Punishment in Dalston*, London: Arcola Theatre.

Fekete, L. (2009) *A Suitable Enemy: Racism, Migration and Islamophobia in Europe*, London: Pluto.

Geschiere, P. (2009) *The Perils of Belonging: Autochthony, Citizenship, and Exclusion in Africa and Europe*, London: University of Chicago Press.

Gilroy, P. (2004) *After Empire: Melancholia or Convivial Culture?* London: Routledge.

Hall, S. (2000) 'Conclusion: the multicultural question' in Hesse, B. (2000) editor, *Unsettled Multiculturalisms: Diasporas, Entanglements, Transruptions*, London: Zed Books.

Hill-Collins, P. (1990) *Black Feminist Thought, Consciousness and the Politics of Empowerment*, London: Harper Collins.

Michaels, A. (1998) *Fugitive Pieces*, London: Bloomsbury Paperback.

Reilly, N. (2008) *Women's Human Rights: Seeking Gender Justice in a Globalizing Age*, Cambridge: Polity Press.

Squire, V.J. (2009) *The Exclusionary Politics of Asylum. Migration, Minorities, Citizenship*, Basingstoke: Palgrave.

Stoetzler, M. and Yuval-Davis, N. (2002) 'Standpoint theory, situated knowledge and the situated imagination' *Feminist Theory*, Vol. 3, No. 3: 315–334.

Yuval-Davis, N. (1994) 'Women, ethnicity and empowerment' *Feminism & Psychology*, Vol. 4, No. 1: 179–198.

Yuval-Davis, N. (2006) 'Human/women's rights and feminist transversal politics' in Ferree, M.M. and Tripp, A.M. (2006) editors, *Transnational Feminisms: Women's Global Activism and Human Rights*, New York: New York University Press.

Yuval-Davis, N. (2011a) 'The dark side of democracy: racism, xenophobia, autochthony and the radical right' *Open Democracy*, June.

Yuval-Davis, N. (2011b) *The Politics of Belonging: Intersectional Contestations*, London: Sage.

doi:10.1057/fr.2011.60

open space

100 | blossom time

Catherine O'Flynn

No one caught the bus out there; it wasn't that sort of area. He'd catch glimpses of people getting into cars at the retail parks or moving behind the plate glass windows of the car showrooms, but never a soul at the bus stops. The pavements had disappeared along with the pedestrians; Dermot wasn't sure which had gone first. Now there was just a strip of neatly mown grass between the dual carriageway and the perimeter hedges of the car parks, but somehow the bus stops clung on as forlorn remnants of another time. An empty bus suited him well enough. Eamonn Rooney was doing his Irish Country hour on Radio Shamrock and Dermot listened on his portable transistor. He tapped his big hands on the steering wheel in tense rhythmic counterpoint, occasionally bursting into song when he knew the words.

This stretch always reminded him of visiting Michael and the grandkids in Houston, and the ghostly walks he had taken along the road there each morning trying to find a newspaper. Whenever he drove this way with Bridie he'd say: 'I remember when it was all fields' and she'd laugh, because of course she knew he did. Every Summer, the buses would be packed with families heading out to the Pick-Your-Own strawberry fields. They had taken Geraldine there a few times when she was little. She had found it hard though, all the bending and stooping. All she really wanted to do was eat the strawberries and all Dermot had wanted to do was let her.

Once the bus reached Shirley, the passengers started to flood on, pensioners mainly, taking last minute short hops before the off-peak curfew sent them scurrying indoors. Dermot was 12 months away from retirement. He looked at the small, neat men in their cream caps, pale grey windcheaters and stone coloured trousers. The tones seemed chosen to render their wearers barely visible against the pavements and street furniture around them. Some of the men had women's shopping trolleys. He imagined their wives sending them out for things they didn't need. He saw a man emerge wide-eyed and empty-handed from Iceland. Dermot looked away and burst into song again.

At 3.30, everyone over the age of 60 vanished. Their replacement by schoolchildren was so rapid and so complete that sometimes Dermot had the strange sensation that he was seeing the same people at an earlier stage of their lives. It sometimes helped to make him feel more tender to the school kids, to understand why they should make so much noise, why they should be

(161–164) © 2012 Feminist Review. 0141-7789/12 www.feminist-review.com

anything but invisible. Only sometimes though, most of the time he felt murderous towards them.

'You're not getting on with that'.

'You blind? It's a daysaver'.

'I know what it is son. It's a week out of date'.

'Nah I bought it this morning mate. Machine's bust, ain't my problem'.

'You can pay £1.20 or you can get off the bus'.

'Fuck you man. I bought my ticket'.

As the bus moved in from the suburbs to the inner city, the school uniforms gradually disintegrated, from blazers and ties to sweatshirts and hoods, but the attitude remained the same. At the stop ahead, he saw a jostling mass of boys — Nike bags and razored haircuts — pushing each other into the gutter. As the doors opened, all he saw was their teeth.

A riot appeared to be in full swing on the top deck. He heard the hammering of feet, shouts and howls. The boys charged off the bus in their twos and threes, thundering down the stairs, calling to friends and victims. They hurled bags of chips and empty coke cans at the side of the bus in salutation or threat at those still on it. Dermot wondered how the small terraced houses the boys returned to could contain them; he wondered how they didn't burst apart at the seams. Neither Geraldine nor Michael had been any trouble as teenagers. Michael had been busy with his athletics and before him Geraldine had always been quiet. She spent most of her time in her room, drawing pictures of horses. It was only a modest semi but it always seemed too large for the four of them. Dermot remembered his brother Jack visiting from Ireland, big and loud as ever. He'd said that it was like they had mice in the house, not youngsters. Bridie had left the room upset.

In Sparkbrook, the bus's progress was slowed by the surrounding traffic before finally grinding to a halt. Dermot's shift was over when he got to the city centre, but how long that might take was impossible to guess. He always got stuck there and it always caused him stress. He was hungry and wanted to be home with his tea and his paper. He remembered the café that used to stand on the corner ahead of him. It did decent sized breakfasts with white pudding and soda bread and good brewed tea. He remembered the smell of the bacon. Now he wasn't sure what it was — some kind of place for making phone calls abroad. Every other window was one of those, the rest were barbershops. Some seemed to combine both functions. Why did they need so many barbers? Somedays the area seemed unrecognisable from the place he used to know, on others he looked right through the new signs and strange languages and saw the street as it was when he arrived 40 years ago. He'd got off the coach at Digbeth station and headed for the address of the boarding house he'd been given. He remembered walking along with his big suitcase, sweating in his woollen suit. He looked at the block now and saw where Murphy's bar used to be. Beyond that had been the Roscommon

Lounge, then O'Rourke's the grocers and Frank Sweeney the bookie, though Dermot thanked God that he'd never been one for the horses. Above Murphy's was a big room where Dermot used to box and had got his nose broken by his friend Frank Tumelty.

He thought it was sometime in the 1960s that the area started to change. Strange ramshackle shops set up selling gaudy fabrics and vegetables that looked fearsome to him. One by one, the old names went and were replaced by restaurants selling curry and soon there was nowhere to get a plate of bacon and cabbage. As each new wave of immigrants arrived at the coach station and drifted up the road, the neighbourhood would change again. Dermot looked out now at the current uneasy hybrid of Mogadishu and Krakow – ghettos within a ghetto.

The bus inched along under the shadow of the Holy Cross, the one landmark unchanged through the years. It was an ugly building resembling a factory more closely than a church. It had somehow lasted through the long, lean years with a parish consisting only of the handful of derelict old drunks and penniless widows that never managed to move out with everyone else. On Sunday shifts, Dermot had sometimes seen men he recognised from the old days as he drove past. He remembered one with whom he'd shared a room. When he'd seen him again, he had the ruined face of a drinker, his nose swollen, hands shaking, making slow progress along the road towards the church, followed by a lame dog. Dermot imagined him still living in the same boarding house feeding the dog bacon rind and whiskey on the cracked brown lino.

Now the church car park was full again every Sunday, the pews swelled with the new Polish arrivals. Dermot didn't know who the priest was anymore. He wondered if he too was Polish. Back in his day, the priest had been Father Dempsey who'd always been arranging parish dances and socials. Dermot remembered some wonderful St Patrick's nights, everyone in a charabanc travelling off to other parishes for the big night. He remembered very clearly the first time he'd seen Bridie, laughing with some other girls while Tommy Fitzgerald's Showband played 'Black Velvet Band'. He loved to hear her laugh. Father Dempsey hadn't seemed like the priests Dermot had known back in Ireland. They had been all sin and penance and bare knuckles on the back of your head when you spoke out of turn. You could have a joke with Father Dempsey. He'd spent all his time organising social events, helping out families, setting up youth clubs and promoting community spirit. He'd done a lot for the Irish in the parish. He was dead now, but there was a mural of him done some years ago by local children on the wall of the Church car park some years ago. Dermot passed it each day on the bus, the peeling paint revealed patches of dark brick in the priest's face.

The bus moved forward 30 yards and then came to a halt again. On a scrap of land between the side of the church and the petrol station was a single cherry blossom tree. Yesterday there had been nothing much to see, but the tree had bloomed overnight and the bus was stalled beside it.

For their tenth wedding anniversary, he and Bridie had booked to go to Brean for the weekend. There was more to it than a simple celebration. It had been 8 years since they'd had Geraldine and they couldn't understand why they hadn't had another two or three since then. Bridie had thought it might do them good to go away. Dermot was beginning to think that Geraldine might be an only child, but he was more than happy to have a break with just the two of them. Bridie's sister was going to look after Geraldine, but fell ill at the last minute. Father Dempsey heard of this somehow and phoned them up. He insisted to Dermot that they should go, he said it was important, and Dermot remembered blushing at this indication of the things Bridie must have discussed with the priest in the confessional. Father Dempsey said that Geraldine could stay in the Presbytery for the weekend and help Mrs Connor the housekeeper. Dermot and Bridie decided to cancel, but Geraldine got wind of Father Dempsey's offer and was delighted at the idea. She'd not long made her communion and was going through what Dermot termed her 'Holy Joe' phase, to such an extent that Bridie was worried her daughter might have a vocation. In the end they went.

They'd arranged to meet at the station on their return. Dermot and Bridie got off the train and saw them waiting beyond the gate, Father Dempsey with his hand on Geraldine's shoulder. Dermot and Bridie were still in high spirits, giggling about the woman they'd sat opposite, as they walked along the platform. Then Dermot looked up and felt as if he had taken a punch to his stomach. Bridie too had stopped laughing and was stood quite still beside him. Ahead of them Geraldine was dressed from head to toe in new clothes.

It was a long time ago. Geraldine was married now with children of her own. Father Dempsey was quietly moved to another parish in an even poorer part of the city. It was never passing the church that reminded Dermot, but the blossom tree. The tiny pink flowers fluttering against black branches that took his breath away.

At the next stop, the passengers snarled at him as they got on, blaming him for the traffic. He'd be home in an hour. He tried to sing again but found he couldn't remember the words.

author biography

Catherine O'Flynn's debut novel, *What Was Lost*, won the Costa First Novel Award, was shortlisted for the Guardian First Book Award, and longlisted for the Booker and Orange Prizes. She was named Waterstone's Newcomer of the Year at the 2008 Galaxy British Book Awards. Her second novel *The News Where You Are* was published in 2010 and shortlisted for the Bollinger Everyman Wodehouse Prize. Her short stories and articles have featured in *Granta* magazine, *Good Housekeeping* and on Radio 4.

doi:10.1057/fr.2011.68

open space

100 | in exile

Laleh Khalili

Here

My mother grows lemons and mint

    in the periphery of her exile garden

    paved with the grid of planned stones

My mother drinks her bitterness down with microwaved tea

    and finds joy in pistachio green

My mother, she used to want me to find myself

    a rich physicist or a family friend

    who knew the contours of my discontent and her sorrow

My mother, she reads self-improvement manuals daily and watches *The Young and the Restless* to her heart's content.

Here 2

He says

    But *we* were legal

He says

    But *we* are modern

    In the confines of the commuter train

    our sweat doesn't smell of fenugreek

    (even if we eat ghormeh sabzi)

    and turmeric

He says

    But *they* want the caliphate (*we* are modern seculars; *we* are not Arabs)

He says

    But *we* are modern

    even in the loneliness of our exile in the bright shopping centres of glorious

(165–166) © 2011 Feminist Review. 0141-7789/11 www.feminist-review.com

clean streets in their perfect geometry

We *are* modern

author biography

Laleh Khalili is a member of the *Feminist Review* Collective and a senior lecturer in the Politics of the Middle East at the School of Oriental and African Studies. She is the author of *Heroes and Martyrs of Palestine* (Cambridge, 2007) and co-editor of *Prisons and Policing in the Middle East* (Columbia, 2010).

doi:10.1057/fr.2011.64

open space

100 | acrid text: memory and auto/biography of the 'new human'

Joan Anim-Addo

In response to Avtar Brah's insistent question: 'What do you think?', this piece draws on auto/biographical fragments in an attempt to further probe concerns with 'the figure outside of the narratives of humanism', and the related significance of memory and re-memory. It should be declared at the outset that this is not an essay. It is interested in the spaces that Brah has opened up for 'graffiti' in which I intend to begin by writing.

Gendered   Classed   Racialized

No

GENDERED   CLASSED   RACIALIZED

yes capitalised

yes huge lettering

jarring gold

shadowed black

leaking black

new-in-*dis*-place

weare survivors people

thisisnot an essay

have YOU seen the newhuman

SEEN THE NEWHUMAN

in your space/life/graffiti

HEARD her

notanessay

(167–171) © 2012 Feminist Review. 0141-7789/12 www.feminist-review.com

a kindof genealogy

alongside Haraway

and truth

Graffitti is a meditation. The first time I wrote on a wall, that was more than a response. The graffiti writer had stated: 'Shit to J ... '. Since ours was a small, school community, I knew who J was, and that she (Wall Writer) was talking to me. Correction: about me. To the community. I see afresh that that was a community of females. Nothing new there. Importantly, though, this was predominantly White working class, and I was not only *the* Black presence, but incredibly (for too many), a figure of authority. Well, a teacher and Black! A diminutive 5 ft 1-ish, Black, teacher, female, and working in 1960s east London. With hindsight, I sympathise. How could White parents accept such a being as not only fully human, but fully intelligent enough to be teaching their offspring? What inner turmoil for the students! What memories of double lessons with 3F first thing on a Monday! Speaking from the *dis*comfort zone, I ask YOU: A Black teacher teaching English?

What language do you speak where you come from, Miss?

NigNog

Are you a proper teacher? I mean, you do look young, Miss.

Wog Coon

Miss, why don't I ever see coloured people on holiday?

OUT OF PLACE! But reading you (reading Jean), Avtar, what figures we must have cut! Blindly building new lives in spaces with histories that we did not know. 'Other' native women pounding East London streets. Black women oblivious! Black oblivious women!

BOW

Bow Bow

immigrant woman

whodoyouthinkyouare

Nobody had warned that a new human would appear in Britain in an era when the concept of racism itself was yet to become current. In those days, Black people carried chips on their shoulders if they noticed *difference*. Head teacher, psychologist and author of *Black Teacher*, Beryl Gilroy, would be among many African-heritage new-in-*dis*-place testifying to being asked whether Black people had tails.

My reply to Wall Writer was simply ambiguous: 'And to you babe!' What identification across 'difference'! So much said; so few words. Of course, the words were not spray-painted. If they had been, I like to think I would have chosen a jarring golden yellow banked against stark black, a signature in its becoming. Of course, there had been a film 2 years earlier: *To Sir with Love*. How would Sidney Poitier have fared gender-bending in *To J with Shit*?

OUT OF PLACE! In 1981, Brixton erupted. All local Black family life was touched by the riots. Attempting to be *in place*, I lived and worked in Brixton at the time. On the day of the riots, I waited anxiously for my 4-year-old to be dropped off at my place of work as usual by a friend after school. Eventually, calling the school, I found that my son was still there. Half-crazed, I negotiated the many road blocks to finally reach the school and collect him. The deputy head was not pleased. He needed to get back to suburb safety and home. Apologetic, I explained that I had no idea why X had not collected my son and why there had been no contact from him whatsoever. His response indicated that the riots had sparked keen observation, for my teaching colleague took the opportunity to ask in confidential tones:

But are there any middle class coloured people? I mean, I've just noticed: you don't see middle class coloured people, do you?

You don't see middle class coloured people. DO YOU?

Who do you see when a Black person comes into view? Where does the cross-racial gaze lead? (My son's middle name is Frantz — after Fanon). Ah, I recall Rich's words, 'the white eye does not always see from the center'. This particular colleague and I had worked together in that same school. I had certainly seen Black middle-class people in the playground regularly dropping off their children. I could even guess which among them were law professionals in their uniform three-piece suits. Why had my colleague not noticed? How are we reading the masquerade of clothing inhabited by Black people? Hoodies today. And yesterday?

You don't see middle class coloured people, do you?

There was good reason why X had not delivered my 4-year-old. Operation Swamp! The police saturation in the local area prior to the riots would give every other Black male a story to tell and to pass on to their Black family and community for generations. Such oral methods have been a primary way of learning history. In X's case, while driving during the morning of the riots, and before any rioting had begun, he had been stopped, searched, arrested and held in a cell without communication. The charge was SUS. He was released after the riots when he could no longer be detained. No charges were pressed. Consider the anger generated within that one case study. Consider the anger waiting to explode.

ANGER

In the school in which I was teaching, not a single teacher spoke in the course of the next day to their class of 5- to 11-year-olds in their classrooms about the riots. No teacher asked the usual questions, did you get home alright? Did anyone have problems? These are all normal teacher questions indicating care in primary schools. No one encouraged the children to write about the event. I am straining to maintain a type of truth by which this 'new' figure might become knowable. I am speaking again of *difference*. Remembering, too, the New Cross fire after which the Queen was silent.

Out of place? Edging. EDGING! Words from a Black (African-heritage) London University student, 2011, the year declared 'International Year of People of African Descent' by the United Nations:

> In year one, a seminar leader called me 'coloured'. I find this an offensive term although I know a lot of people don't. I asked her what she meant by 'coloured'. She said; 'anyone that isn't white'. I said, 'my best friend is Trinidadian and Arab, that girl over there is Chinese, I'm black, do we look the same? Do you think it's fair to posit white as the standard, as the norm, as something you either are or you aren't?' She sputtered a bit and told me that in North America it's okay to say 'coloured'. I reminded her that she was teaching in London.

I had provoked her. I had asked my students: what evidence is there to be found in our universities that British-African-heritage women think?

Can YOU point to such evidence? Where are the books? Where are the professors?

Do African-heritage women in Britain write autobiography? Cite me one that you have read. My student, above, is a writer. I hope she will one day write her own story. This is a narrative of NOW that she has written:

> My writing style has also fallen into the category of misunderstood. I find that because I am not integrated into the language of British politeness, hedging and not saying what you really mean, I tend to come across (to white British people) as sharp, blunt, unfeeling, cold, ruthless (I could go on). So when I'm writing I find my tutors think I am skating over subjects, not discussing them at length, using words that signify to me but not to them. It is interesting to see that my work has been understood how I have intended by the black and Caribbean people that have read it but not by my classmates or tutors all of whom are white.

JUST WHY IS SCARY SPICE SCARY?

She looks to *me* like any mother's daughter. I am relaying my student's story because I recognise it as my own. Been there. So, the 'new' human arrives on the Bow Road, Toxteth, Southall, as teacher, researcher (in the making), at university as student, professor (the latter one or two only, to be sure), but are our humanist institutions ready for her?

Pursuing D. Haraway

Let us go then. Lewwe go.

But after all those years, do you KNOW me?

Found: a figure of critical subjectivity

and still

I carry hope, Donna.

Tings haffe change.

This is not an essay. This is graffiti. In words that take up some of your questions, dear Avtar Brah, and also asks its own. It speaks from Sylvia Wynter's demonic ground, and Joan Anim-Addo's *dis*comfort zone. It is an acrid text smelling still of riots 1930s, 1981, 2011(!) and of times much further back, still teasing memory. Tempting rememory.

author biography

Joan Anim-Addo is a professor of Caribbean Literature and Culture and Director of the Centre for Caribbean Studies at Goldsmiths, University of London. Her recent publications include *Interculturality and Gender* (co-edited 2009), *Caribbean-Scottish Relations: Colonial & Contemporary Inscriptions in History, Language and Literature* (co-authored 2007), *Touching the Body: History, Language and African-Caribbean Women's Writing* (2007), *I Am Black White Yellow: An Introduction to the Black Body in Europe* (co-edited 2007), the poetry collections: *Haunted by History* and *Janie Cricketing Lady* (2006), and the libretto, *Imoinda: Or She Who Will Lose Her Name — A Play for Twelve Voices in Three Acts* (2007), first published bilingually (English/Italian, 2003). She is a member of the *Feminist Review* editorial Collective

doi:10.1057/fr.2011.58

afterword

100 | some fragments by way of an afterword

Avtar Brah

I

This is the hundredth issue of *Feminist Review* (*FR*) and much has changed since its inception in 1979, yet there are some important continuities. As before, the journal maintains its commitment to prioritise work that seeks to further theoretical and political debates that animate variegated forms of feminism. In 1979, the journal was produced by a group of women who explicitly described themselves as socialist feminist, although they welcomed contributions from any point of view within feminism. The project of socialist feminism has metamorphosed into many different formations. Some would say we have seen its demise. But for me, some of the critical questions it raised about global socio-economic inequities and inequalities still remain hugely pertinent in the face of neo-liberal globalisation that we face today.

But the overarching theoretical frameworks — the grand narratives as they were called — would not brook the demands of intersectional analysis. Eventually, they could not withstand the pressures of fully addressing questions of race, class, ethnicity, gender, sexuality, disability and gene-ration in their *relational* forms. These grand narratives were challenged by developments in poststructuralist theory, queer theory, the language and cultural turn in analysis, postcolonial theory and psychoanalysis. This contestation in theory and politics has been reflected in the articles published in the journal. Late capitalism in its various guises as globalisation has spawned its own plethora of analysis, as has environmentalism. The 9/11 attacks in New York and the 7/7 attacks in London introduced cataclysmic changes in the political scene and unleashed the so-called 'War on Terror' and wars in Iraq and Afghanistan, which have demanded urgent attention, as have the ecological disasters that have led to famines in different parts of the world. The journal attempts to stay abreast of such develop-ments and encourages submissions that attend to feminist analysis of such phenomena. The crisis in higher education with funding cuts and the introduction of debilitating tuition fees has made the academic members

(172–180) © 2012 Feminist Review. 0141-7789/12 www.feminist-review.com

of the collective reflect upon the potential impact of these changes on entrenching educational inequality further. Who will or will not be able to benefit from university education in the future? Will the instrumentalist objectives in education submerge the value of education as a creative force for developing human potential? What happens to pedagogical imperatives associated with projects such as feminism, where education is a modality designed to contest hegemonic asymmetries of power? How do we defend certain threatened subject disciplines, especially within Humanities and Social Sciences, which do not fit neatly into the rubric of narrow conceptions of utility? Such issues continually foreground questions of social relevance and encourage political activism and solidarity within and across educational institutions. *FR* is committed to mapping and addressing such socio-political and cultural questions.

II

FR has been one of my intellectual 'homes' for a long time. There have been moments when I felt like an outsider. But in time, I felt at home. What makes a place, a context, a circumstance 'feel like home'? How is nation figured? A number of articles here highlight the ways in which the contested site of Englishness/Britishness is struggled over, proclaimed or disavowed. Who is accepted as British/English, and who is constructed as the Other? There is a sense in which 'home' is a key underlying theme of this special issue. Here I reflect briefly on questions of home and belonging in terms of the personal, the social and the political (Yuval Davis, 2011). How do we think through the local and the global dimensions of home?

The current local, national and transnational migrations are creating new displacements all over the world. Many new diasporas are created and questions of home and belonging acquire critical importance. Home is where you are from, but it is also what you move towards socially, politically and psychically. It is not a fixed node, but a moving signifier constructed and transformed in and through social practices, cultural imaginaries, historical memories and our deepest intimacies. The concepts of home and diaspora are intrinsically interconnected. As I have argued elsewhere, home and diaspora as theoretical concepts are better understood as historically contingent genealogies in the Foucauldian sense. Hence, they serve as investigative technologies that address their historical trajectories across fields of social relations, subjectivity and identity. But Foucault would need to be refigured through the lens of psychological analytic, including psychoanalysis. (See also the collection by Ahmed *et al.*, 2003; Hall in this issue.)

The concept of home as mobilised in my concept of 'diaspora space' (Brah, 1996) is a critique of fixed origins while taking on board the concept of homing desire, which is distinct from the concept of 'homeland'. This is important because not all diasporas sustain an ideology of return, while all groups are affected by the affect, emotion and memory inscribed within homing desire. Importantly, home is a political category. Wars are fought over it and debates over it engage our deepest emotions. Home raises the contradictions of the 'indigene' subject position. It is a position that is on the one hand mobilised by right-wing groups such as the British National Party (BNP), and on the other it is raised by First Nation peoples such as the aboriginal peoples of the world. What position we take in relation to such discourses and debates is a question of politics, which focuses on the power dynamics that inscribe so called 'indigeneity'. The BNP is a racist organisation, whereas the First Nation people are dispossessed groups. Yet some of the arguments are sometimes similar and in the case of BNP, for instance, their views can appeal to what Gramsci calls the everyday commonsense of the people. With all its contradictions, commonsense is critically embedded in our deepest emotions about home. Hence, when taken to extremes, seemingly patriotic discourses can lead to all manner of severe conflict. In other words, there is a precarious relationship between indigeneity and nativist discourses. The problematic that faces us is whether the question of origins is treated in essentialist terms or conceived as a historical genealogy.

In home and travel, we carry different images of what we construct as home. These memories are deeply personal, but they are also structured by social relations constructed around social differentiations across such factors as social class, gender, age, sexuality and so on. Feminists have argued that these are all intersecting modalities and these intersecting realities should be taken account of in thinking about home. Women will have different memories marked by the patriarchal cultural formations of which they are a part. The new contexts in which they may find themselves may offer them more options or provide greater restrictions compared with those at the place of origin. Similarly, if you are gay, your experiences are likely to be marked by the cultural views about homosexuality, as well as state policies and practices about issues on sexuality. Class position or economic situation is crucial to formations of home in both the country of origin and that of destination. Therefore, discourses of home and diaspora foreground contexts of location and the regimes of power that produce these contexts. Home, location, displacement and dislocation have long been debated in feminist discourses. Feminists speak of politics of location as locationality in contradiction. That is, a positionality of dispersal, of simultaneous situatedness within gendered spaces of class, racism, ethnicity, sexuality, disability and age. Simultaneous situatedness entails movement across shifting cultural, religious and linguistic boundaries, and journeys across geographical and psychic borders. Importantly, such conceptualisations fore-ground a multi-axial concept of power. These debates are sometimes subsumed under the heading of 'intersectionality'. Home, whether in the sense of a nation, a transnational belonging or a residence, is a site of intersectionality where contradictory realities are experienced (Brah and Phoenix, 2004). For example, home can simultaneously be a place of safety and terror. Abused children know this all too well.

In my writing, I have described diaspora space as a site where 'genealogies of dispersal' intersect and interact with those of 'staying put'. Home is the node where genealogical intersection takes place. Processes of homemaking are markedly contested for migrants, often due to racism and economic discrimination (see Gedalof, 2009). Discourses of home have a close relationship with discourses of nation. In fact nation is frequently figured as 'home'. Discourses of Britishness are singularly about who belongs and who does not belong to the British 'nation'. Infamously, Enoch Powell argued that people of colour could be 'in' Britain but not 'of' Britain. Since the attacks of 9/11 in New York and 7/7 in London and the subsequent War on Terror, Muslim cultures have become the Other par excellence. The garments of Muslim women are seen to be particularly pernicious. They are attributed to Islam as a religion and as an ideology that is considered to be predisposed towards anti-liberal values such as violence, intolerance, authoritarianism and so on. Such constructions of Islam are construed as the antithesis of Britishness. Will the events of August 2011 go some way towards interrogating this image of Islam and Muslim people, since the families of the three young men killed in Birmingham during the disturbances were represented in the media as models of rationality, calmness and community spirit as they urged everyone to stay united and not take revenge?

III

The idea for this special issue of FR emerged at the symposium held in 2009 to mark my retirement from my post at Birkbeck College. As a keynote speaker at the symposium, Stuart Hall singled out my essay, 'The Scent of Memory', for comment. At the end of the symposium, members of the FR Collective who were present came up with the idea of a special issue in which members of the Collective as well as other speakers on that day would write, using 'The Scent of Memory' as a point of departure. This hundredth issue of FR is the result. I feel hugely touched by this honour. I have been a member of the Collective since 1988, and have seen FR go through many different phases. FR has been a very significant companion during my intellectual journey. The debates conducted on its pages have exercised a major influence on my work. 'The Scent of Memory' itself was framed through a series of questions prompting the reader to 'write back' in the hope of starting an open-ended conversation. The articles published here have been worth waiting for. They are rich, multilayered, nuanced nuggets that take the themes of 'The Scent of Memory' to a new level. I thank everyone involved.

This is a different moment from when 'The Scent of Memory' was written. Many things have changed, socially and politically. But some things, such as the riots of August 2011, remind one of the protest demonstration in Southall in 1979, and the riots of the early 1980s. For some segments of the population, as for example young people, especially black and minority ethnic young people, the life chances have not improved significantly. In the academy, cuts in education are wreaking havoc. But creative intellectual energy is still very much in evidence and this is demonstrated by the contents of this special issue. A number of articles draw upon methodologies that are new and innovative. The irreducible simultaneity of the social and the subjective threads through all articles and the personal and the political are imbricated in a powerful way. The analyses not only address the 'social' and the 'cultural', but also the 'affective'. And this makes the essays particularly special for me. Autobiography and memory is a key resource in the writings, taking us deep into the dynamics of self with the social. The intricate, theoretically complex, emotionally marked, collective imagination found here is cutting edge.

Stuart Hall's contribution is a transcript of his speech at the event mentioned above. It was a great privilege for me to have him speak there and now to have his presentation published here. Stuart has been my intellectual guru since the days that I was a PhD student. I remember that a couple of my fellow students and I went to meet him at the Centre for Contemporary Culture Studies at Birmingham University where he was then the Director. We were nervous that we were meeting such a great intellect, but we were immediately put at ease. The warmth with which he greeted us and his generosity was remarkable. I have closely followed his work ever since, and learnt much from it at every stage of my intellectual journey. Stuart is one of the foremost thinkers of our time, and to have him comment on my work gives me great pleasure. It is a profound honour. The piece is not simply a straightforward commentary. It contains some powerful analysis of his own, speaking of the 'moment of the diasporic' and the 'moment of the subject' as key double inscriptions of contemporary knowledge formations. He writes about the 'politics of the subject' and the contestations between those who subscribe to the psychoanalytic framework and others who draw upon the discursive analytics, and argues that while the two cannot be read off against one another: 'The challenge is nevertheless to find ways of thinking them in their interconnections'. Like other contributors here, there is an emphasis on the psychic and the social.

The mother is a key figure in 'The Scent of Memory', as is my emphasis on the importance of psychosocial analysis. Irene Gedalof and Ann and Aisha Phoenix undertake such analysis with the mother, as a central motif. Using and elaborating upon the analytical framework of Lisa Baraitser, Irene Gedalof rethinks the figure of the mother, and the physical and cultural work of reproduction that mothers do, which tends to be thought of in western thought as sameness. She links Baraitser's understanding of an individual subjectivity to the more collective work of reproducing social or cultural identities. 'What happens', Gedalof asks, 'if we think about this kind of reproduction as being framed by interruption instead of repetition'? Here, both the mother and the migrant become a figure of interruption – a moment 'of the appearance of difference that dislodges the Same from itself ... the moment in which we are interrupted by the other, something happens to unbalance us and open up a set of new possibilities'. Thereby she develops new ways of thinking about identity and belonging, and challenges the assumptions underlying contemporary discourses of social cohesion. Aisha Phoenix and Ann Phoenix focus upon a first-time mother in the maternity ward in a hospital in Tower Hamlets. This insightful piece analyses her experience of becoming a first-time mother, and the emotional resources and conflicts she brings to mothering, and how she negotiates her new identity in intersection with ethnicity, religion, culture and social class. Aisha and Ann demonstrate how racialised difference is foregrounded, when she constructs her maternal identity by highlighting her difference from Bangladeshi mothers. Indeed her feelings about Bangladeshi women and Tower Hamlets are akin to Jean Lott's about Southall. The paper engages with the psychosocial concept of interpellation and explores the impact of her biography in helping explain the ways in which her experience 'interpellates her into racialised positioning'. It uses a new 'psychosocial' methodology. The paper also examines the media responses to riots in the various English cities in August 2011. It analyses three sets of commentaries by well-known figures and shows how they essentialise black cultures as pathological. They remind the readers of how the concept of 'new racism' of the 1980s, which disavows biological racism but in turn constructs a cultural racism, is relevant in understanding these discourses.

The contemporary rise in the activities of right-wing organisations such as the English Defence League and the BNP echoes the demonstration of the National Front in Southall in 1979. What kind of boundaries do such groups construct between themselves and those they regard as the 'Other'? Nira Yuval- Davis reflects upon how to theorise the process of boundary maintenance amongst these groups. She draws upon the concept of 'autochthony' to address the racist discourses that mark the imagination and practices of these groups. Autochthony uses origin, culture and religion as a signifier of immutable difference that is bounded across spatial/territorial boundaries. It is distinguished from indigeneity in that this concept defines marginalised racialised people in settler societies, whereas autochthony is concerned about the discourses and practice of privileged hegemonic majorities defending access to what they see as threatened neighbourhoods.

'The Scent of Memory' is inspired by an autobiographical book. Two articles here are based on auto-ethnography. Lyn Thomas deconstructs 'the previously unmarked whiteness of the self narrated in my auto-ethnography, exploring the absent scenes of learning (about) race'. She writes about growing up in Wolverhampton, an area that, like Southall, has been transformed by post-war migration of postcolonial migrants. She analyses her 'working class culture of origin' providing an intimate analysis of the racialisation of gendered class subjects and subjectivity. She vividly depicts the 'defensive Englishness' that marks Enoch Powell's discourses of the period, and traces the impact of Powell's speeches on the culture she grew up in through a series of interconnected memory scenes. The essay is also an account of the changing class structure during the period when the manufacturing industries were decimated and replaced by jobs in the service sector. Her culture of origin, she argues, was one of resignation rather than resistance. In analysing the intra-differentiations of class, she challenges those accounts that treat class as homogeneous.

A second article that focuses on autobiographical details and memory work is the one by Suki Ali. It uses narrative analysis and memory work as a methodological tool to unearth the interconnections between psychic and social accounts of memory and history. This methodological use was part of the 'auto-biographical moment' in the UK feminist cultural studies of the 1980s and 1990s. The article is a touching account of interviews with family members as they look back on their experiences when they were growing up 'mixed race' during the 1960s and 1970s in a mainly white seaside town in the South of England. She demonstrates how this experience was differently remembered by members of the family: some events were clearly remembered by some members, while there were disavowals by others. Like Lyn Thomas, Suki Ali is a class migrant with a working class background and she addresses the psychological hurt of racism and class injuries. However, this was a racism that was different from that of 'swamping', as in Southall and Wolverhampton of the 1970s. This, she says, 'was born of a much vaguer kind of exoticism and novelty'.

Two pieces focus on the cultural and political dynamism of the first generation of South Asian women in Post-war Britain. Nirmal Puwar writes about a video produced by a group of elderly Asians in a day centre in Southall. The video emerged as part of an educational project that was designed to extend educational opportunities to adults who were not in education, employment or training. The project was undertaken by Jasbir Panesar and myself, and the video was one part of the larger project with different age groups of South Asians. It was produced over 20 years ago, at a time when the use of media technologies with elderly Asians was very rare. The participants were trained to use the equipment and the art of making the film by Creative Media Group, Vipin Kumar and Jasbir Panesar, but *Aaj Kaal* was made entirely by the participants through mutual collaboration. The article details the production process and analyses its content as part of the oral history of Southall. Although the video-making was offered to both men and women in the event, the actual filming was done entirely by women. There is a vivid description of the performance of *Giddha* and *Bolian* – Punjabi women's dances and exchange of repartee in poetic form – by the women. The women also speak of the activities of the right-wing groups around Southall and what happened in 1979, and they recount their memories of the Partition of the South Asian Subcontinent. The article documents the trials and tribulations of their lives, as well as the vibrancy of their cultures. In a similar vein, Navtej Purewal describes the singing career of her maternal aunt, Mohinder Bhamra, during the 1970s and 1980s. It charts her journey from reciting religious music in East Africa and Southall to becoming a singer of popular Punjabi music. Some of her songs speak to the double burden of full-time shift work in factories and domestic responsibilities at home. Lyrics, Bhamra says, were all important then, but the beat to which one could dance matters much more today. She is a pioneer in the field of post-war Punjabi music.

Joan Anim-Addo's and Laleh Khalili's poetic pieces are close to the bone. They play on the strings of a heart that knows pain and sorrow, like Jean did from a different vantage point. Joan speaks of her experience as a black teacher in a predominantly white school where both pupils and parents question her authority. Now a successful academic, she uses the testimony of a student to point to the struggles black students and academics face in institutions of higher education. And there is anger, but also an ongoing struggle for justice. And there is dignity and serenity. Laleh's 'In Exile' touches the soul. How does one live life in exile? Well, 'bitterness is drunk down with tea', there is frustration at the news that does not cover the 'wars and genocides' in the world, but there is joy in 'pistachio green', and dreams for a daughter. There is gentleness and ironic peace.

May the conversation carry on.

author biography

Avtar Brah is Emeritus Professor of Sociology at Birkbeck College. She writes on race, ethnicity, gender, identity and diaspora. Her publications include: *Cartographies of Diaspora/Contesting Identities* (1996, Routledge); *Hybridity and its Discontents: Politics, Science and Culture* (edited with Annie E Coombes, 2000, Routledge); *Global Futures: Migration, Environment and Globalization* (edited with Mary J. Hickman and Mairtin Mac an Ghail 1999, Macmillan); and, *Thinking Identities* (edited with Marry J. Hickman and Mairtin Mac an Ghail, 1999, Macmillan).

references

Ahmed, S., Castenada, C., Fortier, A. and Sheller, M. editors, (2003) *Uprootings/Regroundings: Questions of Home and Migration*, Oxford: Berg.

Brah, A. (1996) *Cartographies of Diaspora*, London and NY: Routledge.

Gedalof, I. (2009) 'Birth, belonging and migrant mothers' *Feminist Review*, Issue 93: 81–100.

Yuval-Davis, N. (2011) *The Politics of Belonging: Intersectional Contestations*, London: Sage.

doi:10.1057/fr.2011.69